Printed in England by Flexipress Printing Ltd., Ormskirk, Lancashire.
Tel. 01695 576839 I www.flexipress.co.uk

About This Book

Thanks to all who purchased my third volume of *The Hidden History of St Helens* and said they enjoyed reading it. This fourth edition follows a similar format – although one chapter that I call 'Those New Fangled Ideas!' comprises almost one-quarter of the book. It describes the introduction of such innovations as the bicycle, the motor car, aeroplane, telephone, traffic lights etc.

The chapter does not concern itself so much with the technologies but with how the people of St Helens took to these new developments. That was invariably with fascination but usually as observers, rather than as users. Unlike today when the pace of change can be rapid, it was many decades after the introduction of bicycles, motor cars and the telephone before the vast majority of the St Helens' population could afford them.

However, there are fifteen other chapters containing fascinating stories that I have uncovered from the local newspaper archives. Did you know that the first savings bank in St Helens had to be shut down due to a giant fraud by those that ran it? The chapter called 'The Brothers That Broke The First St Helens Savings Bank' explains all. Or that some hairdressers used petrol on their customers' heads? 'The Petrol Shampoo At A St Helens Hairdressing Salon' tells of one shocking outcome.

And 'The Sectarian Riot Of 1910 – St Helens' Own Bloody Sunday' describes the last time religious hatred descended into mob violence on the town's streets. 'The Tragedy And Heroism Of The Sandbeds Disaster' relates how an unofficial playground amongst sand dumps off Borough Road took the lives of three children and how others were saved by courageous rescues.

And 'The Coroner's Poor Box' describes how the misery of extreme poverty compounded by bereavement was alleviated by small gifts of cash. But there's lots too that should make you smile! 'The

Gorgeous Carnivals And Pageants Of The Past' revisits the celebrations of the 1930s when most people possessed very little but knew how to enjoy themselves.

There are some comical tales amongst 'St Helens Dogs That Have Made The News' and there's a reminder when Ena Sharples ruled the roost in the chapter titled 'Coronation Street Stars' Visits To St Helens In The Early 1960s'. And to end the book there's more 'Weird & Wonderful Things St Helens Folk Have Said', which, hopefully, will also make you chuckle.

Most of the content has been sourced from newspapers stored on microfilm at Eccleston Library and I would again like to thank their ever-helpful and cheerful staff and those at the St Helens Archive Service in the Gamble Building for their kind co-operation. **SRW**

Contents

The Cruel Treatment Of Paupers By St Helens Relieving Officers

"You came to Mrs. Cliff's house, where I live, about eight o'clock. You came in whistling, and said, "Where's the sick child?" and I said "It's no use coming now, it's dead".... You said nothing, but whistled and laughed and walked out."

Whiston Workhouse

The Guardians of the Prescot Union were the men who administered the Poor Law within the districts of St Helens and Prescot. Whiston Workhouse was at the heart of their operations having been built in 1843 to replace much smaller workhouses in Sutton, Prescot, Windle and Bold. But it was expensive housing the destitute and it was a lot cheaper to maintain so-called paupers within their own homes.

That was the job of a Relieving Officer who, after investigating each application for what was called parish or "out relief" *(meaning provided outside of the workhouse)*, made small, subsistence payments that were often in the form of food coupons. That was if the applicant was successful and there was certainly no guarantee of that! If the family did pass the impoverishment test and officially were classed as paupers, then they could also qualify for free treatment from a doctor, known as medical relief.

Of course, Relieving Officers did not completely relieve a claimant's state of poverty. Their small payments of out relief simply made life a bit more tolerable for the recipients – although their intervention could be the difference between life and death. In one week in 1869 only £64 9 shillings was spent within the St Helens' district assisting 1,119 people, which averages a little over one shilling for every claimant. At a meeting of the Guardians in 1870 it was stated that over the previous six months the average cost of relief per pauper had been 20s 4d – the equivalent of just £2 per year, when the average weekly wage was around £1. However, some relief payments would only have been provided on a very temporary basis.

The money for this "relief" came from the Poor Rate that the town's ratepayers had to pay. There was pressure on the elected Prescot Guardians to be economical in their spending in order to keep the Poor Rate levy low. Only what were considered to be the deserving poor were expected to receive financial assistance, with many ratepayers objecting to their cash going to the families of men that were able to work – even if they could not find a job.

And so a Relieving Officer that paid out as little as possible to the poor would be congratulated for his wise management of taxpayers' money – and so had a motivation to be stingy. That said, if severe cases of suffering were not supported, the Relieving Officer could be heavily criticised for his negligence.

Constantly dealing with cases of extreme poverty could also desensitise Relieving Officers to the grim situations of those they were supposed to assist – and some may have even enjoyed the power that they held over desperate folk. That, at times, could even be the power of deciding life and death and William Robinson seems to have fitted into that category.

John Fidler was an estate agent living at Lugsmore House in Eccleston and the Guardian and former councillor was quite a critic of Robinson. In 1879 he told a meeting of the Prescot Guardians:

> "The complaints about this relieving officer are loud and numerous, and the clergy of all denominations are under the impression that Mr. Robinson is omnipotent at the board [of

> Guardians], and that it is of no use to make any complaint against him."

Two years earlier William Robinson and John Fidler had crossed swords over the case of Ann Lyon. On July 16th 1877 the Relieving Officer stopped the 67-year-old pauper's relief payments and within hours the woman was dead. Fidler brought a complaint against Robinson and stated that he had other charges of an "equally grave nature" to bring.

A special committee of the Board of Guardians was appointed to investigate the cases but concluded that the charges could not be proved. However, they considered that Robinson had been guilty of undue harshness to paupers and so admonished him. In other words, he only received a slap on the wrist.

Robinson came from Liverpool and had been appointed a relieving officer in September 1876. Then he was one of two successful candidates for two vacant positions out of a total of 69 applications, with Sutton, Rainford and Eccleston being his territory. The latter township then included part of Westfield Street and the Greenbank district of St Helens.

There appeared to be some truth that Robinson had much support amongst the Board of Guardians, who probably thought well of his penny-pinching approach. John Fidler's comments from 1879 that made that claim arose as a result of a written complaint from Dr James Ricketts. He had a surgery in Cotham Street in St Helens and was the district medical officer for Sutton. This is how the Prescot Reporter of January 4th of that year described what was revealed in Dr Ricketts' letter:

> The writer stated that he visited a man named Gallaker, of 19, Appleton-street, Peasley Cross, who was suffering from spasmodic pains. The man and his wife were without food, she said, and without the means for procuring any. He gave an order for the relieving officer. The relieving officer said he

would see the doctor about it first; but he had not seen him nor communicated with him. On the following day (Friday) the poor woman stated she called on Mr. Robinson again and asked him if he had seen the doctor, and he replied that he had not, and did not intend to relieve her.

On the Saturday he [the doctor] found the man sinking rapidly for want of food. He then gave the woman an order marked "urgent," and also sent a verbal message that unless relief was administered at once it would be too late, and an inquest would be the result. The woman returned shortly afterwards in great distress saying Mr. Robinson said he would give her no relief – but he would come to the inquest. It would be seen from the order that the demand made on the rates to keep life in the man was most meagre – for bread, butter, tea, and sugar. Seeing there was no other way of relieving these people he gave them money to buy food, a bottle of brandy, and some soup. On the Monday he called upon the overseer, Mr. Boyle, who kindly and promptly visited and gave relief, pending the decision of the Guardians.

The kindly Dr Ricketts concluded his long letter by saying how reluctant he had been to bring his complaint against Robinson. But he felt that if he did not do so he would have been failing in his duty to the poor – and from what he had heard of the relieving officer's behaviour, this case was not the only one of its kind.

In response Robinson stated that much of the doctor's report was "founded on fiction" and he denied receiving his orders requesting relief for the Gallakers. Guardian John Fidler wanted the claims investigated calling Robinson's behaviour a "gross neglect of duty" – but he received very little support from the other Guardians and so the matter was dropped. However, at the board meeting of the Prescot Guardians a week later, a letter was read out from John Fidler that suggested that Robinson had not been telling the truth.

Dr Ricketts had now informed Mr Fidler that Mrs Gillaghan *(as the Gallakers name was now being spelt)* had definitely given Mr Robinson the second order for relief. And the woman had also confirmed the Relieving Officer's comment about attending her husband's inquest. Mrs Gillaghan was prepared to swear that had been the case and Fidler said he was considering proposing a vote of "want of confidence" in the man at the Guardians' next meeting.

Then on March 1st 1879 the Prescot Reporter described another serious allegation that had been made against William Robinson. A 3-year-old child called Catherine Sherdine of Liverpool Road in St Helens had been gravely ill and was badly in need of medical assistance. After the child had suffered a very bad night, her mother Mary had gone to Dr Patrick Donnellan's surgery in Westfield Street at 6am to request his help. But he had refused to attend the little girl unless he received three shillings as an advance payment of his fee. As many doctors had difficulty in getting paid for their services, such demands were not uncommon.

Mrs Sherdine had no money and so she went to William Robinson's home to request a 19th century version of a sick note. These were not written by doctors but instead given to them as a guarantee that the Prescot Union would pay for a patient's treatment. However, Mrs Sherdine stated that the relieving officer had behaved in a very off-hand manner and had sent her away without a note – even claiming that he had shut the door in her face. Within an hour her little girl was dead and an angry Mrs Sherdine wanted justice.

Of course, medical intervention at such a late stage was unlikely to have saved the life of little Catherine, whose actual illness was never known. But her parents were denied the consolation of knowing that everything possible had been done for their child. Mary Sherdine had a witness who had accompanied her on her abortive 7:20 am trip to Robinson's house and who backed up her statement. But the receiving officer had his own version of events, which was supported by his wife – although as the Coroner at the end of the second inquest hearing stated, the couple's account had not fundamentally "shaken" the bereaved mother's claims.

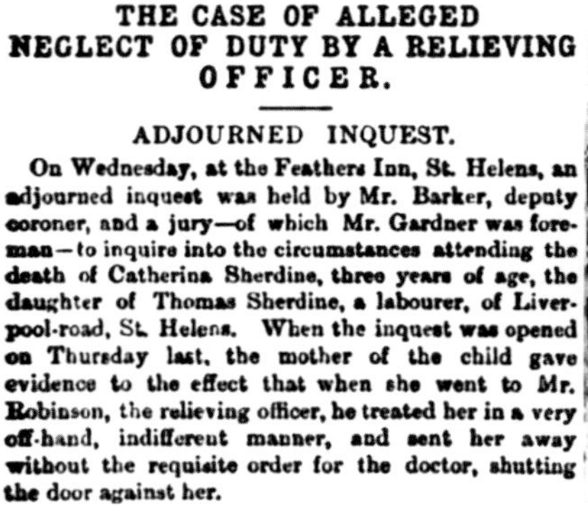
THE CASE OF ALLEGED NEGLECT OF DUTY BY A RELIEVING OFFICER.

ADJOURNED INQUEST.

On Wednesday, at the Feathers Inn, St. Helens, an adjourned inquest was held by Mr. Barker, deputy coroner, and a jury—of which Mr. Gardner was foreman—to inquire into the circumstances attending the death of Catherina Sherdine, three years of age, the daughter of Thomas Sherdine, a labourer, of Liverpool-road, St. Helens. When the inquest was opened on Thursday last, the mother of the child gave evidence to the effect that when she went to Mr. Robinson, the relieving officer, he treated her in a very off-hand, indifferent manner, and sent her away without the requisite order for the doctor, shutting the door against her.

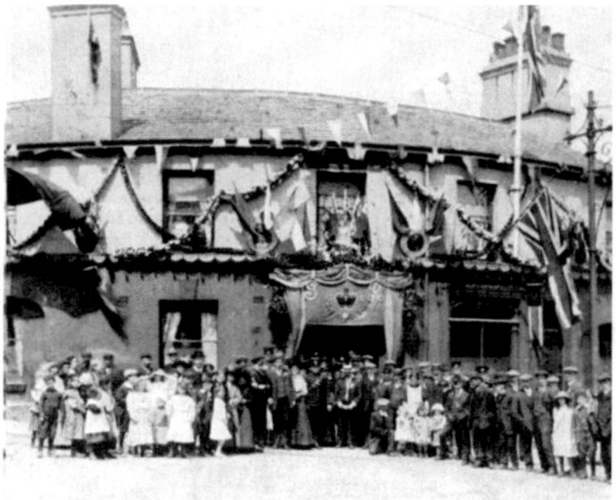

Prescot Reporter March 1st 1879 and the Feathers Inn

The inquest hearings were held at the Feathers Inn – which used to be at the bottom of Westfield Street in St Helens – and Mary Sherdine told the Coroner what occurred at Robinson's home:

> "I told the officer [William Robinson] I wanted a note for the doctor, but he banged the door, and said, "I have no paper here, so go on." I said "I'll see your betters about this." He said I was to call again at nine o'clock, and I told him the child was so bad it would never live till then."

During the inquest hearing Robinson denied having spoken to Mrs Sherdine at his house and he chose to question the bereaved mother himself. The Relieving Officer asked her many trivial questions as he attempted to catch her out. But Mrs Sherdine was reported as having given a good account of herself, explaining how she had been "that stubborn" about obtaining a sick note for her dying child. This is some of the reported dialogue:

Robinson: "After you had been at my house at 7-20 when did you next see me?"

Mrs Sherdine: "You came to Mrs. Cliff's house, where I live, about eight o'clock. You came in whistling, and said, "Where's the sick child?” and I said “It's no use coming now, it's dead”. I was going to say something to you, but you said “Talk to the officer.” The police-sergeant was writing down what I was telling him when you came in. The child died a few minutes before eight."

Robinson: "Did I not ask you to speak the truth, when you were saying something?"

Mrs Sherdine: "No, you said “Talk to the officer and don't speak to me.” You said nothing, but whistled and laughed and walked out."

Robinson then attempted to prove that Mrs Sherdine's circumstances had not qualified as a pauper case. He claimed that shortly before their child became ill, the woman's husband had been working at Liverpool docks and had given his wife thirty shillings wages. But Mrs Sherdine insisted that her husband Thomas’s employment on the docks had been some time since and she had then only received eight shillings, which she had immediately given to her landlady as back rent. The Coroner then confirmed that no work had recently been undertaken at the docks, seemingly because of severe weather.

After thirty minutes of private discussion, the inquest jury returned a verdict that the child's death had been from natural causes and they exonerated the Relieving Officer from blame. What their rationale had been for coming to that conclusion was not stated – but it may have been that Robinson's actions or inactions were unlikely to have made any difference to the child's survival.

As well as doling out small amounts of money to the destitute, Robinson had also been expected to collect poor rate payments from ratepayers and complaints had been received that he was not giving receipts. Within a few weeks of the inquest hearing, the Prescot Guardians were informed that Robinson had gone missing and so they suspended him from his position as Relieving Officer while enquiries took place. Then at their meeting held on April 24th 1879, this letter from William Robinson was read out:

"I am very sorry to have to say that I cannot possibly produce my cash balance, and therefore I beg most respectfully to tender my resignation, thanking you for past favours and kindnesses, and hoping that you will give me a testimonial, and thus enable me to support my family respectably. I should not forget to mention that I am very much indebted to Dr. Ricketts and Old Barney for their scurrilous treatment towards me, and I can assure them that I shall never take any physic from the former, or notice of the latter."

should be inquired into, and he would report at the next meeting.

MR. ROBINSON, THE RELIEVING OFFICER, MISSING.

The Clerk informed the board that on Tuesday he received information from Mr. Harrison, a Guardian, that Mr. Robinson, the relieving officer, had not been attending to his duties since Saturday. He (the Clerk) felt it incumbent upon him to proceed to St. Helens, and make arrangements for the relief of the poor, and he at once instructed Mr. Houghton's son to proceed with Robinson's work, and take care that none of the poor people were neglected. He now wished the Guardians to suspend Mr. Robinson, as he had received no information regarding him except the following from Mr. T. Houghton :—"I paid over £4 for Eccleston poor in Mr. Robinson's account, and I fear that the Rainford poor are not paid. I am sending

Prescot Reporter March 29th 1879

The Prescot Guardians were informed that Robinson owed them just under £50 – the equivalent of around a year's salary for many labourers. But despite his fraud the man cheekily wanted a testimonial – what we would call a reference – and he criticised Dr Ricketts and someone called Old Barney for reporting his failures.

The Guardians owed Robinson £10 for fees previously earned and that sum would now be deducted from his £50 debt, with the balance covered by insurance. However, it was also revealed at the meeting that on the previous day Robinson had buried an "idiot son" – as he was described – and another of his sons had TB and was not expected to live. It was possible the insurance society in making good the missing £40 would apply for a warrant to seize Robinson's possessions and some sympathy was expressed for his situation, even from his critics like John Fidler who said:

> "However blameable Robinson might be in the discharge of his public duties, these circumstances require sympathy. I should he very sorry if the society did take his few goods for so small an amount, and thus probably send him to the workhouse."

Some might say if that had occurred, it would have been a case of his chickens coming home to roost. But Robinson was not alone as a Relieving Officer in treating the poor severely – and, at times, seemingly, with contempt. At the same meeting of the Guardians a 20-page foolscap letter from Dr James Ricketts was read out criticising the behaviour of other officers. And Thomas Houghton – whose relieving office was in Tontine Street in St Helens – was very much in his sights. This is what the Prescot Reporter wrote:

> Dr Ricketts' letter stated that the conduct of the relieving officer in the Sutton district, in the administration of outdoor relief, was characterised by an amount of harshness and want of consideration for the poor at variance with the spirit of the poor law system, and in many important matters it was in direct opposition to the orders of the board. ...The poor people were prepared to prove their case, but they had no opportunity. Cases such as those to which he referred were of almost daily occurrence.

An elderly couple called Parr were quoted as an example. The doctor said the husband had been in a very critical condition and he had prescribed for him the drinking of beef tea. Although the relieving officer had allowed it, the tea needed to be fetched from a hotel in St Helens and the person that delivered it demanded 4d for making the 2-mile trip.

The impoverished couple could not possibly find fourpence and a clergyman had to come to their rescue and bring them the tea, or the "man must have died", as the medic put it. That was probably unlikely but doctors often then prescribed beef tea as somewhat of a panacea for illness.

Alana Farrell, UK Medical Heritage Library project coordinator, explains why on the Royal College of Physicians website:

> It [beef tea] was a type of broth – made with beef and water – given to patients to drink if they were suffering from digestive problems, fever or weakness. People believed that the tea was nutritious and easy on the stomach, which would help patients to return to their former fortitude.

The point, of course, was not the dubious efficacy of the beef tea on critically ill persons but that the relieving officer had not arranged for its free delivery after it had been prescribed. The doctor was also critical of officers that did not regularly visit the poor who were in receipt of medical relief. That was something they were obliged to do and Dr Ricketts said he knew of cases in which a relieving officer had not made a home visit for six months.

The doctor also claimed that persons considered troublesome were despatched to the workhouse without his authority in order to get them off the relieving officer's books. The Reporter wrote:

> Having given an instance of a sick woman who had been ordered into the workhouse, although, as a matter of fact, she was not fit to be carried there, the letter went on to say that the poor applying for relief were refused attention at the relieving officer's house, and told they could only be attended to at his office at certain hours, and the relieving officer would not condescend to listen to complaints in the streets.

The Guardians subsequently held an inquiry into Dr Ricketts' claims against Thomas Houghton, with the case of Mary Flaherty from Parr causing particular concern. The woman's husband and their young children had been sick – seemingly all suffering from scarlet fever – and 40-year-old Mary had been heavily pregnant. In order to satisfy the relieving officer, Mary had on one occasion been forced to walk back and forth from Houghton's office in Tontine Street to the coal mine where her husband worked.

In total the woman had walked ten miles on that day to try and get some relief for her family. Her husband only earned 9 shillings a week as a labourer and as soon as he became sick, the family's income completely dried up. They were in a parlous state without funds to buy food or pay for medical help. However, the kind-hearted Dr Ricketts again came to the rescue and to prevent the family's starvation gave Mrs Flaherty some small sums of money out of his own pocket.

Thomas Houghton denied all the accusations that were made against him, although he acknowledged he had not been accepting applications for pauper relief at his own home. At the conclusion of the hearing, the Guardians discussed his case and mixed views were expressed, with some lending the man a measure of support.

However, John Fidler said his experience had taught him that relieving officers became "used to human suffering" and added that it had been with "deep feelings of pain" that he had listened to the proceedings. He said he had known Houghton for some years and had been one of his strongest supporters when he had applied for his job and thought he could be relied upon to act "with feelings of charitableness towards the pauper". And a Guardian called Edwin Birch called for Houghton's suspension, saying:

> "I have watched this inquiry and I have come to the conclusion that he is not fit for the office of relieving officer. He is not actuated by a sufficient amount of kindness, and having acted as he has done in the cases which have come

before us, we should be wanting in our duty if we did not do our utmost to remove him from his post. I therefore move that he be suspended."

And William Tyrer, a Prescot solicitor, thought Houghton "stood a good deal too much on his dignity and forgot that he was the servant of the guardians, and the servant of the public." But in the end the Guardians decided to give Thomas Houghton only a ticking off for refusing to accept applications for relief at his own home. A letter was also sent to the relieving officer that advised him to exercise a more "kindly consideration in dealing with the unfortunate creatures who are required to seek help, through you".

The Prescot Reporter in an editorial summarised the findings of the inquiry as "Not proven but be more careful", after Houghton had denied the claims against him and blamed overwork. The paper added as an understatement: "It would appear that the officer's mode of dealing with the poor was not open to the charge of being excessively sympathetic and kindhearted".

But like William Robinson, his fellow relieving officer, Thomas Houghton did not last long in his job. Three months after his ticking off for the way he had been dealing with the "unfortunate creatures" that had badly needed his help, the Prescot Guardians suspended Houghton. That was after some smart detective work by their Clerk had revealed that the man had been on the fiddle.

In his other role as a collector of Poor Law payments from ratepayers, Houghton had been entitled to claim his expenses. But he had been deducting his costs from the cash that he had been receiving and then claimed the same amounts again off the Guardians. Although anyone who entered Whiston Workhouse claiming to be a pauper without declaring the few coppers in their pockets would likely be prosecuted and possibly imprisoned, neither Houghton nor Robinson appear to have faced justice.

Those New Fangled Ideas!

"The introduction of the bicycle as a mode of locomotion was looked upon for a time, as are most innovations, with disfavour by many people."

Innovation today tends to be accepted rapidly. But in the past new ideas could take a long time to be implemented, with many people suspicious of them and even abusive of their early adopters. Many advances have only been fully recognised in hindsight with newspaper accounts at the time of their introduction being minimal. This chapter is devoted to examples of how St Helens' newspapers reported on what proved to be important technological and social changes in the town and how local people embraced them. These include the motor car, the aeroplane, telephone, traffic lights, hearing aids, blood donors and beginning with the bike.

a) THE BICYCLE

On April 3rd 1869 the St Helens Newspaper published this report announcing how "curious vehicles" were set to come to the town:

> We understand that a bicycle will soon be produced in St. Helens, on a new principle, that can be run at the rate of thirty miles an hour. The owner will be willing to back it against any other in England, for £100, in a trial of speed. We may soon expect to see these curious vehicles running through our own streets as freely as they do in Liverpool.

The brief piece was a reference to John Christian whose main business was as a coachbuilder in Ormskirk Street and who traded as the St Helens Carriage Works. Christian made bikes to order to "suit any height of rider" but they were not cheap, costing at least £8 10 shillings to purchase.

In 1869 most workers earned around 20 to 25 shillings a week and so bicycles were initially the playthings of the middle and upper classes. Custom-made bikes were rather like a made-to-measure suit. They were a better fit with the correct inside-leg measurements important for both. With the bicycle a better fit was important for comfort, stability and greater speed and increased in importance once the "penny farthing" bikes with their high front wheels became popular.

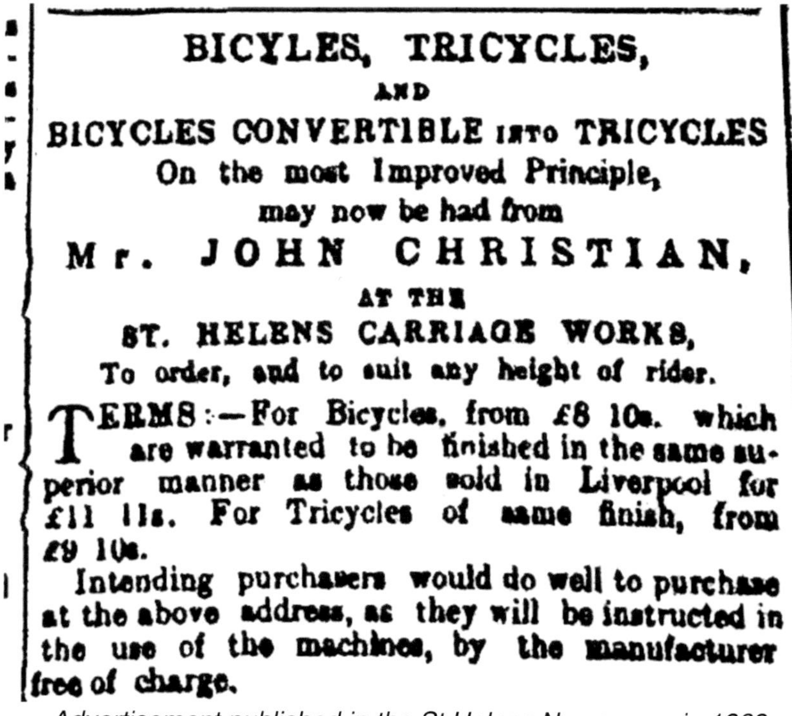
BICYLES, TRICYCLES,
AND
BICYCLES CONVERTIBLE INTO TRICYCLES
On the most Improved Principle,
may now be had from
Mr. JOHN CHRISTIAN,
AT THE
ST. HELENS CARRIAGE WORKS,
To order, and to suit any height of rider.

TERMS:—For Bicycles, from £8 10s. which are warranted to be finished in the same superior manner as those sold in Liverpool for £11 11s. For Tricycles of same finish, from £9 10s.

Intending purchasers would do well to purchase at the above address, as they will be instructed in the use of the machines, by the manufacturer free of charge.

Advertisement published in the St Helens Newspaper in 1869

Pedal bicycles had only been developed in the early 1860s and during the later years of the decade, the French Velocipede *(or "boneshaker")* briefly became fashionable with some well-off folk. A cyclist writing to the Liverpool Mercury in January 1869 was far from convinced of the machine's utility and safety:

> Setting aside the great unsteadiness of the bicycle on a straight road or up hill, and its utter uselessness after rain, when the rider has the full benefit of the splashes from both wheels, the exertion, even after he has thoroughly learned to balance himself (no small task), is such an effort upon both mind and body that all benefit attaching to a ride into the country would be quite lost, and pleasure would be made a toil. Another great inconvenience in this machine is the requirement of a constant speed to preserve the balance. In fact, these inconveniences and others are now being found out in France, where the number of accidents serve to render it apparent that the bicycle is only fit for racing on level ground.

John Christian was advising prospective cyclists to buy their bike from him so they could be taught how to master it. This would have been essential in reducing the number of bruises that riders received through falling off the rickety machines! In April 1869 Christian gave a demonstration of his new bicycle at the Volunteer Hall in Mill Street in St Helens where the local volunteer regiment were based. In a short article entitled *"The Bicycle In St. Helens"*, the St Helens Newspaper of April 24th 1869 wrote:

> On Thursday evening a number of gentlemen, including several of the officers of the 47th L.R. V., assembled in the Volunteer Hall, to witness a trial of the bicycle belonging to Mr. John Christian, who attended and worked the machine with considerable skill. Many of the gentlemen present tried to follow his example, but invariably came to grief, to the amusement of the others. It is in contemplation to start an association, with Mr. Christian as instructor, and we may expect soon to see the bicycle mania in full swing here.

When in 1870 the inaugural St Helens athletics meeting took place on the cricket club's ground in Dentons Green, a bicycle race was included. However, cycle races at athletics festivals were for some time treated as comic novelties – like the sack or egg and spoon races – and occupied a very small part of the programme.

According to the 1871 census John Christian employed five men and seven boys at his carriage works at 25 Ormskirk Street. However, he appears to have soon dropped his manufacture of bicycles, presumably through poor demand and returned to focus on carriage making. Later in 1871 he was advertising his "St Helens Cart" that could accommodate four persons.

The founding of the St Helens Bicycle Club in 1876 provided an impetus to cycling in the town – although only having 9 members at first suggests interest was still low. However, within ten or so years its membership had risen to eighty and in 1878 the Liverpool Mercury described how racing events were a staple of the club:

> The bi-annual race for the championship of this club, including the handsome silver cup given by the mayor (Mr. Joseph Cook), came off on Saturday afternoon, the course being from Sankey Bridges to the Bird-i'-th'-hand, St. Helens, about eleven miles. The cup has to be won three times, when it becomes the property of the winner. In all 15 started. The winning time was 46 min. 50 sec.

By the late 1870s the construction of cycles had improved and in an article called *"The History of the Bicycle"*, the Northwich Guardian in 1878 wrote:

> The earliest bicycles, it is true, were clumsy machines of wood, the hind wheel of which was almost the size of the front. Improvement, however, has rapidly succeeded upon improvement, until in the modern racing bicycle we have almost reached perfection. The driving wheel has grown larger and larger, and the running wheel smaller and smaller. Wooden spokes have been abandoned, noiseless india rubber tires adopted, and a Coventry bicycle of the

best kind is now a really marvellous piece of mechanism, combining with a positive minimum of weight a maximum of strength and durability.

BICYCLE SUITS. BICYCLE SUITS.

STURGIESS' 30s. BICYCLE SUITS.

STURGIESS' 30s. BICYCLE SUITS.

FOR STYLE, COMFORT, AND DURABILITY, GO TO

STURGIESS, 54, BRIDGE STREET.

Advert in the St Helens Newspaper of August 19th 1879

The so-called "penny farthings" with high front wheels were fast machines but they were not particularly safe, with riders positioned high up and travelling at great speed on dodgy road surfaces.

St Helens Cycling Club pictured in 1889 when they numbered 80 members

The photograph on page 17 shows members of St Helens Cyclists Club at Hoo Green, near Warrington. It was the club's opening run of the 1889 season and the event led to this report being published in the St Helens Reporter on April 27th of that year:

> The introduction of the bicycle as a mode of locomotion was looked upon for a time, as are most innovations, with disfavour by many people, but step by step the art of cycling gained in public favour, and it is pleasing to note that the cyclist can now undertake his peregrinations [journeys] without "provoking the envious gibes of each pedestrian churl" [receiving insulting remarks from rude folk].
>
> The truth of this was fully manifested on Good Friday, when the members of the St. Helens Cyclists' Club kept up their time-honoured custom of formally opening the season upon that day. The cyclists wended their way down Duke-street and Boundary-road, and proceeded via Rainhill and Bold to Warrington, on nearing which place their arrival was announced by many blasts from the bugles, and as a proof of the truth of the proverb that "Music hath charms," it may be mentioned that a large number of persons turned out to witness the arrival of the cyclists.

In 1939 the Reporter reproduced the Hoo Green photo and under the headline *"Knights Of The Road 50 Years Ago"* wrote:

> This picture was taken fifty years ago. That was in the days before lightweight racing bicycles, pneumatic tyres, electric dynamo lighting, and long, long before the era of sports girls in shorts and shirts. In fact, it is very doubtful whether a modern cycle "miss" could have ridden some of the machines in this picture, for they had solid rubber tyres and weighed up to and above forty pounds each.

By 1904 the club had 161 members, some probably riding the Duke cycles that were sold by Topping Brothers of Duke Street. According to John Seed of Henderson Drive in Rainford, The Duke – and its female version known as The Duchess – were actually made by Toppings. Mr Seed had this note published in the St Helens Reporter on January 4th 1985:

The Duke as depicted in a 1905 advert

> Does anyone remember the Duke and Duchess of St. Helens? If you do you are getting on a bit, for these were cycles made by Toppings of Duke Street, before the First World War and for a time afterwards. Toppings – three brothers, and a sister – were in business as cycle dealers at the corner of Rigby Street and Duke Street, but later moved across the street to Duke Street.

The St Helens Newspaper July 23rd 1907

During the early years of the 20th century the bicycle in St Helens became more affordable for the working class who increasingly used bikes to get to work. The St Helens Cycling Club had been created when better-off folk only rode bicycles for leisure and with the growth of the motorbike and motorcar organised cycle rides lost much of their appeal. In 1920 the club was dissolved through lack of support and at that time it was said to have been one of the oldest surviving clubs in the country.

SOME CYCLING STORIES IN BRIEF:

~ One can understand nervous horses being frightened by the tall penny farthing bikes that whizzed past them and on May 18th 1876 the Liverpool Daily Post described such an incident:

> Mr. Stones, of Liverpool, who had been on a visit to Prescot for the purpose of strewing a few flowers on the grave of his wife, recently buried in the parish churchyard, was returning home on horseback the other evening, when he was met by two young men on bicycles, at which the horse took fright, and threw its rider. He was severely injured on the head, and rendered unconscious for some time.

~ In the early days of cycling the working class had no chance of buying a bike that might have cost eight weeks' wages – but that did not stop them from being curious about the machines. Under the headline *"Unprovoked and Dastardly Attack on Bicyclists"*, the Wigan Observer on April 12th 1878 wrote:

> Several members of the St. Helens Bicycle Club had a run to Wigan on Saturday week, and on their return made a halt at Billinge. Whilst there several labouring men who, after their work had been accomplished, meddled with the bicycles, and tried to mount them. On being requested to desist, they commenced a perfect onslaught on those members present, and in the general melee which ensued, the young gentlemen got severely handled. Before assistance could be obtained the fellows endeavoured to make good their escape, but their names and places of abode having been

ascertained and they have been summoned to answer for their alleged wrong-doings.

~ On October 14th 1892 when the "mania" for cycling was approaching its height, the Liverpool Mercury published this article:

> A cyclists' lantern parade took place at St. Helens last night in aid of the funds of the Providence Free Hospital. About 150 members of the various cycling clubs of St. Helens and district gathered in front of the Town Hall, and after being marshalled into processional order paraded the principal thoroughfares, which were crowded with sightseers. The riders were attired in character costumes, and from their machines were suspended many-coloured Chinese and other lanterns. As a spectacular display the gathering was a great success. Collections were taken from the bystanders as the novel procession moved along.

Advert for William Corbett in the St Helens Reporter of 1898

~ A court case in Prescot Petty Sessions on August 17th 1897 became a national news story because of the unusual means in which a constable had halted a cyclist. Liverpool bootmaker Arthur Evans had been riding past the Royal Hotel in Derby Street in Prescot at what the police said was a "tremendous pace" and they claimed that he had failed to stop when ordered. PC Johnston had a stick in his hand and he used it to grab Mr Evans' arm and as a result both he and his machine were brought crashing to the ground. The rider was injured and spent two weeks off work. Despite witnesses claiming that Evans had been travelling at less than 10 mph, five constables claimed it was more like 20 mph. Mr Evans was fined but appealed against his conviction, as reported by the Edinburgh Evening News on November 3rd 1897:

> At Liverpool County Sessions to-day, an appeal by Arthur Evans against a conviction by the Prescot justices for furiously riding on a bicycle was heard. This was a case where the cyclist was hooked off his machine by a constable and seriously injured. The public subscribed liberally towards the expense of the appeal. The police evidence was that Evans was riding down Prescot Hill at twenty miles an hour. Independent witnesses swore that the pace was ten miles. The bench quashed the conviction, amid applause from a crowded court.

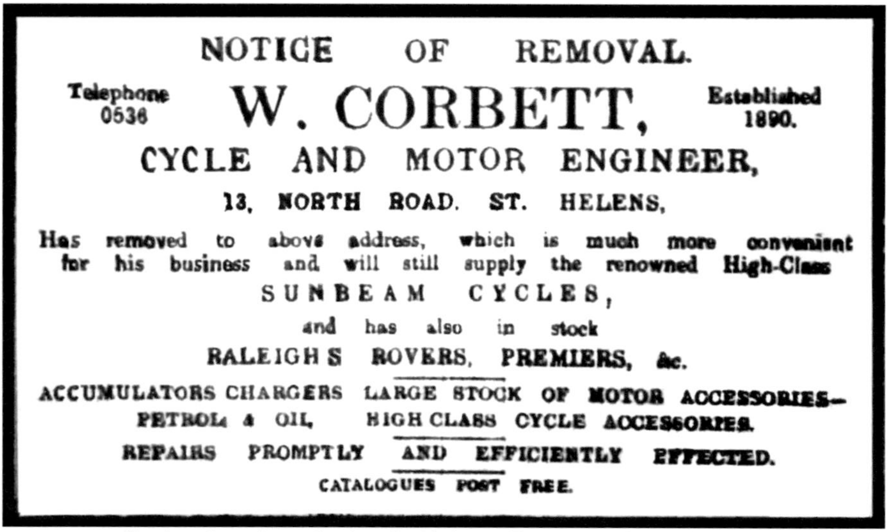

Corbett's advert in the St Helens Reporter July 4th 1905

~ This article concerning cyclists riding their machines too fast was published in the St Helens Newspaper on August 8th 1919:

> Residents in Duke-street are asking if that thoroughfare is being converted into a cycling track. Those who keep an observation upon the street note that despite the fact that there are many cross streets, many cyclists race down the street as if they were on a track. This is particularly noticeable about half-past five, when many young men are on their way home from work, and they race away at top speed, a positive danger to themselves, and to people who desire to cross the street. When a serious accident occurs some notice will be taken of the matter.

b) THE MOTOR CAR

I wonder if a St Helens newspaper could have been the first to use the term "motorist"? That is probably doubtful but on October 31st 1896 the St Helens Examiner commented on some new measures that would soon affect such drivers:

> The regulations for motor cars issued by the Local Government Board are regarded as fairly satisfactory by the motorists, if I may coin a new word.

The writer did, however, comment that the need for the name and address of car owners to be displayed on their vehicle under the new system was unnecessary, adding: "...but, in the judgment of the shrewd, this naming will gradually lead to registration". And so it did seven years later, when all cars had to bear number plates.

The regulations were introduced on November 14th 1896, which the Liverpool Daily Post dubbed "Motor Car Day". What were officially known as "light locomotives" no longer needed a man with a red flag to walk in front of them. A maximum speed was also set at twelve miles an hour, which was then considered quite fast.

The Daily Post also called motor cars "self-propelled traffic" as they described how the great day of motor liberation had arrived. But the paper pointed out that although there was a Liverpool branch of the Motor Car Association, there was a scarcity of cars in the city. And if there were few vehicles in Liverpool, then St Helens would have fared far worse.

On December 24th 1896 a feature writer in the St Helens Examiner wrote:

> As yet motor cars are objects of curiosity, serving little purpose except as something to talk about. Only very few have seen a mechanically propelled vehicle, but there has, however, been time enough for accidents. The other day one of these contrivances when speeding along a leading thoroughfare in London, suddenly caught fire, and the day before a similar accident occurred in Paris, the flames from the oil tank bursting out to a great height. The unfortunate individual in charge of the London motor car was of course greatly chaffed by the passing omnibus and cab drivers, and it was "the jokes finally put out the fire."
>
> But what many people are seriously asking is, what is going to happen when motor cars come into general use, and the roads are crowded with them? So long as they only burn it does not matter much to passers-by, especially in the cold weather, it is their liability to blow up that is the more terrifying, and unless there is to be some official check to carelessness and recklessness, a considerable number of us stand an excellent chance of fervently wishing the motor car had waited another century or so before careering wildly about the streets.

On May 24th 1898 a short series of trials of motor vehicles for heavy traffic began in SW Lancashire. These were essentially lorries that were being tested as to their usefulness in transporting goods from Liverpool docks. The routes out of the city varied on different days and although the procession of vehicles did not appear to have travelled through the town of St Helens, it certainly passed through Rainford, Prescot and Rainhill. The St Helens Reporter had a journalist on board during one of the trips and on May 27th 1898 the paper published this account of his journey:

> A series of interesting trials of motor vehicles for heavy traffic were commenced on Tuesday at Liverpool, under the auspices of the Self propelled Traffic Association. The chief object of these trials was to arrive at a type of heavy motor waggon suitable for trade requirements in Liverpool and neighbourhood, which should be capable of economically taking the place of horse haulage, and of competing with the existing railway rates in the transport of heavy loads of goods over a considerable distance. A great deal of interest was centred in the competition which occurred on Tuesday between four heavy motor freight cars, over a distance of 30 miles, and besides a number of prominent citizens who accompanied the cars on vehicles propelled by the force of petroleum, there was present the Lord Mayor of Liverpool.
>
> A start was made at the Prince's Dock depot in the early morning, and following the actual competing vehicles there were half a dozen or more light self-propelled cars. Seated amongst some six or more passengers on board one of the light vehicles, our representative was whirled along with ever increasing speed towards the old town of Ormskirk. ...The country surrounding the old-fashioned "gingerbread" town looked at its best. The natives turned out in their full strength to view the novel procession, and as it whirled past the highway and entered the pretty country road to Rainford, the keen interest of the villagers found expression in hearty cheering. At Rainford a halt was made, and the several passengers on board the cars assuaged their hunger with a homely but substantial meal. At this place an opportunity was afforded of inspecting the four competing vehicles,

which up to this point had worked with perfect success. A smart run took place after leaving Rainford, and at a swinging pace the pleasant villages of Mossborough and Knowsley were traversed, and after leaving Old Swan the cars, without relaxing speed, quickly sped away over the granite setts and entered the city.

Chauffeur George Berryman on the Rainford Hall estate at Crank

Then in an editorial on November 24th 1899, the St Helens Examiner wrote:

> What is to be the future relationship of the cycling and motor-car trades? For the present, it is true that cycle makers do not need to fear competition with the rival industry. Cycles are cheap, while motors are absurdly dear, and can only be purchased for pleasurable purposes by the moneyed classes. Two or three years hence, however, a great reduction in price is bound to come, and the cycle trade will probably feel the effect of it in two ways. Shareholders will be anxious to put their money into motor-

car companies, and large numbers of people, having had time to be tired of cycling, will take up the new amusement with avidity. At first there will be not a little amusement and personal danger to be derived from motor-car driving. To master the art is as difficult and dangerous for the novice and his beholders as was the art of cycling. The public will have to be protected by stringent police regulations.

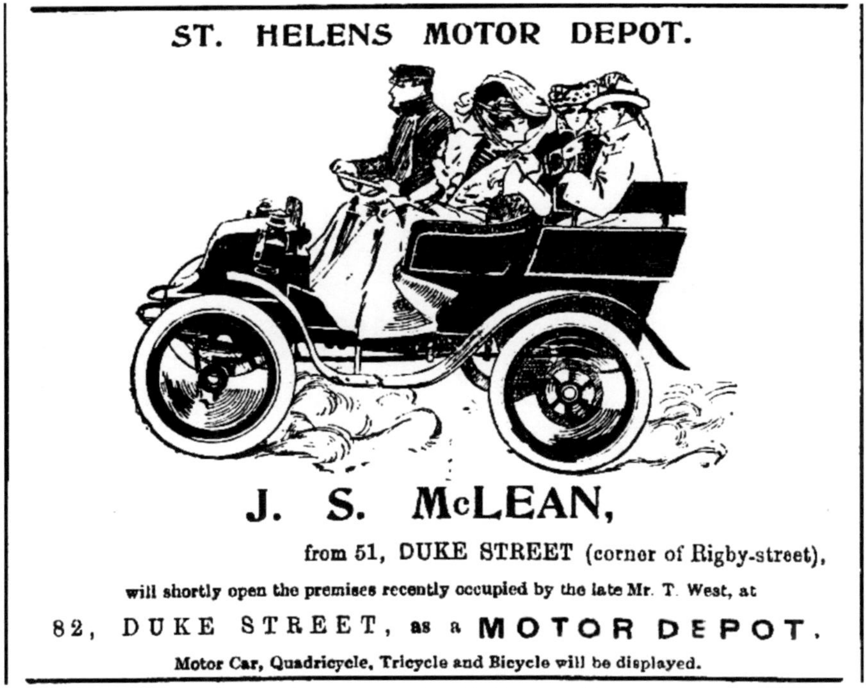

Advert for John McLean from the St Helens Newspaper in 1902

According to an article in the St Helens Reporter of April 4th 1930, Charles McLean and his brother John had introduced the motor car to St Helens, while the St Helens Newspaper's obituary described Charles as having been "a prominent person in the cycle and motor

Part of the Central Motor Co's ad in the St Helens Reporter of July 1925

business, in which he was one of St. Helens pioneers". The brothers initially owned a cycle shop in Duke Street and selling cars became a natural extension of their business. C. A. McLean was the first firm to become Ford dealers in St Helens and they had a garage built in Rigby Street to service vehicles. By 1925 Charles McLean was advertising as the Central Motor Company of Corporation Street.

Just whether the McLean brothers were the first to own a car in St Helens, I cannot be sure. The St Helens Reporter on March 11th 1932 thought motor car dealer William Corbett deserved credit as the pioneer who had introduced “the then wonderful invention” to the town. Mr Corbett was mentioned earlier in my cycling section and had bought a Sunbeam Mabley car c.1900 for his personal use and later built his own model for sale called "The North Road".

And to confuse matters even further, the St Helens Reporter of October 14th 1927 considered builder Fred Brown to be "about the first motorist" in St Helens. "Motorist" was the operative term as Fred initially drove a motorcycle as opposed to a car but he did own the registration number DJ 1.

However, that only meant that Fred was the first person in St Helens to register his vehicle when the Motor Car Act came into operation on January 1st 1904. That said the well-known builder certainly did much motoring. When Fred appeared in court on October 10th 1927 after being prosecuted for dangerous driving, it was claimed that he had over a quarter of a million miles under his belt. This is how the Reporter described the case:

> The famous owner of "D.J.1" – Mr. Fred Brown – appeared at the Police Court on Monday on a summons for driving to the public danger, though he was not then driving his famous motor-cycle, but its successor a Wolseley two-seater. About the first motorist in St. Helens, Mr. Brown has during the past 25 years covered nearly 300,000 miles on the road without an accident.

"D J 1 'S" RECORD UNSMIRCHED

QUARTER OF A MILLION MILES IN 25 YEARS

NO CASE AGAINST MR. FRED BROWN

The famous owner of "D.J.1"—Mr. Fred Brown appeared at the Police Court on Monday on a summons for driving to the on the footrest. Mr. Davies expressed surprise that he could so ride at 1 m.p.h. and with a pillion passenger.

St Helens Reporter October 14th 1927

Joseph Ellison – the owner of a motorbike involved in a smash with Fred's car at the junction of Westfield Street and Eccleston Street – had brought the prosecution. But Ellison's claim his bike had only been travelling at 1 mph when the collision occurred was ridiculed in court and Fred was subsequently cleared of the charge.

I shall conclude this section with a couple of reflections on the early years of motoring. The first comes from William Corbett:

> "It was no rare occurrence to be stopped twenty times on a long journey. As soon as the rider of a horse heard the sound of a car he would halt and lift up his hand as a signal for me to stop. Of course, I did so, but it often occurred to me that it was the man and not the horse who was nervous."

And the memories of Tom Reynolds, the St Helens Newspaper's longstanding editor writing after retiring in 1937:

> "How time flies! Thirty years ago, in 1907, St. Helens streets were quiet and peaceful. The taxi fleets of to-day had still to be launched. Old Fraser's nag, and his fourwheel cab, still camped in St. Helens Station. You could walk in the roads if you wanted to. Motor cars were so few and far between they were looked upon as freaks that would never come to anything. They had to be towed home too often by the village nag, or repaired en route by the village blacksmith."

Dr Henry Baker Bates pictured outside Sutton Hall c.1908

c) THE TELEPHONE

The suggestion that speech could be transmitted over long distances must have sounded preposterous to many in the 1870s. On April 21st 1877 the newspaper known as the Liverpool Mail wondered whether what appeared to be "one of the most wonderful discoveries in practical science" was for real:

> For we are told that by this same "telephone" it is possible, not only for one man to carry on a conversation with another at a distance of two or three hundred miles, but that the speeches made in a room may be heard distinctly by an audience assembled in a hall in a remote town, that musical performances can be given at one place and be listened to elsewhere, and that almost every day some improvement in the invention is being made which renders it capable of

> greater extension. Is all that we hear about this "telephone" true, or is the whole thing a hoax?

It was not until the founding of the Lancashire and Cheshire Telephonic Exchange Company (L & C Tel Ex Co) in 1881 that the telephone came to St Helens – and then it was in an extremely limited form. In October of that year the L & C Tel Ex Co obtained permission from the Postmaster General to open an exchange in Hardshaw Street in St Helens, as well as operate in thirty-five other towns within Lancashire and Cheshire.

At first the phone was a bit of a novelty. On December 7th 1881 a Swiss bazaar was opened in St Helens Town Hall to raise funds for St Paul's Church. A telephone line was set up to a property in Hardshaw Street *(probably the exchange)* and for a shilling those attending the bazaar could call the house and arrange for a message to be sent to any address within a half-mile radius.

The telephone as depicted by the Illustrated London News of December 15th 1877

Telephone poles began appearing on St Helens streets during 1882 and these were installed and operated by the L & C Tel Ex Co. Of course, telegraph poles and their associated wiring had existed for some time but those were operated by the Post Office and were limited in number. Commenting on the similarity between the two, the St Helens Examiner of July 15th 1882 wrote:

> We have now a new feature in the landscape, to wit, the telephone [poles], in no respect distinguishable from the telegraph, but whether it is an improvement or not is of course a matter of opinion. There can, however, be no doubt but that it will facilitate the business for which it was erected,

and probably the cost of £50 will not be seriously felt by the ratepayers now that every day increases their number.

In a separate article in the same edition the Examiner wrote:

> Those accustomed to walk along the road from Earlestown to Newton, or Crow-lane as it is called, during the last few days, will not have failed to notice a new object – or, rather, objects – placed at intervals along the road. These are posts, on which are placed a telephone wire from Mr. Brierley, [surveyor Newton Commissioners] C.E., Town Hall, to the gas works, near to the glass works. Such a handy means of communication has long been wanted, and it will, no doubt, prove of much use and benefit. The entire distance from the clerk's office to the gas works is a little under a mile.

That was a good example of the main utility of the telephone during the early 1880s – i.e. voice communication over short distances between known parties. In that case it was a council official being able to talk to his gas works and vice versa, greatly increasing the efficiency of his department's daily contacts with the plant.

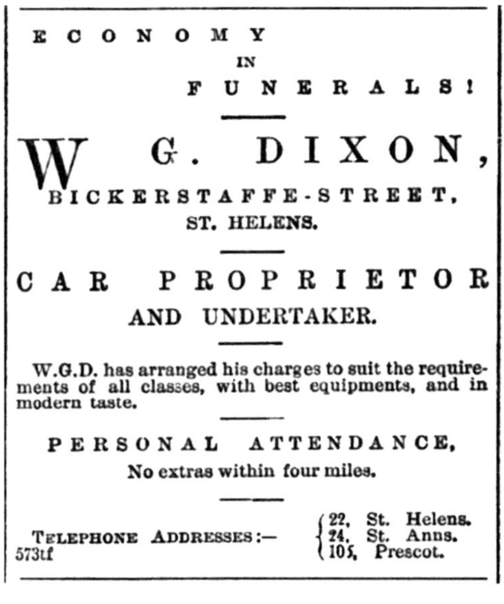

Dixons were early adopters of the telephone – Advert in the Prescot Reporter in 1889

Many head offices of large firms also became connected by telephone to their own works – which might be situated a mile or two away. However, the head office's telephone was probably the only one that was connected to the local exchange and so be able to contact other subscribers.

Before long the L & C Tel Ex Co fell foul of the strictness of St Helens Corporation. In February 1883 the council's Paving and Highway Committee complained to the firm that they were installing telephone poles and cables on the streets of St Helens without permission. The L & C Tel Ex Co responded that they had been allowed to run telephone wires across the streets of Liverpool without needing any council consent and had assumed St Helens would similarly have no objection. After discussions were held an agreement was reached in which the L & C Tel Ex Co would in future apply to the Corporation for permission for each installation.

The mid-1880s saw an expansion of telephone use by organisations. For example, in May 1884 it was decided that Whiston Workhouse would be connected to its relieving office in St Helens where the very poor applied for help. The workhouse had its own horse-driven cab and upon receiving a telephone message could despatch the vehicle to St Helens to collect new inmates. Around the same time St Helens Town Council's Water Committee agreed to replace its telegraph service – that ran from the Town Hall to the water pumping stations – with a telephone facility.

Beecham's Pills advert from 1896

There was an ongoing debate about whether overhead telephone wires should be allowed – but for an odd reason. On July 16th

1884 St Helens Council's Paving and Highway Committee considered an application from the L & C Tel Ex Co to install 26 telephone poles along the road from Broad Oak railway to the boundary stone in Broad Lane. Committee member Dr Jamison objected to the erection of such poles in the town because of the noxious St Helens' atmosphere.

Overhead wires, he claimed, were very liable to corrode and break and a very serious accident could happen at any time. Dr Jamison suggested that in future all wires should be taken underground but Councillor Hanson remarked that if such a course was adopted it would practically put an end to the development of telephonic communication in St Helens because of the huge costs involved.

A couple of years later it was decided that the risk of corrosion to the telephone wiring because of acid in the atmosphere was minimal – a far greater threat was the stormy St Helens weather! On September 6th 1884 two telephone poles in Prescot Road, near the Toll Bar, were blown down by a high wind causing disruption to road traffic and there would be many similar instances in the future.

Although the L & C Tel Ex Co had permission from the Postmaster General to operate three-dozen telephone exchanges in Lancashire and Cheshire, they had one big drawback. They were not permitted to connect to each other. The Post Office had banned phone companies from allowing calls to be made out of each town. In fact the reach of each town's exchange was limited to a maximum of five miles from its centre.

However, this restriction was dropped in the autumn of 1884 and quickly the L & C Tel Ex Co linked up all its exchanges to create a 297-mile network. On October 7th 1884 the Manchester Evening News described how the L & C Tel Ex Co had been conducting tests along its new system:

> Experiments have now been made which have proved that a conversation can be successfully carried on through the

> whole length of these wires, which clearly demonstrates that messages can – and in a very short time, doubtless, will – be transmitted to any town in England. Last evening Mr. R. Heywood Claxton (Liverpool manager), without the slightest difficulty, communicated with the chairman of the company (Mr. Charles Mosley) at Manchester, and also sent and received a number of messages from people in St. Helens, Wigan, and Bolton.

Note how telephone calls were described as "messages", as that was how the invention was then portrayed. It was not seen as a device to enable persons to chat to their family and friends but as a means of communicating a short, verbal business message and then receive an instant reply – a more efficient version of the telegram, in other words.

On December 11th 1884 when the St Helens Literary And Scientific Association met at the Town Hall they were able to celebrate this communication liberation with what the St Helens Examiner called a "novel and exceedingly interesting feature". The Town Hall was connected to St George's Hall in Liverpool where a "large soiree of working-men" was being held. And telephonic communications were also made with the Alexandra Theatre in Liverpool and the Theatre Royal in Manchester with performances being heard with "singular distinctness".

Just how many subscribers there were in St Helens by 1885 I cannot say – but it was far fewer than in Manchester and Liverpool. An article published in the Stalybridge Reporter on March 28th 1885 stated that both cities then had around 1,100 subscribers. But as well as business customers, the L & C Tel Ex Co was encouraging the general public to use the telephone by visiting "call stations" or "offices", as the Stalybridge Reporter described:

> Offices have been opened in tradesmen's shops and other places where any passer-by may call and for 3d. speak with any subscriber to the local exchange, or for 6d. with a

subscriber in any distant town included in the system. Manchester already possesses 15 of these call stations, Liverpool a similar number, and new stations will be opened shortly. They are also in operation in a score of other towns in the district. Only three minutes can be allowed, and at the commencement of the conversation a clockwork arrangement slowly moves an index finger (visible to the user) over a graduated arc. At the expiration of the stipulated time the connection is automatically severed. If further conversation should be necessary the payment must be renewed.

The tranquil Moss Bank / Carr Mill district was soon pockmarked with poles

The increasing proliferation of telephone poles on the streets of St Helens soon provided an extra target for mischievous, missile-throwing boys! On August 7th 1885 eleven lads appeared in court charged with throwing stones at the telephone wires and insulators that had recently been positioned in Sutton Road and which belonged to the L & C Tel Ex Co. It was stated that 15 to 20 insulators had been smashed during the previous three weeks.

As it was the first case of its kind in St Helens the magistrates said they hoped that a small fine would have the effect of "deterring boys from indulging in this kind of amusement". As a result George Bradshaw, Alfred Parnell, John Parnell, Edward Southward, John Seddon, Henry Battersby, George Tickle, William Johnson, John Jackson, Samuel Cunliffe and John Gee were each fined 7s 6d.

In 1886 there was a dispute in Rainhill over the proposed installation of telephone poles in St James Road. Homeowners claimed they would cause "injury to the place and so reduce the value of property at Rainhill". Extremely few private homes were connected to the telephone network and so there was no advantage to homeowners in having telephone poles and wiring down their street – but that also meant the company might be able to choose an alternative route if residents objected. The dispute led to the chairman of the Prescot Highway Board saying Rainhill people had "peculiar notions" about telephone and telegraph poles.

In a lengthy advert published in the St Helens Newspaper on September 10th 1887, the L & C Tel Ex Co listed many towns in Lancashire and Cheshire that St Helens subscribers and the users of call offices could now telephone. A shorter list of places in Yorkshire that had recently been made available was also listed. It may have looked impressive to prospective subscribers at that time but to our eyes it illustrates how

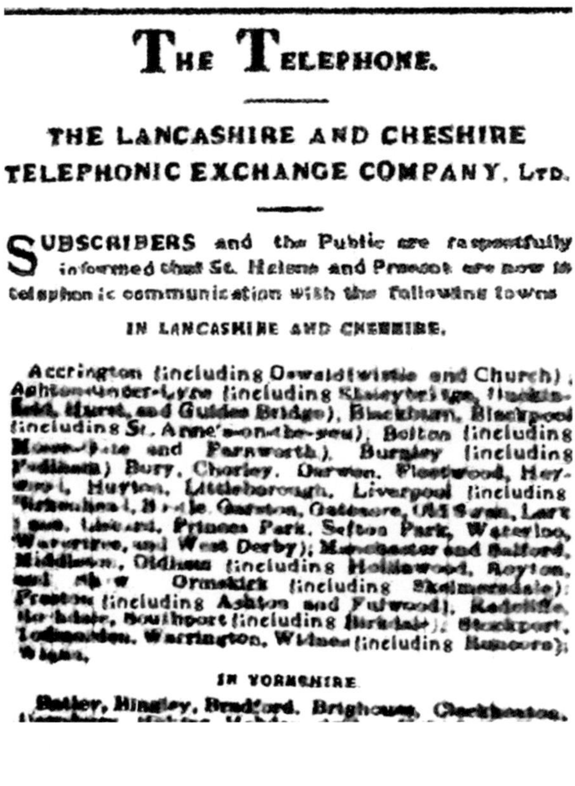

THE TELEPHONE.

THE LANCASHIRE AND CHESHIRE TELEPHONIC EXCHANGE COMPANY, LTD.

SUBSCRIBERS and the Public are respectfully informed that St. Helens and Prescot are now in telephonic communication with the following towns

IN LANCASHIRE AND CHESHIRE.

Accrington (including Oswaldtwistle and Church); Ashton-under-Lyne (including [illegible], Hurst, and Guide Bridge), Blackburn, Blackpool (including St. Anne's-on-the-sea), Bolton (including [illegible] and Farnworth), Burnley (including [illegible]) Bury, Chorley, Darwen, Fleetwood, Heywood, Huyton, Littleborough, Liverpool (including [illegible], Garston, Gateacre, [illegible], Princes Park, Sefton Park, Waterloo, [illegible], and West Derby); Manchester and Salford, Middleton, Oldham (including Hollinwood, Royton, and [illegible]) Ormskirk (including [illegible]); Preston (including Ashton and Fulwood), Radcliffe, [illegible], Southport (including Birkdale); Stockport, Todmorden, Warrington, Widnes (including [illegible]); Wigan.

IN YORKSHIRE

Batley, Bingley, Bradford, Brighouse, Cleckheaton,

St Helens' folk could only be in telephonic contact with a portion of the North of England – never mind the rest of the country!

Earlier in the year the annual meeting of the L & C Tel Ex Co had stated that there was no likelihood in the immediate future of telephone calls being made to London and other distant places. However, I expect most people didn't mind this limitation too much. Few large businesses had works and depots scattered around the country and for those that did long distance telephone calls would have been very expensive and so not for everyday use.

Two types of telephone subscription were on offer in the advert. Doctors, cab proprietors (i.e. taxis / funeral firms), shopkeepers and private addresses could have a phone installed for £9 per year. Other businesses were charged £12. What were described as "messages" spoken to towns in Lancashire and Cheshire were charged at sixpence for three minutes, with the rate to Yorkshire being a shilling.

A call office was inside Dromgoole's in St Helens at 4/6 Hardshaw Street

There were two call offices in St Helens available for any member of the public to use – but both were in the same street! They were located within the Telephone Exchange and inside Dromgoole's Public Hall / stationers. These were both in Hardshaw Street, with the latter owned by the St Helens Newspaper. Prescot users had a sole call office inside the premises of surveyor William Goldsworth in Bank Buildings, Derby Street.

Call office charges were threepence for three minutes if made to another number within St Helens or Prescot. Telephoning to other towns in Lancashire and Cheshire cost sixpence and to Yorkshire it was a shilling. I expect very few calls were made from these call offices as there were very few people whom callers could talk to.

The advert did point out that prearranged calls could be made from one call office to another and so couples separated, say, by work might have taken advantage of it. But in their paper during 1887 the St Helens Newspaper heavily promoted the goods and services available from the shops that it owned – but did not bother mentioning their call office, suggesting demand was very low.

In February 1888 the L & C Tel Ex Co was granted permission to erect telephone poles to provide direct communication between Prescot and Rainford police stations. Then in December 1892 – with the L & C Tel Ex Co now part of the National Telephone Company – the debate over whether telephonic cabling in St Helens should go underground surfaced again.

The St Helens Paving and Highway Committee served notice that in the near future all telephone wires would have to be installed beneath the surface. But over time as more private homes obtained the telephone, there was less resistance to tall poles and their wiring within neighbourhoods and it appears that the underground instruction was never widely implemented.

In early 1892 the old exchange in Hardshaw Street was transferred to 11 Cotham Street, near St Helens Town Hall. At the time it was revealed that the exchange only carried fifty-seven private wires, ten trunk lines and twenty wires connecting Liverpool with Manchester.

Slater's Directory of 1895 states that the Cotham Street premises also served as a public call office. The 1901 census lists four persons that were then resident at 11 Cotham Street, including Agnes Heaphy and Margaret McGuire who were both listed as telephone operators.

In December 1907 when Rainford Council was considering whether to install a telephone in their new Village Hall for their own use at a cost of £10 per year, Cllr Richardson said: "We should not have a new building and make it like a dog with one leg; it would be rather silly not to have a telephone."

However, Cllr Pennington was against the installation and called for the question to be referred back to the council's Management Committee where he hoped it would be "thoroughly thrashed out". He was not the only councillor against having a telephone but his motion was lost and the phone was approved.

In January 1912 the Post Office took over the National Telephone Company and the public were consequently able to make calls from several St Helens post offices. Then from 1924 the roll out of telephone kiosks on the streets of St Helens began. On October 15th of that year the council's Highways Committee granted the Post Office permission to install two kiosks as an experiment.

One was to be sited to the right of the entrance to the Town Hall and the other in front of the Black Bull in Church Street. The Borough Engineer told the meeting that he thought the boxes would prove useful and not get in the way of pedestrians and they had the advantage over other public phones of allowing 24-hour access. But it would take until the 1960s and '70s for most people in the town to have telephones installed within their homes.

SOME TELEPHONE STORIES IN BRIEF:

~ **Making Doctors Busy** – When Dr Tom O'Keefe was interviewed in 1939 he said: "The telephone has definitely increased a doctor's night work. Relatives of a patient think twice about getting out of bed and walking a couple of miles to bring a doctor. But they will leave the blankets to go to the telephone kiosk at the end of the road."

~ **Early Telephone Numbers** – The generally low take-up of the telephone amongst the people of St Helens – even by the 1920s – is reflected in the low phone numbers of shops and businesses at that time. For example, Dixons undertakers had the number 22; the

Co-op Cinema in Baldwin Street was 37; Slinn's wallpaper shop in Peter Street had 38; Burchall's butcher's in Westfield Street had 48 and the Theatre Royal was 114. The 1932 automation in St Helens saw the end of very short two or three digit numbers as the new exchange was constructed to work only on four-figure numbers. In August 1931 in explaining the change, the Reporter wrote that: "...all local telephones with a present number of three figures or fewer will be promoted to the thousands."

~ **Hoax Calls** – The introduction of private telephone kiosks in St Helens in the 1920s led to a new phenomenon – hoax telephone calls. Although public call offices had been in existence since the mid-1880s, the kiosks provided the privacy needed to make bogus calls. On February 13th 1931 the St Helens Reporter wrote:

> Chief Constable Ellerington is determined to stamp out the mania for raising false fire alarms in St. Helens, and is offering a reward of £5 for information that will lead to the conviction of the offenders.

The police then ran the Fire Brigade and recently hoax calls had been made from call boxes claiming that Clock Face School and the Elephant Hotel in Thatto Heath were on fire.

~ **Police Boxes** – In October 1930 St Helens Council's Watch Committee decided to install eight police telephone boxes in various locations on the outskirts of the borough and in 1932 that number was increased to fourteen. But some members of the Town Council were against the idea. Even the Mayor was not in favour but he did recognise that they could have advantages:

> "On occasions urgent requests come from other towns for the interception of people proceeding on the roads towards St. Helens. Then the police could be given the opportunity of having their meals in the boxes, and 'clock' on and off duty. They would be able to telephone to the central office that they had come on or were going off duty."

~ Automatic Exchange – Knowsley went automatic in early 1930 and became the first exchange in SW Lancashire to introduce direct dialling to its subscribers – instead of callers going through an operator. St Helens followed two years later and on January 20th 1932 the Liverpool Daily Post published this article:

The automatic St Helens Telephone Exchange

> I had, yesterday, an opportunity of seeing work on the installation of the automatic mechanism in the new £30,000 building behind St. Helens Parish Church. Some 1,300 subscribers on the Prescot and St. Helens exchanges are immediately affected by the change-over, and there is provision at the exchange for several times that number of lines. Calls will be able to be "dialled out" to the exchanges at Rainford, Rainhill, and Newton-le-Willows. Ten lines or more each way connect the new exchange with Liverpool. For subscribers' aid operators will sit at three "inquiry positions" in the switchboard room, and a permanent watch is mounted in the instrument room.
>
> Compared with the new apparatus St. Helens' old equipment is looked upon as somewhat of a museum piece. One of the most fascinating new devices is a switchboard capable of handling almost any number of calls an hour. One point is that a subscriber's completed call is registered automatically, so that disputes over the bill need not arise. The exchange has been planned for the next thirty years' use. The actual change-over, once prepared for, is the work of a few seconds. In the meantime, each subscriber is being

communicated with, having the working of the new system explained to him, and after the transfer, each line will be tested. Operators are being trained to conduct the new exchange. They are confronted at the boards with an array of flashing lights and handy switches, much more efficient in use than the old boards.

~ The Introduction Of STD – But the new automatic system only allowed callers to directly dial telephones on up to a dozen relatively local exchanges. That was until 1963 when St Helens adopted the STD system. This is an extract from the St Helens Reporter's article on STD published on November 16th 1963 under the headline *"'GRACE' – The Robot Operator Takes Over":*

St Helens Reporter advert

> Eight o'clock next Thursday morning will mark the advent of a new era in the history of St. Helens Telephone Exchange, with the introduction of Subscriber Trunk Dialling. The friendly operator's voice on the other end of the line asking for "Number please," will be heard no more. Instead, local subscribers will receive the more impersonal touch of GRACE – the robot operator

whose name stands for Group Routing and Charging Equipment. GRACE will deal personally with all local and trunk calls. Although ingenious, she is an operator without a voice. St. Helens subscribers will miss their telephone exchange operators. The Mayor (Coun. J. Hand) emphasised this when he opened a three-week exhibition at the Gamble Institute on Thursday which is being held for the purpose of instructing local people in the use of S.T.D.

"We will miss the voices of the girls at the other end of the line," he said. "It will take some people a long time to get used to. But this is progress and St Helens must move with the times." What may be lost in personal attention will be made up for by quicker, cheaper and easier telephoning with S.T.D. GRACE is an amazing invention. She will give local subscribers dialling access to 750 exchanges in comparison with 12 under the present system. St. Helens exchange has grown from the 400 lines existing in 1906 to a figure which now exceeds 5,700, making more than 11,000 calls a day.

d) THE HEARING AID

In their obituary on Fred Brown on March 13th 1931 the St Helens Reporter wrote:

> The name of Mr. Fred Brown was literally a household word in St. Helens, and his stalwart form and striking features were familiar to everybody in the town.

The Reporter some years earlier had described Fred as a Goliath when profiling the burly builder from North Road who later had premises in Corporation Street:

> Goliath is big in every sense. He has a big voice and a big hand. When he shakes hands with you, you feel your bones

grind one against the other; you screw your eyes up and draw your breath sharply through your teeth. He has a grip of iron and it is honest.

Fred Brown

Fred Brown was able to claim two firsts. As stated in the previous section on motor cars he had been the proud owner of the first registered motor vehicle in St Helens and his vehicle bore the prized registration number of DJ 1.

But Fred was also very deaf and he became the owner of the first electrical hearing aid in St Helens called the Akouphone. Miller Reese Hutchinson had invented the device by adopting the technology behind telephones to convert weak signals into stronger ones. The ear trumpets that some deaf persons used funnelled sounds into one ear but did nothing to amplify them.

The cumbersome Akouphone was most definitely NOT an invisible hearing aid!

And so the American Akouphone hearing aid was revolutionary but like most new inventions of the past, it was expensive and bulky. Although deemed portable, it needed to be housed on a table leaving the user tethered to a large box.

However, Fred Brown was extremely proud of his new hearing aid and he invited anyone who was interested to come and see him demonstrate his device. That was revealed in this St Helens Newspaper article from March 13th 1903, under the headline *"A Remarkable Invention – Electric Treatment For Deafness":*

The friends of Mr. Fred Brown, builder and contractor, North-road, having during the past few days been congratulating him upon being the happy possessor of a wonderful instrument which is enabling him to overcome the deafness with which he has been afflicted for many years, and to participate in a conversation carried on in an ordinary tone. The incident in question is the Akouphone, and, like the telephone, hails from "the other side," and the principle underlying it is based upon the fact that electrical sound waves have a penetrating power far in excess of ordinary sound waves. The instrument consists of a receiver, an electric battery and an ear piece connected with wires, similar to a miniature telephone, and one of our representatives had a practical demonstration of its great utility to the partially deaf.

By its means a conversation was carried on with Mr. Brown in a very low tone, but Mr. Brown heard every word, the great feature of the instrument being that while it does not increase the volume of sound it renders it more penetrating, and it is claimed for it, that it will aid the deaf in quite 90 per cent. of cases, there being, of course, some forms of deafness which cannot be even slightly benefited. The Akouphone is a radical departure from the time honoured trumpet, which it is said has the effect of gradually increasing deafness, whereas the use of the new instrument has a curative effect, a fact, which Mr. Brown is only too ready to affirm. In fact, he is quite enthusiastic over it, in which he is perfectly justified. The instrument he has is one of the first half dozen to come to England, and already there have been numerous inquiries with reference to its utility, one of the latest inquirers being Mr. W. T. Stead, editor of the "Review of Reviews." Mr. Brown will be glad to show the instrument to anyone who calls upon him

e) AEROPLANES

It's impossible to say with any certainty when the first aeroplane landed in St Helens. But it was probably on December 29th 1909 when the biplane piloted by Colonel Samuel Franklin Cody landed at Eccleston Park. The pioneering aviator had been attempting to become the first person to fly between Liverpool and Manchester and win a £1,000 prize – but he was beaten by fog. Cody was forced to land his machine in a ploughed field on Valencia Farm, near to Portico, and he became the guest of Alderman Frederick Dixon-Nuttall at his nearby home in Ingleholme.

Colonel S. F. Cody after making his emergency landing at Eccleston Park

It was not until the summer of 1911 that Henry Melly and his pupil pilot, a Mr Dukinfield-Jones, became the first to fly non-stop between Liverpool (Waterloo) and Manchester (Trafford Park). Two years later Samuel Cody was killed in an air crash near Farnborough underlining the dangers for the early aviators.

Seeing what was often called a "flying machine" in the St Helens' skies was clearly still a novelty by 1916. On May 29th of that year an aeroplane caused what the St Helens Newspaper described as "considerable excitement" when it flew high over the town.

AEROPLANE OVER ST HELENS

On Monday afternoon there was considerable excitement in the town as an aeroplane was seen flying over. It was at a considerable height, but there was a clear sky and the machine was visible for some little time, until it disappeared behind a bank of clouds.

St Helens Newspaper June 2nd 1916

Three years later on July 18th 1919 the St Helens Reporter wrote that the first regular aeroplane flights from Southport to St Helens had begun. It was the initiative of a charabanc firm called County Carriers of Boundary Road who each week was giving away two free seats on Sopwith planes.

The names of all the passengers that had booked charabanc trips with the company were being entered into a weekly raffle, with the two winners of the draw taking to the skies. The Reporter said:

> The popular feeling of reticence at the thought of engaging in a mid-air flight is gradually passing away, and many who, but a comparatively short time ago, would have at once dismissed the idea of their participating in one, would to-day have no scruples at all in doing so.

However, as there was no suitable place for the craft to land in St Helens, the planes would only fly over the town and then return to Southport. Two aircraft had flown on County Carriers' inaugural service during the previous weekend, which had been more of a test flight carrying staff that worked for the charabanc firm.

It had taken just seven minutes to travel from Southport with one of the craft performing a double loop over St Helens, which, according to the Reporter, had "caused many persons to hold their breath at the sight of it". The St Helens Newspaper's description of one of the flights that had been piloted by L. G. Clapham said:

> Mr. Clapham is a well-known stunt aviator, and he treated the spectators to a fine display of flying. He did a double loop the loop, a spiral dive and other evolutions that sent a thrill through the spectators, who were held spellbound by the display. The machines flew gracefully over St. Helens for some minutes, and then made their way back to Southport, which was reached in fourteen minutes. The difference in the time is largely accounted for by the fact that they had a thirty miles wind with them in coming, and it is interesting to note that when flying over Rainford and Ormskirk they attained a height of 5,000 feet. Mr. Marshall [County Carriers MD] says they are exceptionally good machines for passenger flights. Speaking of his experience he said "We seemed to have no sooner left Southport than we saw the chimneys of St. Helens. It is particularly interesting to fly over a place you know, as you pick out familiar spots in a surprising manner, and I would advise anyone who is going on the first flight to fly over their own town if possible. The panorama below is simply gorgeous and the flight is a glorious sensation, once you are sailing at a good height."

According to the St Helens Reporter the first actual customers that were set to receive a birds-eye view of their hometown were a Miss Lowe of Parr Stocks Road and a Miss Fisher of Ramford Street. Perhaps Miss Lowe changed her mind as the St Helens Newspaper of July 25th 1919 reported that a girl called H. Skeath had flown instead.

The 1921 census lists her as 15-year-old coal miner's daughter Hilda Skeath from Morgan Street in Parr with M. Fisher seemingly being May Fisher of Park Road. The two Parr schoolgirls sent a letter of appreciation to Walter Marshall, the managing director of County Carriers, which the Newspaper reprinted:

> Being lucky enough to be drawn for the free flight from Southport to St. Helens and return, given by the County Carriers, Ltd., to their char-a-banc customers, we would like to thank Mr. Marshall for the businesslike way the arrangements were carried out. We reported to the County Carriers, where a taxi awaited us and conveyed us to the Sopwith Aviation Company, Southport. We started from Southport pier [at] 5-30 p.m., and we felt a little excited at first but after a few minutes we were quite calm and began to enjoy our flight. The view below seemed funny at first, but as we became accustomed to it the buildings seemed to be models.
>
> As we approached St. Helens our pilot came so low that we could pick out the position of the victory fair in the Queen's Recreation Ground, also the garage of the County Carriers. We then picked out the Parrvilion [cinema in Jackson Street] and our own homes, and then made our way back to Southport, which was reached at 6 p.m. When descending the pilot made a dive which frightened both of us for the moment. The flight is a glorious sensation, and we are proud to think we are the first two girls to fly over St. Helens. The G.N.O. is a fine machine, but the pilot's motto "Safety first" is a credit to the Sopwith Aviation Company. Thanking you for a glorious free day.
>
> We are, yours sincerely:
> Miss M. FISHER (aged 15 years),
> Miss. H. SKEATH (aged 14 years).

The girls' plane was actually the Sopwith GNU *(as pictured above)* not the GNO, which could only carry a maximum of two passengers. The inability of the early aeroplanes to carry more than one or two members of the public was one of the main problems that held back the commercial development of flying and so for some time such flights were little more than novelties.

However, their future possibilities for business and tourism purposes were recognised quite early on. This is shown in an editorial published in the St Helens Newspaper on July 4th 1919 concerning a debate over the location of the proposed St Helens cenotaph. Plans were in place for the Sefton Arms to be demolished with its replacement pub set back a little to allow more space for traffic at what was becoming a very busy spot.

Some people thought that would also be the ideal location for the new war memorial – which would eventually be sited in Victoria Square. But in declaring how ridiculous that suggestion was, the Newspaper came up with what to our eyes seems an even sillier proposal of their own. They wrote:

> The site is absolutely unsuitable [for a war memorial] and the road space should be kept as free and clear of obstruction as possible in these days of fast traffic, and the possible

need for us at some time to provide a municipal landing place for the airplane service between here and Liverpool.

The notion that planes could be landing at the junction of Cotham Street, Westfield Street and Ormskirk Street amongst motorised and horse-drawn traffic does seems a ridiculous one to us. Four years later a traffic census taken over a 12-hour period would reveal that over 4,000 vehicles of all kinds – from bicycles to heavy lorries – passed that point. But the suggestion by the Newspaper demonstrates how the practicalities of flying as a commercial operation were yet to be understood and how aviation was still largely a novelty.

That said passengers could by 1919 pay to be flown on a plane. In the same month that the two Parr schoolgirls were getting the thrill of their lives, Norman Pilkington of Rainford Hall in Crank was credited as having been the first fare-paying passenger on a flight from London to Paris.

ST HELENS
AS A
FLYING CENTRE.

PROPOSED COMPANY.

CAPITAL £1,000,000.

Practical Airmen, Aero-Engineers. Architects, Surveyors, Tourist Agents, and those interested in COMMERCIAL AVIATION, desiring to be associated with THE GREAT NORTHERN AERIEL COMPANY, as

On April 11th 1919 the advert reproduced above was published in the St Helens Newspaper, which promoted the creation of a flying centre in the town. And on another page there was this brief write-up explaining the planned project:

> Flying is so attractive a subject that residents of St. Helens and the surrounding district will be interested in the advertisement in another column showing that a company is to be formed which will develop commercial aviation and create flying centres at St. Helens and other parts of the country.

But it does not appear that such a centre ever materialised. Five months later on September 19th 1919, the advert shown here was published in the St Helens Newspaper.

PUBLIC NOTICES.

LORD JOHN SANGER.

WANTED, Aviation Ground within reasonable distance of St. Helens, suitable for Lord John to land on the occasion of his visit by Aeroplane.

FRIDAY, SEPTEMBER 26th.

Landowners and Farmers are kindly invited to communicate, stating size of ground and locality to

LORD JOHN SANGER,
ROYAL CIRCUS, SEAFORTH.

Lord John will motor over in the afternoon of the day previous to visit of his Circus, to view prospective grounde.

Clearly Lord John Sanger planned to arrive in St Helens by plane as a stunt, with the circus boss coming to the town by car on the day before his planned flight to check on a suitable landing site. No doubt time would have been spent flying over St Helens prior to his coming down to earth to help promote his circus performances in the town.

Another member of the glassmaking family with an interest in flying was Arthur Pilkington who died in January 1921. The 49-year-old from Windle Hall left £386,076 gross in his will – that's the equivalent of around £25 million in today's money.

Pilkington bequeathed to his widow his fleet of motor vehicles and aircraft and it was thought that this was the first occasion that planes had ever featured in a will.

Aeroplanes not using dedicated runways but instead taking off and landing in fields – and even on beaches at the seaside – had the potential for causing accidents to members of the public. In July 1925 Albert Lewis, a 28-year-old Pilkington's worker from Charles Street in St Helens, was sat on New Brighton beach with his lady friend Catherine Tobin, who was also from St Helens.

The couple was watching a pleasure flight taking off but the pilot took longer than usual to get airborne and instead of soaring over the pair, the wheels of his plane ran over them. The tail of the machine also clattered into Charles and Catherine. Her head received cuts and Albert suffered a back injury, with the St Helens Reporter writing:

> The back of his coat was torn into shreds and portions of his trousers were twisted into ribbons.

Fortunately neither suffered very serious injuries and after treatment at Wallasey Hospital both were discharged to recover from their ordeal at home.

Berkshire Aviation Tours came to Prescot in 1926

Post-war austerity during the 1920s led to little further development of aviation. Flights were still largely joy-rides with no more than two or three passengers sat in cockpits, well wrapped-up because of the cold and often wearing goggles. On October 1st 1926 under the headline *"Flying For All – Local People Take First Trip –*

Landings At Prescot", the St Helens Reporter described how Berkshire Aviation Tours had arrived in the district:

> Flying has at last been brought to the "back door" of this district, and yesterday afternoon many Prescotians and not a few from Rainhill and St. Helens made their first aerial journey. They were enabled to do this by one of the passenger carrying machines belonging to the Berkshire Aviation Tours formed by Messrs. F. J. V. Holmes and O. P. Jones (now of the Imperial Airways, Ltd.), which ascended from a field at the back of the bungalows near Portico. Several trips to and from Prescot were made, and the passengers expressed the pleasure their flights gave them.
>
> "The only fault we have to find," said one amateur aviator to a "Reporter" representative as she alighted, "is that the journey was too short. Almost before we got accustomed to the machine we had to get out of it." Earlier in the day Messrs. Williamson (Deane's House Hotel), G. Marshall and J. Stead travelled from Prescot to Warrington by motor car in order to make their return journey by air. Mr. Marshall was in the "H. E. B. K. B." and Mr. Williamson in "The Wasp ", while Mr. Stead was in the stunt machine which may have frightened the most timid of Prescotians owing to the manner it carried out its manoeuvres to their homes. Describing his flight to our representative afterwards, Mr. Williamson spoke enthusiastically of his experience.
>
> "We left Warrington for Prescot," he said, "just before eleven o'clock; but before leaving we circled round some of the most important works in the town. A flight of about ten minutes brought us to Prescot, where we circled round the B.I. and the church. It was beautiful, and I think from a medical point of view it is the best cure for anyone troubled

with bronchial complaints. On a morning like this you feel the flight braces you up. There was no rocking of the machine. You could lie back and feel you were in bed. I never felt anything like it in my life. All I can say is the machine was first class. The pilot Capt. Kent knew his business thoroughly, and the flight was in every way delightful."

It wasn't just the cold that was a concern for passengers in open cockpits. When in 1929 the Deputy Mayor of St Helens, Ald Richard Waring, prepared to go on his first flight he said his wife had wondered why he'd emptied his pockets before leaving home. The alderman said he had told her:

> "I am going for a flight and there may be some looping the loop business and acrobatics in the air, and I don't want my money dropping on the heads of the people."

TUESDAY, APRIL 16, 1929.

UP IN THE CLOUDS

ALD. WARING'S STORY OF AEROPLANE TRIP

A NEW POINT FROM WHICH TO SEE ST. HELENS

You ask me to write of my experience as a flyer, and it seems to me that I have

My main thought was what would happen if the engine broke down while we were in mid-air. But my faith in the

That was when an aviation firm based on the Wirral had spent a fortnight in St Helens conducting pleasure flights and making aerial displays from a field at Glade Hill, near Islands Brow. Lift-offs and landings would certainly have been very bumpy experiences in those days, as the St Helens Reporter's article on the firm's flights published on April 19th 1929 makes clear. That was under the headline *"Hurtling Through The Air – Loops and Nose Dives Over St. Helens – A Reporter Man's Experience":*

Those who saw an aeroplane gliding over St. Helens at a low altitude in the middle of Saturday morning, little thought that the passengers were the Mayor and Deputy Mayor of St. Helens (Ald. T. H. Boscow and Ald. R. Waring), who, at the invitation of the North British Aviation Co., Ltd., who are making a fortnight's stay at the Glade Hill fields, took a "flip" over the town. Following the flight a "Reporter" representative was taken for a trip, which included the various stages of aerobatics, including the spinning nose dive, straight nose dive, spiral spin, and, lastly – but very far from least – looping the loop. His experiences are given below.

The Mayor and Deputy-Mayor stepped from the cockpit after their flight in quite an exhilarated manner. I asked the Mayor what he thought of aerial travel. "Oh, quite fascinating," he replied, "quite fascinating. In fact, I much prefer it to sailing. We had a wonderful view all the time." Turning to Ald. Waring, who appeared to be as "keen as mustard" on flying, I asked how he had enjoyed the trip and what he thought of St. Helens from above. "It looks a very fine town, indeed," was the somewhat surprising reply, "but though we were travelling at 10 miles per hour we scarcely seemed to be moving. Yes, I quite enjoyed the trip." Then came the Pressmen's flight, and it was with little thought as to what was going to happen that my companions and myself donned our helmets and goggles and settled down in the cockpit. Though there was a moderate breeze blowing the visibility and general conditions were good, and the "prop" [propellor] being swung, the engine roared into life and we began to gather speed across the field.

The bumpings gradually eased, the plane's nose elevated and we soared into the blue at an angle of 40 or 50 degrees to the horizontal. A glance over the side assured me that mother earth was left behind and in a very few seconds the railway lines and meandering canal appeared to be mere ribbons. At a thousand feet fields become of postage stamp size, and looking towards St. Helens one saw a bunch of chimneys over which lay a thick, cloudy mantle of smoke. And towards this we dashed at over 100 miles per hour. Smoothness characterised the "cruise," and as I peeped over the side I noticed a small, red doll's house-like building. It was the Gamble Institute. Then I saw two little pill-boxes, which turned out to be the gasometers.

But then came the end, for Pilot Preston signalled that we poor reporters were to be ready for our baptism in aerobatics. Even progress was stopped, the machine now dipped towards earth and we shot down at 100 miles per hour through 1,000 feet. Recovering, the machine straightened out for a breather, and then we climbed to 2,000 feet again. This time the nose dipped again, the machine swung round and we had begun a spinning–nose dive at a terrific pace. The propeller "zoomed," and spinning round we hurtled towards the ground. One thousand feet of this and we became steady again.

The preceding stunts were only an appetiser for the great thrill to come – looping the loop. A download dive, not too steep, at 110 miles per hour, had begun. Back went the joy-stick, up and over went the nose of the 'plane, earth appeared above our heads, and then we regained an even keel again. I must admit that looping the loop is not an experience for the nervous or weak-hearted. The sensation of speed was regained with a thrilling steep dive to earth at over a hundred miles per hour. The engine is shut off, the wind tones you with quadrupled force, whilst fields, trees, and roads seem to be coming up to meet one at a tremendous pace, increasing in size with the rapidity. Diving is a very thrilling and exhilarating pastime.

f) TRAFFIC LIGHTS

I don't think there is much likelihood that a fascinated crowd would gather today to watch a set of traffic lights being installed in St Helens! But in 1931 they were a great novelty and as the first permanent automated signals in Britain had only opened in Leeds three years before, St Helens was fairly quick off the mark in following suit. And the town became the first place to have two sets of coordinated "robot traffic controllers", allowing a smoother transition between a pair of lights.

Point duty policeman on duty at the bottom of Cotham Street

The 1920s was the decade when there was a huge growth in motor traffic. However, cars were out of reach of most people and much of the expansion came from business owners switching to large motor lorries and vans. Alongside the existing horse-drawn vehicles, this created much congestion on the narrow streets of St Helens and at busy junctions point duty policemen were kept busy.

Accidents still occurred despite the bobby stopping and waving on traffic at busy places, with drivers often claiming that they had not seen the point duty officer. Such road traffic duty removed police from other duties and the invention of a system of automation using what the newspapers liked to call robots was seen as the solution to both issues. It was much harder for motorists to claim not to have seen the colourful traffic lights and the point duty policeman was able to take on other policing tasks.

On May 23rd 1930 the St Helens Newspaper described a call from Arthur Ellerington, the St Helens Chief Constable, for a pair of traffic lights to be obtained as an experiment:

> At a meeting of the Highways Committee, held in the Town Hall, on Wednesday, a letter from the Chief Constable (Mr. A. R. Ellerington) was read relating to the need for traffic control signals at different points in the town. Mr. Ellerington expressed his conviction that the value of the signals from the point of view of the police and general public could scarcely be over-estimated. He pointed out that the diverting of the police from their normal duties to such tasks as controlling traffic depleted the strength of the force considerably, and to a certain extent increased the opportunities of the criminally inclined. In St. Helens eight men were continuously employed on point duty, and an increase in that number was more than likely in the near future. In his opinion the erection of traffic control signals in St. Helens was long overdue. A suggestion was put forward that steps should be taken with a view to installing a set at the junction of Duke-street and Corporation-street, and also at the junction of Corporation-street and College-street.

TRAFFIC SIGNALS FOR ST. HELENS

CHIEF CONSTABLE'S SUGGESTIONS

At a meeting of the Highways Committee, held in the Town Hall, on Wednesday, a letter from the Chief Constable (Mr. A. R. Ellerington) was read relating to the need for traffic control signals at different points in the town. Mr Ellerington expressed his conviction that the value of these signals

Alderman Richard Waring told the meeting that he thought the placing of two sets of lights close together near the YMCA corner would prove confusing to strangers, although the Borough Engineer pointed out that they could be connected up to allow more free-flowing traffic. After some discussion it was decided to submit the idea to the Ministry of Transport for their approval. But it took a full twelve months for that to come through and for all the necessary equipment to be obtained.

On March 27th 1931 under the headline *"Robots For St. Helens Traffic"*, the St Helens Reporter published this short article:

> The Robot Traffic Controller has come to St. Helens. Yesterday (Thursday) workmen were busy erecting four of the automatic signals at the corners of the junction of Corporation-street and College-street. The electric wiring has been done, and, apparently, all that is required is that the connections shall be completed, and "Robot" will be ready to function. At any rate these controls will be in operation within the next few days. Another installation will be placed at the junction of Duke-street, North-road, Corporation-street and Baldwin-street. This will be erected to-day, and both sets will probably begin to operate at the same time.

The traffic lights were connected up on March 31st 1931 and were subsequently described by the Reporter as having been functioning well, who commented:

> An interested crowd watched the operation throughout the day, and the smoothness with which traffic was controlled made it evident that the installation was fully warranted.

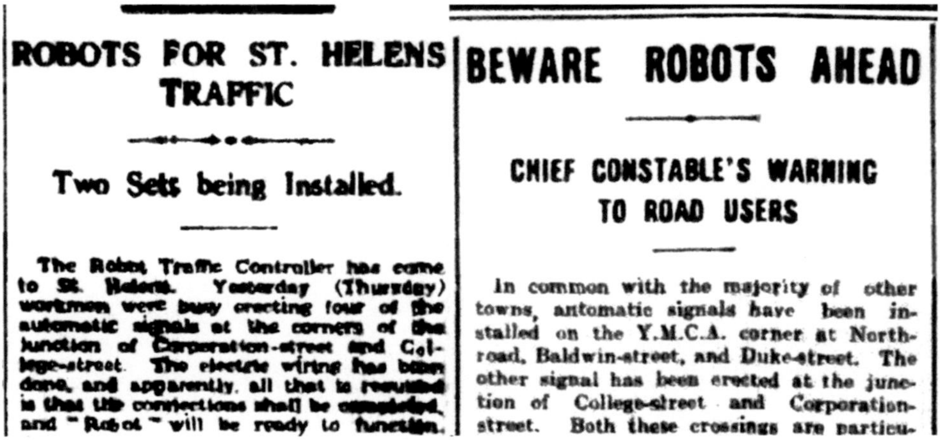

ROBOTS FOR ST. HELENS TRAFFIC

Two Sets being Installed.

The Robot Traffic Controller has come to St. Helens. Yesterday (Thursday) workmen were busy erecting four of the automatic signals at the corners of the junction of Corporation-street and College-street. The electric wiring has been done, and apparently, all that is required is that the connections shall be completed, and "Robot" will be ready to function.

BEWARE ROBOTS AHEAD

CHIEF CONSTABLE'S WARNING TO ROAD USERS

In common with the majority of other towns, automatic signals have been installed on the Y.M.C.A. corner at North-road, Baldwin-street, and Duke-street. The other signal has been erected at the junction of College-street and Corporation-street. Both these crossings are particu-

St Helens Reporter March 27th 1931 & St Helens Newspaper April 3rd 1931

The St Helens Newspaper in their report of April 3rd 1931 headlined *"Beware Robots Ahead"* stated that both places where the traffic lights had been installed were bad crossings where accidents had been frequent. Warning signs had been erected on all four approaches to the "auto signals" and the public were being asked to be as observant as possible. The Newspaper added:

> The Chief Constable (Mr. A. R. Ellerington) is hopeful that the new signals will supply a long felt want and, if successful, it is understood they will be duplicated at other dangerous points in the town. Mr. Ellerington asks that pedal cyclists, especially, should be on the look out. After this warning offenders will be liable to be prosecuted. In one Lancashire town there were over ninety prosecutions in the first week the signals were in operation. The Chief is not desirous of prosecuting until the public have had a fair chance of acquainting themselves with the new devices.

In describing how the two sets of lights were synchronised, the Reporter said the arrangement was unique to St Helens. When drivers from Duke Street and Corporation Street received the green light from the first robot and resumed their journey, the traffic lights in College Street would five seconds later also change to green.

YMCA Corner at North Road / Duke Street

That was designed to allow most drivers time to cover the intervening distance and pass through the second set of lights without having to stop again. However, in an editorial on April 10th reviewing the new signalling arrangement at the YMCA corner, the St Helens Newspaper said it was unsafe and called for the point duty bobby to be brought back:

Time is needed to give the public adequate opportunity to adapt themselves to such innovations. To be frank, however, we do not think that time will make any vast difference to the successful operation of robot signals at this particular point. The site is a badly handicapped one to begin with, and it will require great ingenuity on the part of the local authorities to adapt it successfully to robot operation...The ordinary operation of a robot signal is nothing like so efficient and safe as the fatherly control of a capable policeman.

The paper described how on the previous Monday evening during rush hour there had been a "terrible amount" of confusion with many motorists assuming that the route connecting the two sets of lights was one that they were compelled to follow:

As a result the majority of cars seeking the Church-street and Warrington-road outlet became lost in the tangle of streets lying to the left. The drivers went straight through the robot arrangement, and then dodged back down Cotham-street, Barrow-street, Hardshaw-street, Hall-street, or Shaw-street. Some were to be found down in Parr trying to retrace their progress.... The Y.M.C.A. double crossing at present is unsafe, and it will not be safe again until we have a couple of capable policemen in charge once again.

The point duty police did return – but only for a few hours after a careering lorry had put the lights out of order. In describing how the bobbies had made a brief comeback, the St Helens Reporter's article of June 2nd 1931 was headlined *"Robot Out – Robert In"*.

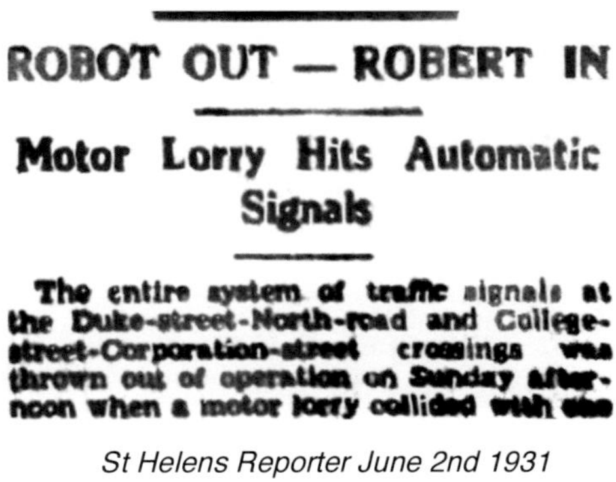
ROBOT OUT — ROBERT IN

Motor Lorry Hits Automatic Signals

The entire system of traffic signals at the Duke-street-North-road and College-street-Corporation-street crossings was thrown out of operation on Sunday afternoon when a motor lorry collided with [illegible]

St Helens Reporter June 2nd 1931

But what was probably the first serious accident connected with the new traffic lights occurred on July 22nd 1931. That was when a heavy lorry collided with a horse-driven milk float that was being driven by Thomas Hankinson from Russell Street, who needed to have an arm amputated. The St Helens Newspaper wrote:

> It appears the milk float was standing outside Messrs. Ryall's and Jones' [piano] shop facing down Duke-street, towards Dentons Green. The driver was at the front of the float. Three petrol lorries came down Corporation-street towards Duke-street. The first successfully negotiated the "automatics," but the second lorry receiving the "stop" sign, pulled up. That forced the third lorry, which was following, to swerve outwards to the right, when the driver attempted to straighten up. Hankinson, seeing the lorry bearing down on to him, ran round the float in an attempt to reach the horse.
>
> Before he was able to reach the horse's head, the lorry struck the side of the float. The latter was jammed between the front of the lorry and a lamp standard. The woodwork was smashed to matchwood, and the driver of the float knocked down. The milk cans rolled about the street, and the contents flowed. The horse escaped unscathed, but the driver's arm was pinned under the rear offside wheel of the lorry, and was severely crushed.

g) TANKS IN ST HELENS

I expect a tank driving down the streets of St Helens would create a stir today. So you can imagine the excitement the machines generated in 1918 when they made their first appearance in the town, after only being developed three years before. Very few civilians had seen a tank and when the metal monster known as Drake left Shaw Street station in St Helens on Monday April 22nd 1918, a huge crowd was waiting to greet it. Drake's appearance was part of a fundraising scheme for the war effort and the St Helens Reporter said those thronging the nearby streets were:

> ...all anxious to get a glimpse of one of the famed monsters which have rendered so much service to our boys at the Front.

After leaving the station the tank proceeded along Church Street and Hardshaw Street and then drove onto vacant land at the top of Bickerstaffe Street where Century House would later be built. Drake then performed a display of the "weird and wonderful things that Tanks can do", under the command of Lieut. Renwick of the Tank Corps. These included a "perambulation over a sandbag parapet" which the Reporter described as "one of the most remarkable sights in the world". This stunt elicited a cheer from the spellbound crowd of observers. The St Helens Newspaper's version of the tank's performance said:

> Slowly it mounted the first lot of sandbags, and then attacked the main barricade. It rose to its full height and then amid the cheers of the assembly, dropped with its nose on the other side, leaving a mass of badly battered sandbags.

Drake at the top of Bickerstaffe Street performing its party piece

After performing its party pieces Drake and its 6-pound gun trundled to Victoria Square where it parked outside the Town Hall. The Newspaper added: "The Square was decorated with bunting, and bore a very bright and animated appearance." There the tank would remain for six days under armed guard, selling war bonds and savings certificates.

The official opening of Tank Week by the Mayor of St Helens, Alderman Henry Bates, took place at 12:30pm on the same day in front of a large crowd. Standing on top of the tank with other dignitaries, the mayor declared his certainty that the townspeople would demonstrate to those at the Front that they were all doing their bit back home.

The opening ceremony of Tank Week by the Mayor of St Helens

A week earlier Ald Bates had met the town's schoolteachers to inform them about Tank Week and invite their pupils to write essays on tanks for which the twelve best would win prizes. Throughout the week the excited children were taken in small groups to see the tank and sing patriotic songs. The local schools were also in competition with each other to see who could raise the most cash. The Reporter wrote:

> Probably the educational arrangements in the schools have been somewhat disorganised this week, but the youngsters have had one of the treats of their lives in being marched down to Victoria-square, and many parents have been unable to withstand their appeals for "more money for the Tank".

There was great fascination for Drake and every day after the opening ceremony many events took place in the Square. The intention was to provide entertainment to draw in the crowds, although the prospect of seeing the tank was probably sufficient inducement for most. A number of brass and military bands performed and the St Helens Glee Club were in good voice.

Wilson Nicholson, a popular local entertainer, gave "elocutionary recitals" and the St Helens Scouts and other youth groups took part in a big parade. On one evening the girls of Sutton National School presented a "beautiful tableau" of Britannia on the Town Hall steps. The Reporter wrote:

> It was a happy idea to allow all the school children of the town to parade to the Square at various times, and the songs they have sung there have been one of the pleasing features of the week.

In another article they said Victoria Square had "worn a gala appearance" all week as "local patriots" enjoyed the rare opportunity of seeing one of the "fighting marvels produced by the British Army. People have come and feasted their eyes on the great steel machine".

Churchmen and councillors gave many speeches on top of the tank. Father Riley of Lowe House Church told the crowd that: "Germany was guilty of a crime for which she would be cursed through the ages". He called for St Helens' people to "give every penny of their means and every ounce of their strength so that England might live."

During the evening of the 24th it was revealed that the St Helens' schools had so far collected over £5,300 of war savings for the tank. Higher Grade School was top of the table having amassed £1,421; Lowe House came second with just over £1,000 and Robins Lane was third with £729. Forty-four schools were listed with St Patrick's RC School at the bottom of the table with only £3 2 shillings having so far been collected.

The highlight of the week was a huge parade held on the 27th, which marked the final day of the tank's visit to the town. The St Helens Reporter said the scenes were unprecedented and would live long in the memory. There was glorious sunshine and what was believed to have been the biggest crowd ever assembled in Victoria Square to view the tank and watch the parade.

Some of the 5,000 female munitions workers in Victoria Square

The procession comprised over 5,000 female munitions workers and there were a number of tableaux representing historic scenes. "And what girls they were!", gushed the Reporter who added:

Such a gathering of healthy, handsome and helpful young womanhood has probably never been seen in Lancashire, and they were all in high spirits, and entered heartily into the day's events.

Pilkington's Cowley Hill Works supplied some of the most elaborate tableaux. Those included 'Britannia and Her Allies', 'Our Fallen Heroes', 'Death of Nelson' and the rather long-winded 'Victory and Peace Crowned and Militarism Subdued'. The women also carried banners such as "We Cannot Make Munitions Without Money", with my favourite being: "The Tank Has a Wide Mouth, Please Fill It"! Several separate processions all met up in the town centre.

About 350 female munitions workers from Forster's Glass processed down Atlas Street and Corporation Street towards the Town Hall. At their head was a decorated steam lorry displaying 13-pound shells. The Volunteer Band came next, followed by workers from Forster's Inspection Department dressed in blue overalls and caps. Other workers grouped in sections and wearing khaki overalls came next led by their respective forewomen. And another lorry carrying 6-inch shells brought up the rear.

The procession was joined en route by women from other firms engaged in some form of munitions work – including the Hardshaw Brook Chemical Works and T. Davies's. Another group of marchers were from the Sutton Bond munitions plant in Lancots Lane.

The St Helens Reporter described the Sutton procession as having been "one of the prettiest and most impressive sights", with over 2,500 female employees taking part. Scoutmaster Holme's Boy Scout Band led the Sutton march for part of the journey and then the Volunteer Band took over. The Reporter added:

> This procession, which was over a mile in length, consisted of all the girls in their various coloured overalls, and their happy, smiling faces showed that not only were the girls pleased to be marching to the Tank with nearly £2,000 for War Savings Certificates, but that they were glad to have the opportunity of showing the inhabitants their loyalty and keenness for their work. They carried themselves extremely well, and their marching was almost equal to a regiment of soldiers. On arrival at the Tank, the Mayoress was presented with a bouquet by the daughter of one of the employees, which was gracefully acknowledged.

Outside the Town Hall the Mayor, Alderman Bates, and the St Helens MP, Rigby Swift, gave speeches from the top of the tank. On the 28th Drake left for Crewe, as Tank Week in St Helens drew to a close. The target of £1 million of war bonds and savings certificates was not met, although the townspeople did well to raise the sum of £507,297 *(about £40m in today's money)*. The St Helens total included £57,300 collected in Rainhill, Prescot and Whiston; £20,700 from Earlestown; £9,000 from Eccleston and Rainford had contributed £1,700.

The schools in St Helens invested a total of £28,087 in the tank bank that was funded by the parents of the children and their teachers. Higher Grade raised the most of the borough's 51 schools collecting £3,186; Sutton National came second with £2,482 and Lowe House School was third having collected £2,005.

The St Helens Newspaper summed up the accomplishment by townsfolk during Tank Week with these words:

> St. Helens made a great and glorious success last week, and every man, woman and child who took part in the investment of half a million pounds in the Tank Bank may well be proud, for it is to the eternal credit of the people, the brightest and best bit of work the town ever did, a proof that the heart of the people is sound.

Advertisements published in the St Helens Newspaper

ST. HELENS TANK WEEK.

TOWN'S MAGNIFICENT RESPONSE.

St. Helens made a great and glorious success last week, and every man, woman and child who took part in the investment of half a million pounds in the Tank Bank may well be proud, for it is to the eternal bers of the firm of Messrs. Pilkington Bros. helped. The Mayor and the officials all acknowledge with gratitude the work done particularly by Mr. Cecil Pilkington, with the support of other members of the firm. The way in which the many thousands of the work-

But the departure of Drake did not end the St Helens' love affair with tanks. On December 19th 1919 the St Helens Reporter published this notice:

> St. Helens is to have a battle-stained tank as a war souvenir, and it is to be placed as a permanent possession of the town in the Queen's Recreation Ground. It will be handed over with appropriate ceremonial some time during January. The matter came up at a meeting of the Parks Committee on Wednesday afternoon. The St. Helens Local Central Committee for War Savings sent copies of correspondence from headquarters re the presentation and installation of a war tank as a memorial of the war savings of the town.

On the same day the St Helens Newspaper felt that the proposed tank in what we know as Queen's Park, off Boundary Road, would have to be fenced off to prevent kids from swamping it. They wrote:

> It is suggested that a concrete bed should be put down in the Recreation Ground on which the Tank can be placed. This will no doubt be necessary, but the Tank will surely have to be securely fenced round with an unclimbable fence or the

> children will absolutely swarm over it all day long, and the martial spirit of the youngsters may lead to the organisation of sham fights and other conflicts which may even endanger the lives of some of the youngsters. The engines will be left in the Tank, and natural curiosity, not to say mischievousness, may lead the youngsters to investigate the interior of the machine, proceedings which may lead to trouble.

On January 23rd 1920 the St Helens Newspaper described the arrival of the St Helens Tank:

> Great interest was aroused, particularly among the juvenile section of the community, by the arrival on Wednesday, of the War Tank....The Tank was met at the station by the Mayor (Mr. J. R. Turner)....and proceeded to the Town Hall....The Tank then proceeded by way of Cotham-street, Westfield-street and Peter-street to the Recreation ground where it was quickly placed in position, and the stores and removable parts were afterwards taken out. The tank weighs 32 tons, and the two six pounder Hotchkiss guns are left in the turret on either side.

The tank behind railings in Queen's Recreation Ground

Railings were installed when the tank arrived and a plaque was later added that read:

Presented by the National War Savings Committee to the citizens of St. Helens in recognition of the readiness with which they lent their money to their country in the financial campaigns carried by the Local War Savings Committee in the Great War, 1914-1918. Coun. J. Heaton, J.P., chairman; Thomas Best, the hon. sec.

By April 17th 1924 at a meeting of the council's Parks Committee the tank was clearly looking worse for wear. "What about the tank, are you going to paint the tank?", enquired the chairman Ald Peet when his committee members began discussing improvement work needed in the parks. In response the Borough Engineer said: "It wants it or it wants taking away." The chairman commented that in a few years time the tank would be more valuable but nobody proposed painting the tank and the matter dropped.

Then in April 1931 the St Helens branch of the Shop Assistants Union wrote to the Parks Committee urging the tank be removed "in the interests of world peace". In a discussion about the letter at a meeting of the committee, Cllr Ellen McCormick declared the tank "an eyesore" and Ald Waring said it should be made more attractive by being polished with blacklead. Just how long the tank remained in Queens Park I cannot be certain. But it was probably removed during WW2 when anything made of metal was salvaged in the hope of being recycled into weaponry.

h) BEING A BLOOD DONOR

The St Helens Newspaper of May 16th 1924 described how a chemist's shop run by John Cotton had previously occupied the site of Woolworth's in Church Street, adding:

> Any of the "old 'uns" will remember the jars of leeches, which were displayed in the shop window, and which were so interesting to the street urchins of those days.

By the early 20th century blood was being put into patients, rather than being sucked out by parasitic worms! I don't know whom the donor and recipient of the first blood transfusion in St Helens was. But the practice was certainly far from common in 1924, when a local boxer donated a pint of his blood and was feted for his act. This is what the St Helens Reporter wrote about the transfusion under the headline *"Glowing Self-Sacrifice Of St. Helens Man – Gives A Pint of Blood For Another":*

> A glowing instance of self-sacrifice for another has transpired in St. Helens this week. William Fairclough, of Woodville-street, who is well known in local boxing circles as "Young" Fairclough, on Tuesday morning gave over a pint of blood in transfusion. Fairclough learned of the critical condition of a man named Atherton through friends, and though Atherton was a stranger to him, Fairclough volunteered himself. The operation took place at the Providence Hospital on Tuesday morning, and we are informed both patients are progressing well.

The newspaper was published on the Friday following the transfusion and the final few words of its report suggests that at the time of going to press the donor was still an in-patient at Providence. There were then issues with storing blood and it wasn't until 1937 that blood banks could be established in Britain.

And so in the 1920s giving blood was a one-to-one transfer between the healthy and the sick. On the one hand it must have been rewarding for the donor to know who had received their blood and got well as a result – but the numbers of people who died in the intervening period from when transfusions became possible and when blood banks were created must have been huge. That was because locating a donor of the correct blood type within a very short space of time was extremely difficult.

Under the headlines *"Blood Transfusion – Remarkable Happening in St. Helens – Young Man's Brave Act Saves Dying Woman"*, the

St Helens Reporter of October 8th 1926 described a further heroic act of blood donation:

> An extraordinary prompt response to an appeal for aid in the shape of a blood transfusion occurred in St. Helens this week. Mrs. Peers, (22) 14, Crawford-street, Clock Face, was in a serious condition and apparently sinking after confinement. Her husband was sent for, and the house surgeon told him that unless the woman had the benefit of an immediate transfusion she would soon be dead. The husband was not a suitable subject, and he left the hospital to seek aid. His distress was noted by three or four men standing near the hospital gates, and two of them immediately volunteered help.
>
> One of them, Edward Burke (18) 11, Sidney-street, St. Helens was accepted by the doctors. Burke was very modest and at first refused to give his name, but said he would willingly give what was required. A transfusion of one and a half pints of his blood was made at once; and the patient, although in a serious condition, has benefited, her life having been saved by this prompt action. Within the last two years two other cases have occurred and have been completely successful.

The Church Street Subway Fire

"When the manhole was lifted great volumes of smoke and gas began to issue, almost blinding and choking the firemen and policemen."

The construction of the Church Street subway

During the 1890s with the prospect of electricity and the telephone adding to the existing utilities of gas and water, there was a call for all cabling and piping in St Helens to go underground. That, of course, would add greatly to their expense and create issues with accessibility when repairs needed undertaking. In the main such calls were resisted in St Helens – but not in Church Street.

There a giant subway was created, not for pedestrian use as such, but to allow pipes and cables to be hidden underground and easily accessed by engineers when needed. It was the first such project in the north of England and only the third one in the whole country after London and Nottingham. The Church Street subway was 6 ft 6 inches high and 5 ft 6 inches wide and stretched for 680 yards from the Raven Street / Shaw Street end of Church Street to Ormskirk Street.

Towards the end of the 1890s – after St Helens Corporation had taken over the town's tramway system and chosen to electrify it –

George Broom designed the Church Street subway

new tramlines needed to be laid. In Church Street there were also plans to lay a new main sewer, as well as relay gas and water mains and install electric cabling. And so it was seen as the ideal time to construct a super subway.

That was on the basis that if you were going to cause disruption through digging up a narrow main street, it might as well be on a huge scale than a moderate one! And once the subway was constructed, repairs should not cause any inconvenience in the future.

In 1898 St Helens Corporation was given sanction by the Local Government Board to borrow £5,000 to construct the subway and work soon began. It was designed by Borough Engineer George Broom and built out of concrete by contractor Peter Tickle from Cowley Hill Lane. At the time concrete was a controversial choice, with some critics claiming that it would not be able to withstand the weight of carts going over it and the argument was made that brick would prove more robust.

Builder Peter Tickle

The work of constructing the subway took place simultaneously with the laying of gas and water mains and tramlines, as well as the paving of Church Street. As already suggested that caused enormous disruption and led to many complaints.

The official opening took place on April 28th 1899 and during the event the councillors and officials walked the length of the illuminated subway. They had to be in single file as the large 18-inch gas main and two water mains that were then present took up much of the room. Electric cables had yet to be installed and telephone connections would come later.

THE NEW SUBWAY AT ST. HELENS.

The new subway which was recently constructed along Church-street, St. Helens, the main thoroughfare of the town, was officially inspected by the members of the town council yesterday afternoon. The length of the subway is 680 yards, and it has been constructed of concrete, 6½ft. high by 5½ft. wide. It is lighted by electricity, and at present contains the large gas main and two water mains. The visitors entered the subway at the Raven-street end, and walked its full length, the arrangements and fittings, including its electric lighting, being greatly admired. The members of the council subsequently proceeded to the town hall, where luncheon was provided, under the chairmanship of Alderman C. J. Bishop, chairman of the highways and sewering committee. Speeches on the success which had been achieved in the construction of the subway, and its evident usefulness, were made by Alderman Bishop, Alderman Cook, and others; and Mr. Peter Tickle, the contractor.

Liverpool Mercury report from April 29th 1899

The Deputy Mayor, Henry Martin, was quoted in the St Helens Newspaper as saying at the official opening:

> "There have, of course, been a great many complaints in the town with regard to the upset the work caused, but now it was completed the ratepayers could congratulate themselves upon having a piece of work in their midst which no one else in the north of England possessed. ...The Paving Committee was one of the committees of the

town which came in for a good deal of blame. They got more kicks than half-pence as a rule, but they were persevering in their efforts to make St. Helens one of the finest towns in the north of England, or even in the country so far as the streets were concerned."

The completed subway which was 680 yards long

Access points were created at each end of the subway and there was also an opening at its mid-point. For several years a dispute with the Post Office delayed telephone cables being fed through the tunnel. St Helens Corporation ran the other three utilities – gas, water and electricity – and so there was no problem in running their pipes and cables through the Corporation's own subway.

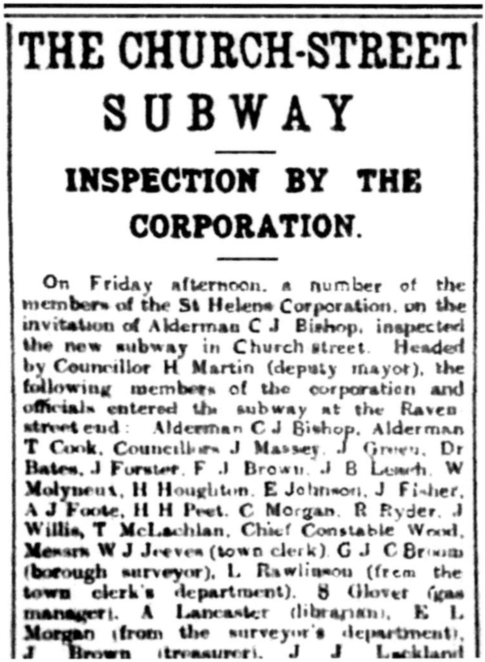
THE CHURCH-STREET SUBWAY

INSPECTION BY THE CORPORATION.

On Friday afternoon, a number of the members of the St Helens Corporation, on the invitation of Alderman C J Bishop, inspected the new subway in Church street. Headed by Councillor H Martin (deputy mayor), the following members of the corporation and officials entered the subway at the Raven street end: Alderman C J Bishop, Alderman T Cook, Councillors J Massey, J Green, Dr Bates, J Forster, F J Brown, J B Leach, W Molyneux, H Houghton, E Johnson, J Fisher, A J Foote, H H Peet, C Morgan, R Ryder, J Willis, T McLachlan, Chief Constable Wood, Messrs W J Jeeves (town clerk), G J C Broom (borough surveyor), L Rawlinson (from the town clerk's department), S Glover (gas manager), A Lancaster (librarian), E L Morgan (from the surveyor's department), J Brown (treasurer), J J Lackland

St Helens Reporter May 2nd 1899

But the council felt the Post Office should contribute to the maintenance costs of the subway by paying £10 per year rent for its telephone and telegraph wires that went through the tunnel. However, the Postmaster General only offered 5 shillings and it took some time for the dispute to be settled.

THE FIRE IN THE CHURCH STREET SUBWAY

SUBWAY FIRE.

EXTRAORDINARY INCIDENT IN CHURCH-STREET.

St Helens Reporter June 10th 1910

What the St Helens Reporter called an "extraordinary happening" in the Church Street subway that had caused "great excitement" and had "possibilities of unaccountable consequences" had begun late on Monday June 6th 1910. The drama started at 11:40pm as a tram was proceeding along Church Street to its depot. One of the five overhead tramway wires broke off and fell into the street "flashing about in a most alarming manner". Shortly afterwards smoke began to issue from the subway's ventilating grids and from its entrance opposite Market Street. The coverings of the entrance began to get red hot and for some time people were mystified as to what was happening. It was not until 1am that a fire was suspected and word was sent to the Fire Brigade. The electricity station and gasworks were also notified and their top officials summoned. The Reporter wrote:

> When the manhole was lifted great volumes of smoke and gas began to issue, almost blinding and choking the firemen and policemen. It could be seen that there was a great blaze down below, and after a good deal of difficulty, the firemen, under Sergt. Shaw, managed to extinguish the flames, great praise being due to the men for the manner in which they adapted themselves to the unusual circumstances...the interior of the subway was like a huge oven, volumes of escaping gas and the fumes of burning pitch adding to the danger.

Samuel Glover was the St Helens-born Borough Gas Engineer who lived in Grosvenor Road. Wearing a smoke helmet loaned by the Fire Brigade, the 52-year-old entered the subway and found that gas was escaping from a service pipe. Ignoring the risk of an explosion, Mr Glover used clay to stop up the broken lead pipe from which the gas was pouring out.

It was subsequently realised that the breaking of the overhead tram wires had discharged electricity into the earth, which had entered the telephone cables belonging to the Post Office. An arc had subsequently been created, which had melted the gas service pipe and caused the fire in the subway.

During the morning there was time for reflection on what had been a narrow escape from disaster. Mr Glover praised the bravery of the firemen that had gone into the subway to quench the inferno and allow him to carry out his inspection. But he himself had also proved to be a hero of the night.

The Brothers That Broke The First St Helens Savings Bank

"St. Helen's rings again with disapprobation of this apparent partiality to the rich delinquents; the defrauded depositors are crying out for further punishment; the trustees of the bank look on in astonishment."

St Helens was little more than a large village in 1819 when its first savings bank was opened. Sponsored by local clergymen and prominent citizens, the St Helens Savings Bank was intended to help the industrious working folk of the town save for that rainy day that inevitably would come. It had only been in 1799 when the first such institution paying interest to savers had begun in England and so the St Helens bank was to some degree a pioneer.

Its growth over the ensuing three decades was slow but steady. In 1830 the St Helens Savings Bank had 367 depositors and by 1844 that number had reached 556. The bank was based in Market Street but was only open for two hours each Monday. A clerk called an actuary handled the transactions with the bank's business being overseen by six trustees. Fifty respected business folk from St Helens also supervised its operations. The tradesmen had a rota and every Monday some would attend the bank to write their initials on depositors' paying-in books to confirm their payments to the actuary.

That office was held by John Johnson from Parr who when appointed to the position at the bank's opening, was aged about 30. Johnson was paid by commission on sums deposited into the bank but had little actual work to do. Despite it only being a part-time job, in about 1833 Johnson persuaded the trustees to appoint his younger brother William – then aged about 26 – as his assistant, or sub-actuary as the term was. The older Johnson had by then become a managing partner in the firm of Johnson,

Worthington and Co – the owners of several coal mines within the St Helens district, including Sankey Brook Colliery – and so had bigger fish to fry. The Wigan Times of January 18th 1850 wrote:

> Of portly appearance, good address, especially hospitable at home, and being connected as managing partner for a period of 25 years with a colliery, well known to be a profitable concern, an almost unbounded degree of confidence was placed in Mr. Johnson, the actuary.

The article was published after it had been discovered that the Johnson brothers had been involved in a massive fraud that went back to 1833 and which totalled thousands of pounds. By 1850 the bank had 600 accounts, the majority containing sums under £20, although few of these accounts had money taken from them.

John Johnson had instead targeted deposits made by friendly societies and a small number of big investors. The friendly society movement had been active in St Helens since the late 18th century and served two purposes. Members' weekly payments provided them with some insurance cover in case of sickness or death and also allowed attendance at certain social functions.

Some friendly societies in St Helens had quite unusual names, such as the Modern Druids, Ancient Shepherds, Free Gardeners, Ancient Order of Foresters etc. None of those appear to have invested in the St Helens Savings Bank but the Backbone Friendly Society did. They met at the Fleece Hotel in Church Street and were described as one of the oldest and richest friendly societies in the town and they had £250 pilfered from their account. To put that figure into some context, £1 was then about the average weekly wage for a working man.

John Johnson, the actuary, lived in what was described as a handsome house in Parr called Delves Cottage and by 1850 appeared to have plenty of resources at his disposal. As well as shares in coal mines, he had investments in Welsh iron mines and he and his brother owned several boats on the Mersey, known as flats. It appeared that John Johnson had borrowed money from the savings bank at certain times during the past seventeen years when in financial difficulties but he had never paid back the abstracted cash when his personal circumstances had improved.

On January 28th 1850 the brothers appeared in court at St Helens Town Hall in New Market Place and full details of how their fraud had been uncovered were disclosed. In December 1849 a similar savings bank deception at Rochdale had been brought to light after the death of its actuary. The government subsequently ordered the trustees of such banks to carry out stringent checks and in St Helens, as the Liverpool Mercury put it:

> Steps were accordingly taken, and placards issued, making it notorious that it was intended to have a rigid scrutiny into the affairs of the bank.

John Haddock told the hearing that in the first week of January 1850, he and his fellow trustee Robert Daglish had been on a train journey into Liverpool with William Johnson. The latter had confessed to them that there were "serious defalcations" in the savings bank books. However, he claimed the stealing had ceased in 1843 and since that time he had not allowed his older brother John to "finger a farthing". William claimed not to have profited himself from the swindle, adding he had covered up the losses by not accounting for all monies that had subsequently been received.

On the following day four of the trustees of the St Helens Savings Bank interviewed the actuary John Johnson who played down what he had done. He said he was "very much staggered" by his brother William's account of the fraud but admitted that depositors' cash had been misappropriated. But he claimed that the deficiency was only £1,500, which was far less than the £6 - 7,000 that William had stated and he blamed his brother for what had occurred.

Trustee John Haddock then told the court that a meeting was subsequently held in the Raven Inn in St Helens in which both

Johnsons signed written statements. But they persisted with their own versions of how the fraud had happened and Haddock said the discussions between the two brothers had got "rather warm".

ST. HELEN'S SAVINGS' BANK.—The Trustees and Managers regret to find that a considerable number of the Depositors have not as yet brought in their pass books for examination, with the bank books, and it being impossible, until such books have been brought in, to ascertain the exact amount of the defalcations, and the liability of the bank, the trustees have arranged with their accountant, Mr. Moubert, for himself and one or more of the trustees or managers to be in attendance, for the purpose of receiving and examining such pass books as may be brought to them at Mr. Moubert's Office, in Market-street, on the following days, namely, Saturday, the 9th day of February instant, and Tuesday, Thursday, and Saturday, the 12th, 14th, and 16th days of February instant, between the hours of eleven and one o'clock on each day; on one or other of which days it is hoped that all the books will be brought in, and the trustees will then be enabled to pay over the present funds of the bank amongst such persons as shall appear to be legally entitled to participate therein, by way of a dividend, without waiting to convert the estates of the late actuary and sub-actuary.—By order,

ANSDELL and HADDOCK,
Solicitors to the Trustees and Managers.

St. Helen's, 4th February, 1850.

This notice was placed in the Manchester Courier on February 9th 1850

William and John Johnson were committed for trial at the South Lancashire Assizes but the light sentences they received caused outrage in St Helens. This was at a time when severe punishments including transportation to Australia were imposed for relatively minor crimes. I have mentioned in a previous book how in 1852 a farm labourer called Thomas Kenwright, a married man with 7 children, was sentenced to transportation for 15 years for setting fire to a barn at Bold. No one had been hurt through his act but he could not afford a defence counsel to plead his case.

However, the Johnsons did have the money to be legally represented at their fraud trial and the judge only sentenced them both to six months in prison. The brothers had agreed for their assets to be liquidated to pay off what they had taken which was now believed to be in the region of £14,000 – roughly £2 million in today's money. There were no St Helens newspapers in 1850 and so we have to rely on the Liverpool Mercury of April 9th 1850 for an account of the fury that the court's decision unleashed:

> Very rarely has there occurred in a small provincial town an incident which caused more astonishment and dismay than the posthumous discovery of the gigantic frauds of Mr. Howarth, the actuary of the Rochdale Savings' Bank; and when, immediately afterwards, the public learnt that the brothers Johnson, the actuary and sub-actuary of the St. Helen's Savings' Bank, had for years been carrying on a system of deliberate fraud and spoliation, to the extent of many thousands of pounds, their case at once assumed an almost national importance. The death of Mr. Howarth, previous to the discovery of his delinquency, did not save his memory from infamy, but it cheated the law of a victim. In the St. Helen's case the wrong-doers were both living.
>
> The elder Johnson had appropriated some £5000 or £6000 of deposits; the defalcations of the younger Johnson amounted to at least £8000, and his fraudulent abstractions had been going on for a period of fifteen years. For half a generation had this gentleman – this man of high standing – been resorting to trickery, to ingenuity, to spoken and written falsehoods, in order that he might despoil the widow, the orphan, the thrifty father, the saving workman and trader of the hard-earned sums on which they calculated for a subsistence, or regarded as a safe resource in old age and difficulties.
>
> This wholesale and prolonged plunder was further aggravated by the fact that it was not caused by pecuniary difficulty, but apparently originated in a heartless determination to secure affluence and luxury in any way,

however dishonest and disgraceful. When this extraordinary case was soon after followed by the discovery of similar frauds, though to a much less extent, in other places, something like a panic spread amongst depositors throughout the country, and a strong and general hope was entertained that an example would be made of the arch-delinquents of St. Helen's. The Johnsons were apprehended; an astounding series of frauds and violations of the law, some of them the most painful in their nature that could well be conceived, were adduced in evidence; the two brothers were committed for trial at the Assizes; and last week they received their sentence.

That sentence was six months' imprisonment among first-class misdemeanants. Now, we hesitate not to say that this result is most extraordinary and unfortunate, and well calculated to cause even as much surprise as the heinous offences of the convicted parties. An ill-educated youth, for two or three petty felonies, committed at long intervals, would in all probability be transported. A single case of embezzlement, committed under the influence of want or the seduction of evil companions, has been punished oftentimes with two years' imprisonment; and here are two educated men, having at their command all the comforts and many of the luxuries of life, converting a situation of trust and confidence into a trap for cheating the poor and unsuspicious, and yet they are punished with little more than a nominal amount of immurement [imprisonment].

St. Helen's rings again with disapprobation of this apparent partiality to the rich delinquents; the defrauded depositors are crying out for further punishment; the trustees of the bank look on in astonishment, and people in other towns join in declaring that so lenient a sentence is only offering a premium for the repetition of such cruel misappropriations. We are forced to believe, when such glaring deception and wrong are perpetrated in different places by men whose characters are deemed irreproachable, that there are, unfortunately, many individuals who, for the sake of amassing or spending luxuriously a goodly fortune, would not hesitate to imitate the criminality of the Howarths and Johnsons, if convinced that they could escape with only six months' duresse in a prison.

The only possible excuse which can be made for the Judge who pronounced such a sentence as that upon which we have animadverted is to suppose that he was ignorant of the scores of cases of appropriation which the prosecutors had ready to bring before a jury. His lordship may have meted out an amount of punishment sufficient for the particular offence to which the prisoners wisely pleaded guilty; but the public at large look at the whole mass of fraud and wrong, and see nothing but an almost ridiculous disproportion between that and the punishment.

THE ST. HELENS SAVINGS' BANK.

Three months have now elapsed since the first intelligence of the vast frauds committed by the Johnsons upon the depositors in the St. Helens Savings' Bank were fully laid before the public in the columns of the *Courier*, and during that time the trustees and managers have been engaged in laborious inquiries into the extent of the fraud, the delinquents have appeared at the bar of their country to answer the serious charges brought against them, and are now suffering that punishment which one of her Majesty's judges thought it right to award them. The investigation into the accounts was necessarily a slow process, from causes which we have before explained; the length of time over which the nefarious transactions extended, their com-

Manchester Courier report of April 20th 1850 on the "nefarious transactions"

The scandal led to the closure of the bank, although it appears that most depositors eventually got their money back. A letter that was published in the Liverpool Mercury on December 28th 1852 from Issacha Edmunds of St Thomas Street in St Helens complained about the time it was taking for full compensation to be made.

He said depositors had been refunded a third of their money in May 1850 but since then...

> "...the managers have not deigned to give the unfortunate depositors, who trusted in their character, the slightest information on the subject...The evil resulting in this town from the failure of the bank has been great. No poor man knows where to invest his savings, except in private hands; and the consequence is that nearly all surplus means are spent in drink. For the continuance of such evils I consider the trustees are answerable."

The biggest asset that the trustees controlled was the Johnsons' large shareholding in Sankey Brook Colliery and they were taking their time to get the best price for it. It was not until June 1855 that the sale was completed and what were described as the "legal depositors" of the bank received the balance of their money back from the trustees, along with some interest.

You may wonder how it was possible to be an illegal depositor of the bank? Well, there was a regulation concerning the amount of deposits that could legally be made in a savings bank during a calendar year, as well as a rule limiting the depositors' own close proximity to St Helens.

And so if you had put in too much cash or lived too far away from the town, you were considered to be an illegal saver and did not qualify for a full refund. The legal depositors felt sorry for the illegal folk and offered to sacrifice their interest payments in order that the illegals got their money back – but ultimately no mechanism to make that happen could be found.

The Liverpool Mercury in their report on the compensation payments said that if the trustees had listened to the "urgent entreaties of many of the depositors" and disposed of the Johnson's property two years earlier they would only have received about 13 shillings in the pound instead of a full refund.

St. Helens Savings Bank.—At a meeting of depositors of the St. Helens Savings Bank, held at the Fleece Inn, on Saturday last, a committee of six was appointed to confer with the trustees in order to ascertain what progress has been made in disposing of the property of the Johnsons, as well as to inquire into what prospect there is of an early liquidation of remaining claims. This measure has been adopted inasmuch as the depositors are not in possession of any definite information as to the actual state of affairs. It is now 16 months since the discovery of the disastrous state of the bank, and but 6s. 8d. in the pound has been paid, although it was at first stated that the trustees and managers had 12,000*l.* in the hands of government. Since that they have received about 500*l.* net by the sale of John Johnson's furniture, and it has been rumoured that William Johnson's property has since been disposed of. The committee are to meet the depositors at the Fleece on Tuesday evening, the 6th of next month, to

London Daily News report from April 26th 1851

Also in 1855 under a much stricter system of supervision, a second savings bank was opened in St Helens. That lasted until 1870 when it was seen off by the growing popularity of the Post Office Savings Bank, which had opened nine years before. It was not until 1930 that St Helens had another savings institution when a branch of the Wigan Savings Bank was opened in Church Street.

The Sectarian Riot Of 1910 – St Helens' Own Bloody Sunday

"We are not going to have St. Helens made into a hell hole by people that incite passions and disgrace not only the town, but disgrace themselves and the towns to which they belong."

"BLOODY SUNDAY": SECTARIAN TROUBLE AT ST. HELENS.

MOUNTED POLICE MAKE A BATON CHARGE.

St Helens Reporter headline from July 29th 1910

In the first volume of these books I describe the 1867 riot in St Helens when a procession of Protestant Orangemen commemorated the Battle of the Boyne. Since then sectarian disturbances in the town tended to be small-scale and involve disputes between individuals.

Liverpool Echo June 26th 1909 – An artist's impression of George Wise in court

However, in Liverpool – where there were more Irish Catholics than in most cities in Ireland itself – the activities of Protestant campaigner George Wise was stirring up sectarian hatred. From the late 1880s, Wise began a campaign against High Church practices in the Church of England and later started holding anti-Catholic meetings that often resulted in disturbances. In 1909 Wise was arrested and the simmering tensions between Liverpool's sectarian communities culminated in riots in Juvenal Street, off Scotland Road, after Protestants had attempted to block a Catholic march. What happened was summarised by the Guernsey Evening Press of June 21st 1909:

> Many civilians and a dozen police were injured in a riot at Liverpool yesterday between Orangemen and Catholics. Houses were wrecked, and swords, pokers, and brickbats were requisitioned. Fifty arrests were made. At Liverpool to-day 54 persons were charged with rioting in connection with the Roman Catholic procession yesterday in which a collision occurred between Orangemen and Catholics. Both men and women were among the accused. It was stated that one man was found stabbing and another brandishing a sword. One woman used a beer jug as a weapon and a man used a murderous looming crow bar.

A government inquiry into the riot dubbed Liverpool the "Belfast of England" and St Helens' close proximity to the city meant another spill-over of violent sectarian prejudice as had occurred in 1867 was almost inevitable. Only a year after the Liverpool riot, the St Helens District of the Loyal Orange Institution of England decided to invite contingents from the city to take part in their annual parade. And so on July 24th 1910 about 150 Orangemen from Liverpool along with two fife and drum bands arrived in St Helens.

The Sunday afternoon event would have been highly provocative at any time but a recent roughing up of a Catholic priest had inflamed passions. That incident had occurred in Southport a fortnight before the parade when Father Daly of Sacred Heart Church in St Helens had taken a group of children on an outing.

What happened at Southport railway station seems to have been little more than horseplay with Liverpool Orangemen – who had been in the town participating in a parade – knocking Fr Daly's hat off and the youngsters being pulled about. But the party needed to be removed to a separate platform and placed on a special train back to St Helens and the children had arrived home frightened by their experience with some of the girls' dresses having been torn.

The incident had infuriated their parents and the prospect of reprisals so concerned the town's priests that they held a special meeting to discuss the situation. That took place at Holy Cross Presbytery in Corporation Street where it was decided that at Mass on the following Sunday they would advise all Catholics to keep well away from the Orange procession. But, of course, passions were so raised and curiosity so great that when the day came the temptation to protest proved too great and the feared violence occurred. The St Helens Reporter of July 29th 1910 wrote:

> It is hard to realise that such desperate sectarian bitterness should be so suddenly sprung upon the town, but the fact remains that a degree of disorder which cannot be appreciated by any who did not actually witness it, existed on Sunday afternoon and evening, and the worst instance is, perhaps, that threats have been made in regard to the future

SECTARIAN STRIFE.

ORANGE PROCESSION ATTACKED.

DISGRACEFUL SCENES.

TRAMCARS STONED. 29 ARRESTS.

MAGISTRATES' WARNING.

St Helens Newspaper July 26th 1910

In total up to 700 persons participated in the procession, with the marchers including 250 local Orangemen representing the Sons of Enniskillen Lodge of Parr and the Ravenhead Orange Lodge. Some women and children also took part. The Liverpool contingent represented various lodges from the city and they arrived by tram or wagonette – the horse-driven predecessor to the motor charabanc. Some of them were known to be firebrands involved in previous disturbances in Liverpool and so St Helens police was well prepared in case of trouble.

The Liverpool party's entry into Victoria Square prompted some minor confrontations. These mainly involved Catholic youths and women shouting threats and making hooting noises – a general sign of disapproval. There were only about a dozen police in evidence at first but once a large crowd of women at the top of Barrow Street began to jeer and hoot, three mounted police officers led by Sergeant George Shaw sprang into action.

Sergeant George Shaw pictured on the left c.1908

The horses were undoubtedly the heroes of the day and their skilful application by Sgt Shaw – who had been in charge of St Helens police's mounted section since its formation – undoubtedly saved lives and prevented many serious injuries. The three officers on horseback drove the hostile crowd down Cotham Street to give the Orange procession the room to begin its journey along Corporation Street to its ultimate destination. That, via Duke Street and Boundary Road, was St Luke's Church in Knowsley Road, which was their old building and not the present-day church that was only built in 1931.

The St Helens Reporter felt that the presence of the noisy protestors in and around the Square was a foreboding of more serious trouble to come, writing:

> ...it was plainly evident on Sunday afternoon before the procession started that there were slumbering fires of excitement which only needed a spark to turn them into heated bitterness...all along the route there were manifestations of hostility, certain portions of the crowd being guilty of insulting behaviour, which in a few instances brought a reply from the men in the procession. It was with considerable difficulty that the police managed to get the procession along, but the mounted men led the way, and at the end of the streets leading into Boundary-road they held the crowds back until the fore part of the procession had passed. There were angry demonstrations at the end of Kirkland-street, Peter-street, and other streets, but the presence of the mounted police had a good effect on the crowd, and in fairly good order the procession continued.

Women and girls marched near the front of the procession with men initially occupying the rear. But as the parade drew near to the upper end of Boundary Road, the men took up positions lining each side of the walk in order to protect the females. Throughout the journey from Victoria Square there had been hooting and jeering from those crowding the sides of the streets. But at the junction of Boundary Road, Eccleston Street and Knowsley Road the hostility was raised to another level and stone throwing took place, with the police needing to re-double their efforts to keep the furious protesters away from the walkers. The Liverpool contingent took the brunt of the crowd's anger and, in particular, their band members who were wearing very distinctive uniforms.

A banner of the local lodges led the procession followed by the band of the Sons of Enniskillen Lodge of Parr and Col. Saunderson's Pride from Liverpool. Sandwiched in between the banner and band were four little girls bearing an open Bible. The children must have been terrified by the reception that the procession received and one wonders at the thoughtlessness of their parents and organisers in placing the girls in such a position. The Reporter continued:

> As the head of the procession reached the junction of the roads there was an ugly rush, and a lot of shouting, and stones could be seen flying over the heads of the processionists. One large stone passed just over the head of a Pressman, and another stone struck a man who was standing by him, on the chest. There were innumerable "incidents" at this part of the route, quite a number of persons engaging in fisticuffs at various points, but still the procession continued. All the way up Knowsley-road to the church the road was lined with an excited throng, and as the procession reached the church a crowd of women and men ironically cheered and jeered at the processionists.

A curious aspect of the procession was the manner in which the bandsmen behaved. During the walk they played hymns, such as Onward Christian Soldiers, and they appeared completely oblivious to the racket that surrounded them. They were clearly, as the Reporter put it, "seasoned veterans" of such receptions. As the Orange marchers entered St Luke's church for a service, it was noticeable that the anger of the crowd was working itself up to a fever pitch. The police realised that even worse trouble would likely occur on the marchers' return journey and so they called in reinforcements, including two more mounted officers.

REAPING THE WHIRLWIND.

Liverpool "Lambs" Cause a Serious Riot.

BATON CHARGE BY THE POLICE.

A Drum-Major's War Dance.

Liverpool Orangemen, having with great care and industry sown the wind, are beginning to reap the whirlwind, and to have brought home to them with painful vividness the consequences of the career of ruffianism which they have so light-heartedly pursued for the past

was not looked forward to with delight by the authorities, as it was known that some of them had insulted a priest, who happened to be in Southport with a children's picnic on the Twelfth of July, and that this was keenly resented by Catholics.

the Orangemen, a
was spoiled.
Inspector Fairh
struck a man on th
several times.

A Dance of

Sergeant Shaw,
mounted police, sai
tom of Knowsley
man was dancing
band and whirling
annoying way nea
crowd, knowing t
very excited crow
Eccleston Street, h
quiet. He refraine
two, but in Boun
to dance and jum
at people with his

Nottingham and Midland Catholic News July 30th 1910

A large-scale effort was then made to clear Knowsley Road and to deal with the disturbances that were occurring on wasteland by the church where thousands were congregating. As orange was the colour of the Protestant contingent, so green was the emblem of the protesting Catholics. The men who were looking for trouble were sporting green caps, ties or handkerchiefs and the women were wearing green ribbons.

The Reporter again: "As time wore on the outbreak became more ominous, and it was easily to be seen that trouble was in store for somebody." And the mob's first target was a boy attired in a glaring orange suit whose appearance acted as a red rag to a bull. He and his father received very rough treatment before the police stepped in and made several arrests.

The five mounted police officers continually rode amongst the crowd to keep a clear route away from the church and as the service ended, the procession was reformed and began to wend its way back to Victoria Square. It was at the Boundary Road junction with Knowsley Road that the main trouble erupted. And the spark that ignited the ire of the crowd was the sight of the drum major in the leading band twirling his baton. The howling mob broke through the police escort from both sides of the street causing a huge commotion, as the Reporter described:

> Sticks and stones were flying in all directions, and fists were used freely. Unfortunately more serious weapons than sticks and fists were used, one of the Orangemen being struck at with a knife which cut a hole through the lapel of his coat. Pieces of iron and hammers were also brought into use, and many persons on both sides received ill-treatment. The brunt of the attack seemed to be centred on the leading band, and for a few minutes there was a seething mass of struggling humanity. The screams of the terrified women could be heard above the yells of the men, and the bandsmen ceasing their music temporarily laid about them right sturdily with flutes and drum sticks on everybody who came within reach.

At this point Sergeant Shaw ordered his mounted officers to charge the crowd with their long batons drawn, which the Reporter said they had made "liberal use". Mounted Constable Hoyle was struck by a stone and blood was seen trickling down his face. A number of constables on foot were also described as having been "knocked about considerably" and many persons in the crowd were hit by stones and had bleeding heads. In summing up the situation, the Reporter wrote:

> It is safe to say there never was such a pandemonium in St. Helens before, and the authorities seemed greatly relieved when the procession had got past this danger point.

Again the employment of horses was pivotal to safely allowing the marchers to return to Victoria Square, via Boundary Road and Duke Street. But then the question arose as to how to get the

Liverpool contingent out of St Helens? Those that had arrived by wagonette were despatched back to the city in their vehicle by a circuitous route that avoided protestors. But for those that remained, it was decided that trams were the best option and so the Orangemen and their followers were given a police escort to the tramway terminus at the top of Bridge Street.

However, there was one big problem with the plan. The tramcars' route to Liverpool took them past the Greenbank district, which was mainly occupied by Irish Catholics. The news of the Orangemen's planned departure from St Helens spread rapidly amongst the residents of Greenbank who collected stones, half-bricks, broken bottles and other missiles ready to give the party the send-off they felt they deserved.

St Helens mounted police pictured c.1908 when George Shaw was inspector

The police recognised the danger and rushed mounted officers and others on foot to Liverpool Road – which the Reporter described as "simply swarming with people" – in order to clear a way for the trams. Foolishly, the Orangemen that were standing on the top of the first open double-decker tram provocatively waived their hats and cheered.

As they drove past the Catholic crowd and at a stop at the end of Liverpool Street, the tram was subjected to a fusillade of missiles. The police ordered the tram driver to leave the danger zone rapidly and, as he did so, his vehicle became the target of more projectiles, as the Reporter described:

> ...for as the car passed the end of the next street there was another "raking fire" of missiles, which completed the destruction of the windows. The inside passengers had miraculous escapes from the broken glass, and those on top quickly "ducked" their heads as they saw the stones coming. One person at the end of Liverpool-street threw a jagged piece of broken glass bottle at the [tram] car, and it struck the top hand rail only a few inches from the face of the passenger, rebounding into the street.

The police began driving the violent crowd down some side streets, although when a second Liverpool-bound tram passed through a few minutes later, it received the same treatment. Statements were made that a man had fired a revolver at the crowd from the top of one tram and it was also alleged that a stone had knocked out a woman's eye – but neither claim could be confirmed.

The Reporter described how two journalists had narrow escapes at the hands of the mob when the Orangemen began to leave:

> A gang of furious women, with missiles in their hands, evidently taking the Pressmen for "Orange spies," advanced with "blood" in their eyes, and muttered threats on their lips; but the sight of a notebook quelled their suspicions instantly.

With the departure of those at the heart of the trouble, the police's priorities changed. They made as many arrests as they could to a backdrop of booing and jeering from spectators. A total of twenty-nine persons were charged with various offences and amongst the prisoners was Albert Kite, the twirling drum major. In St Helens

Police Court on the following day PC Smith told how Kite had used his staff to lash out at some of the Catholic protestors. As the constable had attempted to arrest the man, he said some of the marchers had "hammered" him about.

The much praised Sgt. Shaw of the mounted police told the court that when the procession had reached the bottom of Knowsley Road, Kite had been dancing and whirling his staff in "a most annoying way" near to the heads of the watching crowd. Knowing that there was an even more excited bunch just ahead, Sgt. Shaw said he'd asked Kite to calm down:

> He refrained for a minute or two, but in Boundary Road began to dance and jump about, jabbing at people with his staff. Then there was quite a melee, and the bandsmen were striking right and left with their flutes at the people. I had to order the mounted men to draw their batons, and charge into the row to get the procession on the move again. Constable Smith was right in the middle of the bend holding his prisoner, and everyone was kicking and thumping at him.

Albert Kite told the court that he had only struck back at the protestors in self-defence but the magistrates convicted him and bound Kite over to keep the peace. At the conclusion of the first batch of cases arising from the riot, Alderman Alfred Foote, the Chairman of the Bench who was also the Mayor of St Helens, made this statement:

Ald Alfred Foote

> "The bench are determined to put down rowdyism in St. Helens. We are not going to have St. Helens made into a hell hole by people that incite passions and disgrace not only the town, but disgrace themselves and the towns to which they belong. These sectarian riots will be put down in St. Helens by a very strong hand."

And the final word in this chapter comes from the Reporter who was full of praise for the police's handling of the demonstration – in particular the activities of their mounted section – writing:

> It was the first time the mounted police had had to deal with any disturbances, but they adapted themselves to the unusual circumstances in a remarkable manner, and performed their duties in a way which was a credit to themselves, and a credit to the town. There was not the slightest doubt that had it not been for the mounted police the consequences of Sunday's riot would have been terrible.

The Tragedy And Heroism Of The Sandbeds Disaster

"My attention was drawn to the tragedy by seeing little children running screaming in all directions."

There were several locations in St Helens where sand waste from Pilkington's glass works was dumped. These heaps were the residue of glass polishing and known locally as "Burghy Banks" or "Burgies". The vast sandbeds between Haresfinch and Merton Bank provided lots of fun for children and were also apparently known as "The Alps". They featured in this front-page article in the St Helens Reporter on July 17th 1970 under the headline: *"The Alps are Being Cut To Size":*

> Giant earth-moving machines, generating enough power to propel a 7,260-ton ocean-going cargo ship, are steadily slicing away the towering grey "Alps" which have dominated the Haresfinch scene for years. The "Alps" are the massive "burgy banks," the mountains of sand and ground-off glass from Pilkington's old plate glass grinding process. The machines have been moving nearly half-a-million cubic yards – at about one ton per cubic yard – of the waste to make way for CH2 – the new £21-million float glass line at Cowley Hill. The scheme has been described as "one of Lancashire's major land reclamation schemes," and is a major engineering project.

More sand dumps existed off Borough Road. These were located adjacent to the "Kimmicks", one of several places in St Helens where mounds of ugly chemical waste had been deposited over many years. The area also became a playground for children but on July 30th 1930 three youngsters lost their lives after being buried under sand. Others had narrow escapes as a large embankment containing around 50 tons of sand collapsed upon them after it had been weakened by rain. But as well as tragedy, there were remarkable stories of heroism as a community came together to rescue their trapped children. Some of the rescuers were only kids themselves, who used their bare hands to claw away at the sand that had suddenly rained down on their pals.

GRIM DRAMA OF THE SANDBEDS

THREE CHILDREN BURIED ALIVE BY TONS OF SAND

GREENBANK'S STREETS OF DISTRESS AND MOURNING

PRIEST'S DASH TO SCENE OF DISASTER

St Helens Reporter August 1st 1930

This is how the St Helens Reporter of August 1st 1930 began its account of the disaster:

> "Help! The sandbeds have fallen in and buried our mates." Groups of terrified children came scurrying into Borough-road on Wednesday afternoon sounding the news of the grim drama that was being enacted on the wasteland of the old sandbeds situated near the Ravenhead Glassworks. A few moments before the children had been playing merrily around a pool of water on the sandbeds, little dreaming that stark tragedy lurked so near. Suddenly, there came a crunch, and fifty tons of clay came hurtling through the air, mixed with flying clouds of turf. Looking up, the youngsters had the horrifying experience of seeing the embankment of the sandpit closing down on them. Ere they could move they were engulfed in the debris...The tragedy occurred about

3:45 p.m. in the middle of a large expanse of waste land, on which are rubbish heaps 100 feet high.

The children, between thirty and forty in all, were playing around a large pond on the sand, when, without warning, a great slice of the perpendicular sand wall, which must have weighed over fifty tons, came clean away and fell on them. There are marks which show that the face had been weakened by the heavy rain getting into a rift, and it is believed that the vibration set up by a peal of thunder caused the final collapse.

Those children that were only covered by a thin layer of debris managed to extricate themselves. Some ran to raise the alarm, such as William Burns and Fred Morrison. The 11-year-olds rushed into Phythian Street screaming: "The sand-beds have fallen in. They are all buried." Mothers immediately dashed to the scene, anxious to know the fate of their children. As they climbed up the steep slopes, some of the women missed their footing and rolled back down to the bottom. Men who were in bed following their night shift also rushed out of their houses – some with only their trousers on – to join in the work of rescue.

KILLED AT PLAY.

3 CHILDREN DEAD & SEVERAL SERIOUSLY INJURED.

OVERWHELMED IN A SANDPIT.

BURIED UNDER TONS OF SAND.

DESPERATE RESCUE EFFORTS.

About 20 children were digging into a short steep cliff of sand on the old sand beds near Pilkington's glassworks, St. Helens, yesterday. The cliff, loosened by a storm, collapsed, and the children were buried under many tons.

Lancashire Evening Post July 31st 1930

The first rescuer on the scene was James Maleedy, who was joined by Albert Francis. Both were badly handicapped by the lack of spades but realising that every moment was precious, set to work to claw away the sand with their bare hands in a frantic effort to reach the entombed children. In the meantime messengers were dispatched to Pilkingtons and other works in the neighbourhood to requisition tools. Mr Maleedy said later in an interview:

> "A boy, Freddie Morrison, came and told me that some of the children had been buried by a fall of sand. I ran to the place, climbed over the sand bed, and Freddie showed me the spot. I began scratching with my hands, and after I had worked for some time I found one of the children. Other people came with spades and began digging, and we came across Mary Wright and the other children who were buried. The wall of the claypit had fallen in, and 3ft. of sand covered the children. We kept on digging and got four of them out. We had plenty of assistance, for the police came along and several workmen from Pilkingtons helped to clear the fall with spades."

The eleven-year-old Freddie Morrison had himself been almost completely buried in the sand collapse with only his feet sticking out. William Burns, also 11, had extricated Freddie, who, despite being badly frightened by his experience, pulled several smaller children out of the sand before dashing to James Maleedy for help. Henry Bolton, a miner from Borough Road, was another rescuer summoned to the scene and he described what he saw:

> "I ran to the sand-pit, with half a dozen other rescuers, and we found four of the children had been completely buried. We could not see either legs, hands, boots, or any part of their bodies. Some of the kiddies pointed out where the children lay buried. We hunted around for spades and digging materials, and realising that every moment was precious, we set to work to scoop out the sand with out hands cup fashion until the messengers returned with the shovels. We were badly hampered in the first few minutes by lack of suitable digging implements and although we were working against

> time we succeeded in pulling out Billie Ball after digging for about six or seven minutes. Really the time seemed much longer. It seemed almost an eternity. I supplied artificial respiration to the kiddie and he seemed to breathe again. I put a little mirror to his mouth and it showed steam."

However, the eleven-year-old boy died later in hospital, as did Jennie Wright, aged four of Phythian Street and two-year-old Annie Martindale from Glover Street. Nine other children were injured.

The Rev. Fr. Murphy was in the presbytery of Sacred Heart Church in Borough Road when a youngster ran in shouting "Fr. Murphy, for God's sake, come quick. Lads are buried alive on the sandbeds". Dashing out of the house, he immediately cranked up his car and motored to the scene. Fr. Murphy then seized a spade and joined in the rescue work – but played down his contribution, saying:

> "I did not do much. I just helped a little bit with a spade, at the same time directing the energies of the other men. I tried to see that the digging was done to the best advantage. Digging isn't much in my line."

Fred Rogers also described his experience of the disaster:

> "My attention was drawn to the tragedy by seeing little children running screaming in all directions. I ran up to find out the cause of the trouble. I climbed over the chemical waste heap, which was about 100 feet high, and from the height I looked across on to the sand beds. There I could see a big hole, and I ran down the heap and at the other side on to the sandbank. There were little children scattered about in the sand and two men named Maleedy and Francis were trying to dig them out. Neither of the men had a spade, and they were working frantically with their arms in the soft sand, and in this way freed quite a number of children, who ran away afterwards. I told the children to get assistance,

and then I went down to try to help the men. I saw Fr. Murphy and some other men coming along with P.C. Dillon. They got stuck into the sand with their spades, but they had a difficult job because they could not thrust their sharp spades down into the sand without the risk of maiming those who were underneath. The rescue party took a lot of risk as the side of the cliff of sand was very loose as a result of the rain, and was falling at the time."

James Wright, aged nine, from Phythian Street, was one of the rescued children and he told how ten-year-old Vincent Holden had dragged him out legs first:

> "I was playing in the sand with my play-mates when suddenly the sand buried us. Vincent Holden dragged me out. I ran over the hills and told a lady Mrs. Keenan that the sand pit had buried them."

John Dudley of Pembroke Street was singled out as having worked feverishly to rescue the trapped children. Stripped to his waist, Mr Dudley dug into the sand so energetically that he eventually collapsed and had to be removed unconscious to hospital. A Mrs Grice who witnessed the rescue work of Dudley said:

> "His grit was wonderful…I ran to pick him up. He murmured, “Let me go. I must save the kiddies.” He struggled to his feet and staggered back to the pit, but he fell on his face unconscious when he got there."

The Reporter described the tragic scene when the parents of the victims arrived on the scene:

> Pitiful scenes were witnessed on the sandbeds. Their grief was terrible to witness, and, what they must have felt worse than all, was the fact that they had to stand by helplessly while police and ambulance workers from the glassworks

tried artificial respiration for nearly half an hour. It was the parents' hour of crucifixion.

The inquest on the three deceased children took place on August 6th. The only child asked to give evidence was twelve-year-old Mary Wright who told how they had been playing at shops in a cave on the sandbeds when the whole place collapsed. Perhaps surprisingly, there was no criticism at the hearing of Pilkington's, who were the owners of the land, or of the local authority for allowing children to play in such a dangerous setting. In fact the opposite occurred. The Coroner – who had inspected the scene of the tragedy – went so far as to say that the sandbeds were an "ideal place for children to play in where they could fancy they were on Treasure Island, or with Robinson Crusoe or even shooting Red Indians".

The jury in returning a verdict of misadventure added a rider that there was no blame attached to anyone. And the Chief Constable (Arthur Ellerington) told the hearing that Lord Cozens-Hardy, a director of Pilkingtons, had been in the

THE TRIPLE SAND-PIT TRAGEDY

Witness Tells How It Happened

"SHOP" IN A CAVE

FACE OF THE SAND WALL GAVE WAY

The inquest on the three child victims of the sand-pit disaster at St. Helens last Wednesday was held at St. Helens Town Hall, to-day, by the county coroner (Mr. S. Brighouse). The children were:—

William Ball (aged 11), 60, Phythian-street.

Jennie Wright (aged 4), 47, Phythian-street.

Annie Martindale (aged 2), 74, Glover-street.

The sand-pit where the disaster happened is a shallow cutting on the sand beds at Ravenhead, St. Helens, and for years children from the adjacent congested areas have made the place their playground. The sand-beds are the accumulation of a century of sand and emery used in grinding plate-glass, and they rise in parts to a height of a hundred feet and cover several acres. In addition to its "attractions" as a playground for children, the youth of the district use the flat surface as football grounds and cricket pitches.

Liverpool Echo August 6th 1930

police station when some men had entered requesting permission to collect money for the funeral expenses of the victims. As a result Lord Cozens-Hardy had announced that his firm would pay for all the funerals.

The Coroner's Poor Box

"There are a great many rich people who worry their brains out at breakfast, dinner, and tea as to how they should invest their money, but they never send anything to my poor box. If these people will send me something I will invest it for them and they will get a reward in this world as well as the next."

Coroner Sir Samuel Brighouse

County Coroner Samuel Brighouse presided over thousands of inquests in St Helens during his 55 years in office. For many poor people their bereavement over the death of a breadwinner was compounded by worries over how they would be able to survive. However, in particularly severe cases, Coroner Brighouse was able to dip into what was often referred to as his poor box to give grieving widows or other family members a small amount of cash to help tide them over. The money came from donations made by generous citizens, although the fund never amounted to much.

At the inquest on Alice Parr held at St Helens Town Hall on November 22nd 1906, Coroner Brighouse heard that the five-month-old-child from Brook Street had slept in a bed with three others. Alice would sleep in between her mother and father, with her 11-year-old brother lying across the foot of the bed. That arrangement had led to the baby girl's death through suffocation –

what was commonly referred to as death through being overlain. However, unusually, the child had been suffocated by pressure to her body and not to her face. The coroner asked Detective Staveley whether Mr and Mrs Parr were respectable people. To that the policeman answered: "Yes, very; but they are very poor." In reply Mr Brighouse said:

> "If I have any funds in my poor box I will be only too willing to give Mrs. Parr something. There are a great many rich people in this world who worry their brains out at breakfast, dinner, and tea as to how they should invest their money and get big dividends, but they never send anything to my poor box. There is only presently four shillings in it. If these people will send me something I will invest it for them and they will get a reward in this world as well as the next. However, I will contribute half a sovereign out of my own personal poor box."

The jury foreman thanked the coroner for his sympathy and collected 10 shillings 6d from the other members of the jury. That meant Mrs Parr received just over £1 and she was described as having been overwhelmed by the kindness she had received.

The advent of the wireless provided a means in which the coroner could make a direct appeal for contributions to his poor box and on March 22nd 1931 Samuel Brighouse went on the air. By this time Whiston Workhouse had been rebranded Whiston Institution and the poor box was being called the "coroner's benevolent fund" – although the scale of poverty was just the same, if not worse.

Brighouse's broadcast painted a distressing picture of life in the households of the newly deceased poor as he appealed for donations to his fund. This was the script that he used:

> "The Coroner for Liverpool and myself want assistance so that we can help people in times of distress. Immediate help is needed. Some people are so poor that when tragedy

comes along they do not know where to turn. A man is killed in the mine. His kiddies are playing on the hearthrug. The widow is in the court. I go to the house. “Mind the stairs; they are awkward.” There is no stair-rail. I walk – no I don't – I crawl up the stairs with a policeman behind me. I get to the top and there's daddy, dead. “Do they sleep in these rooms?” “Well, sir,” says the policeman, “they have got used to it.” As we go back the kiddies say, “Hey mister! Where is daddy?” God bless them and the widow. Daddy went off in the morning saying “Now then, mind you go to school and behave yourself.” You can hear his clogs ringing on the pavement. In the afternoon he is brought home dead. A stone fell out of the roof and killed him. He lies dead on the bed in his pit clothes. It gives you a sob in the throat.

The policeman whispers, “Here is a bad case.” Lad drowned; leaves mother with four children. Father blind at an institution in Manchester, learning basket-making. Net income after paying rent 30s. 6d. Trying to keep wife, buying food and clothing and paying for coal. For immediate relief £5 from my fund. One-half of the world does not know how the other half lives. The B.B.C. gives me five minutes to-night – I ought to have five days. God help poor folk in their sorrow. I say, “Please accept this, not from myself, but from compassionate souls who wish to help you over the stile, to give you a lift until you have had time to turn round.” To-morrow and the days that follow I shall face the same tragedies. I shall climb the same stairs; shall see the eyes of the widow who cannot weep. I shall see the kiddies playing on the hearth. I shall again hear them say, “Now, mister, where's feyther?” I have only a sob in my throat. Do not forget the address: Coroner Brighouse, Ormskirk, and endorse your letters ‘Wireless Appeal,’ and the widow and the fatherless will thank you."

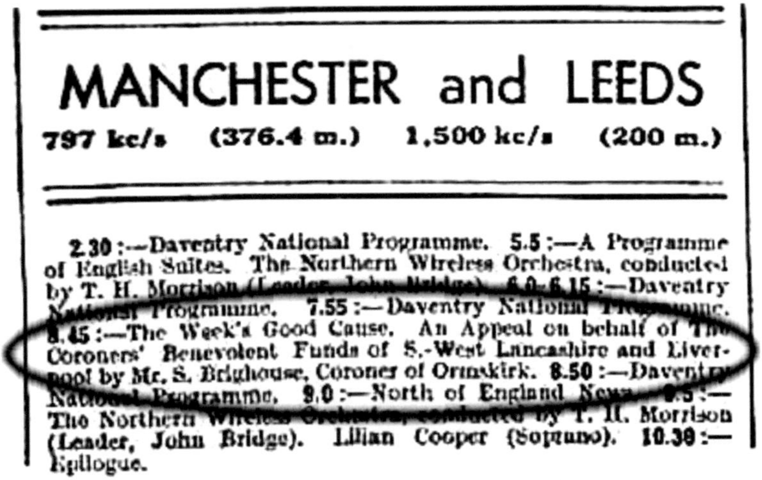

MANCHESTER and LEEDS

797 kc/s (376.4 m.) 1,500 kc/s (200 m.)

2.30:—Daventry National Programme. 5.5:—A Programme of English Suites. The Northern Wireless Orchestra, conducted by T. H. Morrison (Leader, John Bridge). 6.0-6.15:—Daventry National Programme. 7.55:—Daventry National Programme. 8.45:—The Week's Good Cause. An Appeal on behalf of The Coroners' Benevolent Funds of S.-West Lancashire and Liverpool by Mr. S. Brighouse, Coroner of Ormskirk. 8.50:—Daventry National Programme. 9.0:—North of England News. 9.5:—The Northern Wireless Orchestra, conducted by T. H. Morrison (Leader, John Bridge). Lilian Cooper (Soprano). 10.30:—Epilogue.

The Coroners' BBC appeal as listed in the Radio Times

The St Helens Reporter stated that Coroner Brighouse had addressed the largest audience of his career in his wireless broadcast, adding:

> Mr. Brighouse took kindly to the microphone, and the reception was wonderfully clear. His address to his unknown and unseen hearers was just in the manner in which he addresses his juries, and he did not overlay the pathos in his recital of the sufferings of the bereaved poor.

The appeal brought in £274, which is around £25,000 in today's money, of which a third went to the Liverpool coroner for his fund.

SOME STORIES OF THE CORONER'S POOR BOX:

a) The Thatto Heath Fireguard

Coroner Brighouse used to refer to winter as the "burning season" for children because of the countless deaths of youngsters from poorly guarded house fires. The kids tended to wear highly flammable flannelette clothing that once ignited would quickly envelop the child in flames. In December 1903 while holding an inquest at the Griffin Inn in Peasley Cross, Mr Brighouse said it was his 14th burning case of the last four weeks where death was directly attributable to the lack of a fireguard. That would have been in the whole of SW Lancashire and not just St Helens.

One might have thought that a mother who left her children alone in the house would have been criticised, if not prosecuted, for her actions if death followed. That did occasionally occur but Samuel Brighouse took a pragmatic approach, understanding the difficulties of poor parents.

This is exemplified in the St Helens Newspaper's report of March 17th 1916 on the inquest on 3-year-old Thomas Worthington in which the poor box was used to buy the family a better fireguard and give them a small amount of cash:

> On Friday, at the Town Hall, an inquest was held by the County Coroner, Mr. S. Brighouse, on the body of Thomas Worthington, the three-years-old child of a miner named John Henry Worthington, of Fir-street, Thatto Heath, who died as the result of burns received on Wednesday afternoon. Mrs. Worthington stated that the deceased was one of their five children. At a quarter past four on Wednesday afternoon she had to go to a shop in Lugsmore-lane, and at that time the deceased was asleep on the sofa. The baby, five months old, was in the cot in the kitchen, and as she left the house her son John, aged nearly six, told her he would look after the other two. There was a small fire in the fireplace, and it was protected by a fireguard. It was one of those that hung on to the grate. The Coroner: They are not much good. Sergeant Curran: It is a fair one.
>
> Mrs. Worthington said the child was wearing a flannelette shirt. A quarter of an hour after she left the house she met a neighbour carrying the child to Dr. Graham's, and she told her the child had been burned. The child was taken to the

hospital, and at ten o'clock on Thursday night she was told he was dead. She asked John how the child had got on fire, and he said he was reaching over the fireguard lighting a piece of paper, when it burnt his fingers. He threw it on the floor and he stamped on it, and it set his clothing on fire.

The Coroner: The mother has plenty to do with five children. The police tell me she is a very hard-working woman. The husband has not very good health and cannot work full time, and in addition to her household duties she goes out to work so as to keep the house going. She seems to have done everything she could; they cannot be with them every minute. The jury returned a verdict of "Accidental death." The Coroner: Mrs. Worthington, I will buy you a real good fireguard out of a little money I have, and I will also give you £1. Mrs. Worthington tearfully expressed her thanks.

b) The Drowning in the Canal

The tragic circumstances that led to the drowning in the St Helens / Sankey Canal of William Mulvanny were revealed at the man's inquest on October 11th 1921. PC Walter Hall gave evidence that at 3:45pm on the previous Friday he had been watching the siding at the Sherdley glass bottle works when he saw a young man take some coal and place it into a bag. The individual then ran off but the constable said he returned thirty-five minutes later to collect his bag and so he arrested him for theft.

The offender would turn out to be William Mulvanny from Baker Street in Parr but he told the officer he was William Griffiths of Peasley Cross Lane. The constable and his prisoner then began the long walk along the canal bank to the police station at the Town Hall. Suddenly, the 28-year-old dropped the stolen bag of coal and dived fully dressed into the cold water. The officer told the coroner that Mulvanny rose to the surface four or five yards from the bank and then began to swim to the other side.

After a short distance he turned on his back and commenced to float until he reached a bend in the canal where he shouted something that the constable could not understand. Mulvanny then sank and as PC Hall could not swim, he went in search of someone who could. A young man called James Varley immediately went into the water but was unable to find any sign of the drowned man. The police dragged the canal without success but some friends of Mulvanny recovered his body two days later. The coroner said he thought the deceased had been attempting to evade arrest rather than take his own life and revealed what had driven the desperate man to steal the coal in the first place.

William had been an out of work haulage hand at Sutton Manor Colliery with a wife and four children. Nine weeks earlier the authorities had discovered that he had been illegally claiming both unemployment benefit and the "parish relief" from the Prescot Guardians. William's family's punishment for his claiming of both benefits at the same time was to have them both stopped.

His widow Phoebe told the inquest how she had been forced to sell off most of their furniture in order to survive. All they had left was a single bed that all six members of the family slept in and a table. "I have had to do the best I can for the children," she said. Detective Constable Latus told the hearing that since the tragedy the police had arranged for Phoebe to receive some regular relief payments.

The Coroner, Samuel Brighouse, said he was very sorry indeed for Mrs Mulvanny's loss in such sad circumstances and gave her £5 out of his poor box, cautioning Mrs Mulvanny not to spend the money foolishly on an expensive funeral but for the benefit of herself and the children.

c) The Borough Road Jobseeker's Death

As the social security system developed during the early years of the 20th century, there was criticism that some claimants were happy to live off the State and did not look for work. That was despite the very low levels of benefit then available. The Daily Mail, in particular, developed a reputation for taking isolated examples of work-shyness as proving that many persons on the dole were taking taxpayers for a ride. On April 20th 1923 the St Helens Reporter described an unusual death, which clearly touched Samuel Brighouse and led to him digging into his poor box to provide much-needed help:

> The finding of the dead body of a man in the roadway at the top of Borough-road in the early hours of the morning occasioned many enquiries by the police to establish his identity and to endeavour to throw light on the mystery of his death. The adjourned inquest was held at the Town Hall on Monday, deceased being James Coburn, (41) of Rokeley-street, Liverpool. Dr. Reid, who had made a post mortem, spoke of the injuries to face and body and said six ribs were fractured and a lung torn across. Death was due to internal haemorrhage and shock, probably caused by a heavy weight crushing the chest and causing the injuries described. James Ashall, a bottle works labourer, spoke to finding the body in the roadway at ten minutes past five in the morning. Near the body were a tea can and a parcel of food. P.C. Featherstone said there were no signs of a struggle or of the body having been dragged any distance.
>
> Thomas Cook, a Liverpool labourer, stated that deceased and he being out of work, came to St. Helens to look for it. They got a job at Ashton's Green Colliery and had to start next day. They rode on motor vehicles, and usually the drivers neither consented nor knew. Nine drivers out of ten would not let them get on unless they were known. There were no [tram] cars running at night, and they had to walk out from Liverpool to get to St. Helens unless they could get on the back of a lurry [lorry]. On this particular morning witness had not come with the deceased.

> The Coroner: It appeared that deceased might have been riding on the back of a lurry and come to grief on getting off, or he might have been run over by another lurry coming afterwards. There was no evidence to show and he returned a verdict of death from injuries received, but under what circumstances he was not able to say. He handed £1 from his poor box to the witness Cook, who had previously said that he was sick and tired of the dole and of Guardians' relief. He also handed £1 to the widow of the deceased.

The Liverpool Echo also quoted Coroner Brighouse of having made this statement to Mr Cook:

> I think the case of yourself and this poor fellow who came by his death ought to come to the notice of the gentleman who writes about the dole in the "Daily Mail." It not only shows that you [the unemployed] are not all wrong, but that there are genuine, honest, working men who are very anxious to get work if there is only work for them to do. Men who will get up at the unearthly hour of half-past two and set out to walk to St. Helens, taking the chance of getting a lift from a motor, in order to go down a colliery and work there, and then walk back to Liverpool, I think are deserving of every praise.

d) The Premature Smithy Brow Baby

In the days before the National Health Service some doctors would get tired of people not paying their bills for their medical care and would become hard-hearted about providing treatment without cash in advance. A particular irritant were those non-payers who still found the money to go drinking. Reading between the lines that appears to have been the case with John Norman of Flag Street, off Parr Street, in Smithy Brow. On August 28th 1909 the St Helens Examiner published this report:

At St. Helens on Monday, Mr. S. Brighouse, county coroner, held the inquest on the body of Joseph Norman the newly-born child of John Norman, a collier, of Flag-street, who died on Thursday evening. Mrs. Whittle [presumably a neighbour or relative] said as the chid appeared ill she took it to Dr. Bassett. He said he could not attend the baby unless he was paid, and she said she would have to take it back. As she was going to the door he asked what the nurse wanted him to do. She told him she wanted him to look at it, and he said "Very well, I had better look at it," and he looked at it. He then said she would have to tell [John] Norman to take half-a-crown to the surgery at night, and he would attend to it. –

The Coroner: He was within his strict legal rights, but whether he was within his own moral rights I will leave to his conscience. – Dr. Unsworth said the cause of death was premature birth; and if it had received medical attention it would not have had a chance of recovery. —The jury returned a verdict of "Death from natural causes" and the coroner gave Sergeant Staveley £1 out of his poor-box to expend upon Mrs. Norman, remarking that he must let [John] Norman work for his own food.

e) Knocked Down By A Train

It was very common for young children to be tasked with taking food to their fathers at work. Navigating across railway lines and into factories was often dangerous and there were many deaths. On May 16th 1892 the inquest on Catherine McLeny of Albert Street in Gerards Bridge was held in St Helens Town Hall. The five-year-old had been taking her father's supper to him at the Globe Chemical Works, along with her sister Mary.

In order to get to the factory, Catherine and Mary needed to cross over railway lines. This they did via pedestrian gates at a level crossing and the little girl had been knocked down and killed by a passing train. It was common for the workmen to gain access to their works through the pair of wicket gates – but in doing so they were technically trespassing.

A railway inspector told the inquest that the line belonged to his company and they had notices up warning people that if they walked on the line they would be trespassing. To that Coroner Brighouse enquired: "What are those wicket gates for – ornament or use?"

The inspector's reply was that similar crossings were in place all over the country and those who used them did so on sufferance. "We give you every access to the works, but if you go over the line it is at your own risk," explained the inspector.

Catherine's sister, Mary, told the coroner that two trains had been travelling on the line in opposite directions, although Catherine had only seen one. She had run across the line when the first train passed and been struck down by the other engine.

In summing up the case to his jury, Samuel Brighouse said the railway company exercised control over the crossing and that people who went across had no legal right. "In other words," he said, "if the railway company liked to be stupid they could say that if they were to be blamed they would close the crossing altogether."

The inquest jury returned a verdict of accidental death with a recommendation that a footbridge should be erected at the crossing and the railway inspector promised to convey their recommendation to the proper authorities. Coroner Brighouse then remarked:

> "The father of the deceased girl has informed me that he is in very poor circumstances, and has not a penny towards the cost of burying his child. Though my poor-box fund is very small, I have arranged to allow the man 10 shillings."

f) The Man Who Said His Brain Was On Fire

The amount given by the coroner to a grieving relative of the deceased varied depending upon the amount remaining in his kitty, as well as the plight of the individual. Clearly, Mr Brighouse felt great sympathy for the mother of John Cathcart as he awarded the woman from Merton Bank £3 out of his poor box. That was then about a fortnight's wages for a labourer.

Suicide, in spite of the act being illegal, was quite often undertaken by desperate folk suffering chronic pain and enduring other life-limiting conditions. There were few effective painkillers and medical treatments and being unable to work could have huge financial consequences.

The inquest on John Cathcart that was held on February 12th 1914 heard that the 28-year-old had been in a very bad state of health for some years. His mother told the coroner that 12 months ago, with limited income coming into their household, they'd been forced to give up their home and her son had since often slept out. That was, presumably, through lack of room at his mother's lodgings.

Nine days before the inquest John had begged his mother to be allowed to stay with her as he complained of feeling very ill. On the following day his face began to swell and he said he felt as if his brain was on fire. Dr Johnson diagnosed cellulitis of the lip and told him to put a poultice on his face. However, John soon became worse and delirious and subsequently asked his mother to try and get him admitted into the hospital at Whiston Workhouse.

A doctor's note authorising his admission was obtained but John told his mother that he felt he was a hopeless case, saying: "No, mother, they will never make me better. They can't cure me. My brain is on fire."

The hospital admission never occurred as John instead jumped into the canal. His mother told the hearing that on the morning of that day her son had seemed better, although his face was so swollen he could only see out of the corner of one eye. John had left the house saying he was going to see a friend, but instead committed suicide. This was the second such death of a child that Mrs Cathcart had endured, as her son William had returned from the Boer War and used a revolver to blow his brains out. The coroner told the hearing:

> This is a very sad case. The man suffered from consumption, and I understand that the man's father is in feeble health, and altogether Mrs Cathcart has a very hard lot. I want to show some practical sympathy and propose giving Mrs Cathcart £3 from the poor box which I hope will do the father and mother some good.

Spectacular Manifestations And Extraordinary Weather In St Helens

"The oldest inhabitant does not remember anything to equal the amazing visitation. Cattle grazing in the fields were plainly conscious of some strange happening."

Every now and then the newspapers would report claims of bizarre happenings in the skies of St Helens. In Vol 1 of The Hidden History of St Helens, I describe the huge numbers of frogs that twice within a few days were said to have descended on Thatto Heath. And in Vol 2 a chapter covers various reports of flying saucers manifesting themselves within the St Helens district.

But there were many other accounts of strange aerial activities and unusual weather phenomena. This chapter describes several, including bee swarms, freak thunderstorms and gales – and also an earthquake. Some such manifestations were interpreted as signs of foreboding and we begin with one such example:

a) MIDNIGHT DARKNESS AT FULL DAY

The superstitious folk that on October 3rd 1924 witnessed what the St Helens Reporter called "an amazing phenomenon" that was both "eerie and alarming" did not have long to wait for their predictions of doom to come true. These days during wintertime – usually as a prequel to an approaching storm – it is not uncommon for the skies to darken during the day and for lights to have to be switched on. But what occurred in 1924 was considered much more extreme, as the St Helens Reporter described under their headlines *"A Pall of Gloom – Midnight Darkness At Full Day – Amazing Phenomenon":*

> It was shortly before two o'clock that the pall began to gather. It was nothing very unusual at first – nothing, in fact,

very different from the leaden skies to which we have been accustomed for many months past. But slowly the grey sky deepened, first to a darker shade, then to an ominous blue-black, until, within half an hour of the phenomenon beginning it was as dark as some of the typical November days of tradition. Shopkeepers lit up their establishments, though little business was done, as the streets gradually became comparatively deserted, thus adding to the unreality and eeriness of the occasion. The oldest inhabitant does not remember anything to equal the amazing visitation. So impressive was the whole experience that its effect upon some temperaments was distressing in the extreme. People became definitely alarmed, and in more than one instance people have since confessed that they sought consolation in religious devotions.

The depression and gloom lasted close on an hour, and as it passed away, the sky took on a hue that was most unnatural, an indescribable shade of greenish-blue, that bore a closer resemblance to the strange limelight effects of the stage during the production of heavy drama, than anything previously known in the matter-of-fact lives of St. Helens people. In the country the effects were even more pronounced. Women working in the potato fields were compelled to cease work, and the horses attached to the potato lifter, left standing idly by the hedge side, neighed wonderingly.

Cattle grazing in the fields were plainly conscious of some strange happening, and the writer saw a score of cows, when the blight was at its height, calmly lie down as if preparing for sleep, the impression being just as if they had lain down to die. Cocks crowed with unwonted vigour, and some pigs added to the uneeriness [sic] by their alarmed screams. A dog's howling had an almost human note in it, nor could anything be more uncanny than the way in which the birds sought their nests, or seemed to seek to hide from the premature night by fluttering into ivy and creepers.

There were no reports of the blackness being the precursor to a severe storm but something much worse occurred. Later that same afternoon Sherdley Colliery fireman Jon Roberts returned to his home in Robins Lane in Sutton and discovered his wife Agnes dead. Her nephew Frederick Sneyde had bludgeoned his aunt with a hammer, wrote out several notes and then swallowed the deadly poison that he had bought over the counter at Boots in St Helens.

A PALL OF GLOOM.

MIDNIGHT DARKNESS AT FULL DAY.

AMAZING PHENOMENON.

The unprecedented darkness which descended over St. Helens Friday afternoon, shortly before the tragedy was discovered, was a coincidence at once eerie and alarming.

The streets of the town bore an unreal appearance, with the passage of tramcars with their lights full on, and motor cars with headlights in full glare, though the hour was just after two o'clock.

It was shortly before two o'clock that the pall began to gather. It was nothing very unusual at first; nothing, in fact, very different from the leaden skies in which we have been accustomed for many months past.

St Helens Reporter October 10th 1924

It was one of the most mysterious and motiveless murders in the history of the town. The usual reasons for such a crime were all ruled out at the inquest. The shocking attack and suicide were both premeditated and did not take place in the heat of the moment. The 23-year-old seemingly had no ill feeling towards his aunt and was not thought to have been mentally ill. One of the notes that Sneyde wrote said:

> "I did not intend to kill my poor Auntie Agnes, but those who have made crime their whole study will understand why I was afraid that one blow would not render her unconscious. I am now going to cross the border myself and I don't deserve any pity. Fred."

b) THE FREAK THUNDERSTORM THAT CAUSED PANIC AT THE PICTURES

"Freak Thunderstorm Shakes A Town", was the Daily Mirror's headline from April 27th 1934 in which they stated that on the previous afternoon every building in St Helens had been shaken by a "terrific clap" of thunder and vivid lightning.

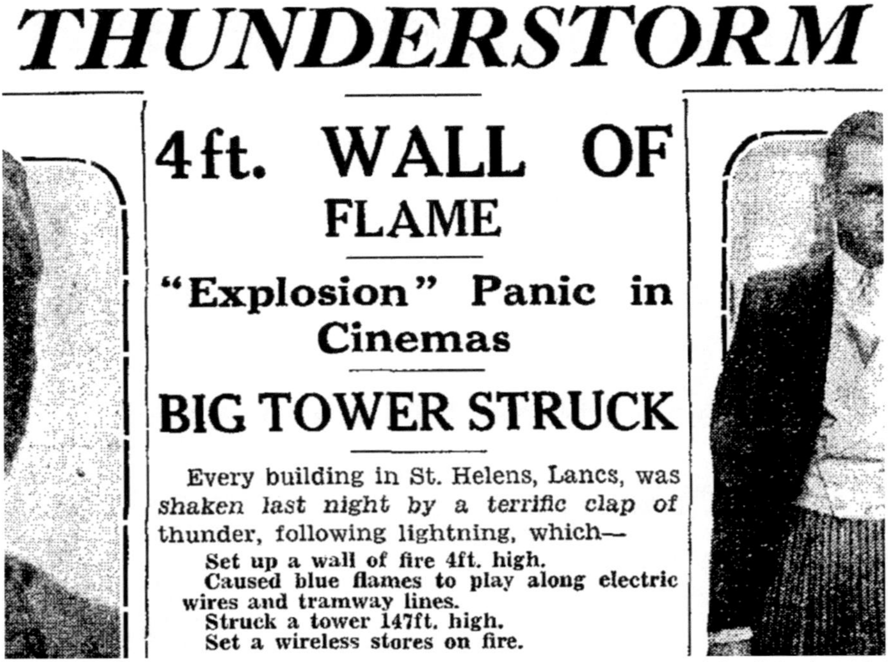

THUNDERSTORM

4ft. WALL OF FLAME

"Explosion" Panic in Cinemas

BIG TOWER STRUCK

Every building in St. Helens, Lancs, was *shaken last night by a terrific clap of* thunder, following lightning, which—

Set up a wall of fire 4ft. high.
Caused blue flames to play along electric wires and tramway lines.
Struck a tower 147ft. high.
Set a wireless stores on fire.

The freak thunderstorm was a big story in the Daily Mirror of April 27th 1934

Panic was caused in the town's picture houses and in other places where people were congregating. The Mirror wrote:

> In cinemas the lightning seemed to pass right through the walls to darkened interiors. Many people fainted and the managers had to explain the cause to avert alarm.

An unnamed cinema manager was quoted as describing how panic had briefly set in amongst his audience:

"For a moment after the flash I thought there had been an explosion. The crash followed the flash so quickly as apparently to rule out any possibility of a thunderstorm. Something like a panic followed, but when I heard the distant roll of thunder I knew what had happened. I informed the audience, who were, fortunately, reassured. We were very busy for some time afterwards, however, attending to the fainting cases."

In St Helens Town Hall a whist drive was taking place and Arthur Birtles, the Town Hall Keeper, told the Mirror:

"I was nearly knocked flat by the force of the explosion. I was attending to a whist drive in the Mayor's reception-room. The blinding light and the crash were just like a big shell-burst. The women at the whist drive shrieked. When the fire bell in the fire station just below began to ring everyone believed that there had been an explosion in the Town Hall itself."

Beecham's in Westfield Street

Beecham's works in Westfield Street was struck and a fire was occasioned in its bell tower. The lightning had put out 200 telephones in the town centre, including that of Beecham's. As a result, old-fashioned methods of communicating the news of the outbreak to the Fire Brigade and preventing the blaze from spreading were adopted. A messenger had to be dispatched to the Town Hall and during the delay before the brigade's arrival, Beecham's staff organised themselves into a line on its roof, passing buckets of water to men in the bell tower. Other parts of the Beecham's building besides its tower also suffered. The covers of fuse boxes were hurled across rooms and a piece of metal several inches long that had been connected to an electric fire was flung a considerable distance. A member of the firm said the metal "flew like shrapnel" and several light bulbs on the ceiling were blown out of their holders. The Liverpool Echo wrote how great alarm was caused among the young women working in Beecham's pill packing room:

> About 200 people were employed on the premises, and many of the girls became hysterical, some fainting, as the passage of the electric current and the terrific clap of thunder affected the building from top to bottom.

The Echo added there had been a number of "terrifying experiences" during the afternoon. The St Helens Reporter described how in Cambridge Road the premises of wireless dealer John Wharton were struck, with lightning shattering the windows of a living room and bringing down large quantities of plaster from the ceiling. It was half-day closing in St Helens and the premises were unoccupied. A neighbour, Owen Brooks, clambered through a shattered window and found an armchair in the kitchen on fire and a nearby wireless set destroyed but managed to move the burning articles into the backyard.

BEECHAM'S STRUCK BY LIGHTNING

"METAL FLEW LIKE SHRAPNEL"

YESTERDAY S STORM

DURING yesterday afternoon's [illegible] thunder storm, the tower of Messrs. Beechams works was struck by lightning, and part of the woodwork of the bell tower set on fire

St Helens Reporter April 27th 1934

Elsewhere the overhead tramway cables in Prescot Road took a direct hit and crashed to the ground just missing a motorcycle dealer from Greenfield Road who was driving his car. Even the Reporter suffered what they called an "alarming experience" during the storm. What was described as a "blinding flash" struck the roof of its printing works and the accompanying thunder caused the building to shake. A Sutton-bound tram almost opposite the Reporter office was so affected by the lightning that it started going backwards, giving the passengers a "severe nervous shock".

Many people in St Helens were subscribers to the Rediffusion wireless relay system, which was a form of early broadcast cable. Most listeners were dramatically cut off as a result of a system fuse box being blown out. One subscriber told the Reporter: "It seemed as though the lightning flashed inside the room." Fortunately, despite the nature of all the incidents, no injuries were reported.

c) MORE SEVERE STORMS AND GALES IN ST HELENS

BUNGALOW ROOF TORN OFF BY FREAK GUST

Workman escapes serious injury

A workman standing on the roof of a bungalow had a narrow escape from death, when a gale-force wind whipped off the roof, and had the incident happened 15 minutes later, a gang of workmen would have been buried beneath tons of rubble.

This photograph was published in the St Helens Reporter on October 12th 1963 and shows what remained after a freak wind had removed the roof off a bungalow in Eccleston. James Lawrenson had been undertaking some tiling on the property in Grange Drive, off Prescot Road, when the gale-force wind struck and told the paper:

"While standing on the roof, I heard a rumbling noise. I then saw the roof began to crack, so I jumped off and ran for my life. I was very lucky not to be killed."

16-year-old apprentice tiler David Swindells also had a lucky escape. The lad was making tea in the bungalow and rushed out as 3,500 tiles and rubble weighing over six tons crashed down. Residents thinking there had been an explosion called the police.

Three years later on September 6th 1966, the St Helens Newspaper described the effects of what they called a "freak gale" and "whirlwind" that two days earlier had hit parts of the town. The paper credited arthritis with saving the life of Thomas Metcalfe of Chapel Street in Haydock. Unable to climb the stairs to his bedroom, the 86-year-old instead slept in a ground floor room and was fast asleep when the wind ripped away the house's gable wall and sent debris into the bedroom. Mr Metcalfe told the Newspaper:

"I never heard a thing. I had a shock when the police told me the wind had blown down half my house."

What the paper called "Sunday's minutes of terror" caused "havoc" on a Crank farm when the roof of a grain shed was blown into a building 20 yards away. At the front of the farm, toppled trees blocked the road and at its rear 20-foot tall trees crashed into the farmyard. Three outhouses had most of their roofs whisked away and two telegraph poles were blown out of line. Farmer Sam Abbott of Greyhouse Farm in Crank Road said:

A damaged outhouse on Greyhouse Farm

"I have never seen anything like it. Around 11.30 a.m. there was a bang. When I rushed out, the clouds seemed to be touching the ground."

And in Sutton the side of a wooden shed was sent flying hundreds of yards across two streets before it crashed on to the roof of 36 Olga Road, tearing down a television aerial and scattering slates. Householder John Birchall was in bed at the time and said:

> "I heard a great scream and a crash. The house seemed to shake for minutes. The side of the shed slipped off the roof, dragging down the aerial and most of the front guttering."

During the 19th century journalists' descriptions of storms were often as vivid as the events themselves. One of the earliest reports was published by the Liverpool Albion on October 30th 1843:

> On Thursday afternoon, about three o'clock, St. Helens was visited with a tremendous thunderstorm; the lightning was awful and the thunder terrifically loud. The electric fluid struck the engine chimney of Messrs. Bourne and Robinson's works, at Broad Oak Colliery, about a mile and a half from St. Helens, completely splitting it in two, about twenty yards down, and leaving one-half standing.

During the evening of Boxing Day 1868 a storm referred to as a hurricane hit St Helens and "raged with great violence" throughout the town for more than 24 hours. Rain fell very heavily and created small lakes on waste ground. Similar events occur today, of course, especially in fields. But the St Helens Newspaper explained how the 1868 storm had a nasty side effect:

> When the storm reached its greatest power it swept this muddy, stagnant water in every direction, raising it high in [the] air, and bespattering things animate and inanimate remorselessly.

A common feature of such storms was that buildings in the course of erection were badly affected, as they had the least protection against the elements. On this occasion a Baptist chapel in Coal Pit

Lane in Parr *(now Merton Bank Road)* was partially destroyed and two partition walls in a new house being built in Hamer Street collapsed. Then on June 22nd 1872 the Newspaper described how earlier in the week a thunderstorm of "exceptional severity [had] burst over this neighbourhood". The report continued:

> The state of the atmosphere on Monday, surcharged with electricity, foreboded thunder, and no change being apparent on Tuesday morning, a thunderstorm of more or less violence was generally anticipated. [By the evening] the rain was descending in torrents. Suddenly a dreadful clap of thunder seemed to shake heaven and earth, and rock the houses to their very foundations. The lightning flashed like sheets of fire, making night for an instant as bright as day. Although the storm winged a fatal and destructive course over most of the country, we are glad to be able to state that it passed harmlessly over St. Helens and vicinity.

However, a separate report in the paper suggested that had not been the case in Prescot where the thunderstorm had destroyed the premises of joiner William Jackson. It was believed that lightning had struck the building's gas pipes and caused an inferno.

The summer of 1872 was an extraordinary one for thunderstorms in St Helens. There were several, which made it difficult for outdoor work to take place, causing farmers to be greatly concerned about their crop yield. But the worst of the lot took place on July 11th 1872 and this is how the St Helens Newspaper reported it:

> A thunderstorm of exceptional severity – even in this season of similar atmospheric phenomena – burst over this town and neighbourhood on Thursday afternoon. About two o'clock the storm commenced with a terrific thunderclap, accompanied by dazzling flashes of lightning, and succeeded by a dense shower of rain. The thunder and lightning continued – now near, now distant – for about two

> hours, and throughout that period the rain continued to fall with most unusual intensity. The busiest streets were speedily cleared, and a regular suspension of out door business seemed to have taken place. The effects of the rain show how unprecedented has been the fall. The sewers everywhere were filled, and in many cases, the water flooded over and along the highway.

Duke Street was particularly badly affected; a beerhouse in Pocket Nook was described as flooded up to the seats of its chairs; a wall in Boundary Road was washed away and the ground floor of a cottage adjacent to Thatto Heath railway station was flooded to the depth of a yard. And this is how the Wigan Observer described the lightning strikes in Rainford:

> Rainford was the scene of a most startling accident. When the storm was at its height the engine of a train from St. Helens to Rainford was struck and disabled, to the consternation of the passengers. At the same time the current caught the telegraph wires, rending them to pieces, and knocking them into fantastic shapes. Several persons were standing on a bridge, when a flash of lightening [sic] struck them, knocking them in different directions, but fortunately without doing serious injury to any.

The crazy summer weather of 1872 continued in St Helens with more heavy storms occurring on July 24th, which again flooded part of Duke Street. The St Helens Newspaper wrote that the storm struck at 2am with "dreadful suddenness, and with a grandeur unprecedented for a long series of years". The lightning flashed with "startling frequency" and the "elemental war" involved rain falling in torrents, which "showered upon the windows until the glass seemed to crack".

On the following day there was another storm which the St Helens Newspaper said had included the most vivid lightning that they had ever seen, with the flashes "blinding in their brilliancy". During the night one flash was so strong that it "made distinct the most minute objects" and the flashes that followed were "terrible to behold". Around 10am the storm returned and the streets "ran with rushing streams of water, which the sewers could not receive fast enough to dispose of as it fell." Water poured from Cowley Hill into Duke Street and with no intercepting sewer, much water accumulated.

Some women in Knowsley had a narrow escape. They had been sheltering under a tree during the storm when a farmer warned them of the danger they were in. Only a few minutes after leaving the spot, the Newspaper said: "The electric fluid struck the tree making it glow as if on fire."

Then on August 7th 1872 there was another severe event, with the St Helens Newspaper writing:

> On Wednesday evening ...between six and seven o'clock the air suddenly grew dark, as if the daylight were dying, and the gloom was lit up by flashes of the most vivid lightning, accompanied by claps of thunder which broke and rolled with dreadful distinctness.

And in describing the St Helens' storm, the Liverpool Daily Post wrote: "The thunder rolled with dreadful reverberations, and the lightning was blinding in its brilliancy." Late at night a 56-ft high foundry chimney in St Mary's Street in St Helens was completely destroyed by a lightning strike. The Newspaper said:

> The chimney was struck by the electric fluid and shattered to pieces. It fell bodily with a tremendous crash, and, strange to say, right out into the yard through the only opening left by the surrounding buildings. It is a most fortunate circumstance that it took this direction in its fall, or one of the sheds must have been destroyed.

Then on July 26th 1873 the Newspaper commented how a "terrific storm" had "burst forth" earlier in the week, writing:

> The thunder rolled in rapidly succeeding peals so terribly resonant that the ground seemed to shake as from an earthquake. The aerial conclusion was something dreadful in its violence, and created a perfect panic. At the same time the lightning, 'the thunder's dread concomitant,' came in flashes following so fast upon each other as to form an almost unbroken illumination. Rain descended in torrents of unusual density. Although the storm lasted less than half an hour, the showers formed a volume of water too large for the ordinary conduits of escape. Consequently the low-lying areas were flooded in a few minutes. Duke-street presented the appearance of a miniature lake, from the rushing streams which poured into it from the higher levels. Bridge-street and a portion of Liverpool-road were almost as bad, and in still the elevated parts of the town the water accumulated with extraordinary rapidity.

The Liverpool Mercury described the gale that struck St Helens on December 22nd 1894 as being "of a most disastrous character" before adding, "it is considered that the hurricane was the most furious ever experienced by the townspeople".

The newspaper described how many of the town's streets had been strewn with broken tiles and chimney pots, and in the more exposed parts of St Helens nearly every building was damaged. At Pilkington's Cowley Hill works there was "considerable destruction" and a loss of life when George Houghton was "terribly crushed" when a 40-foot wall collapsed upon him.

More fortunate was Frederick Bagshaw who survived after a chimneystack at the Corporation gasworks in Warrington Road fell through the roof of his adjoining home and landed in his bedroom. He had what was described as a "miraculous escape" despite his room being demolished. Just over four years later on January 17th 1899 the St Helens Reporter described how a "terrific westerly gale" had struck the district. A football match had been taking place in Haydock and the gale had lifted off the top of the grandstand and blown its corrugated iron sheets over the tops of houses on the other side of the road.

Sixty yards of hoarding around the field was also blown down. The paper described how "great alarm" was caused to spectators in the stand and those living in the houses, although there were no injuries. Roof damage was extensive, with the Reporter writing:

> During the evening the streets were covered with broken slates and chimney pots, and it was scarcely safe for the inhabitants to stir out of doors...A great many narrow escapes from personal injury occurred.

The many recorded incidents included the laundry chimney at St Helens Hospital in Peasley Cross being blown over; a 11-year-old boy suffering a bad cut to his head after being struck by a slate and two "massive" chimney stacks crashing through the roof of Mrs Dutton's millinery shop in Church Street. The pots passed through her kitchen and the place was covered with debris.

Serious damage was also caused to St Peter's Church in Parr. A large Maltese cross weighing half-a-ton that had been placed on the church's gable end was blown over and it crashed through the roof, breaking the rafters and alighting on the church organ.

What was claimed at the time to be the worst thunderstorm in the history of St Helens took place during the afternoon of May 29th 1920. It led to many flooded homes, especially in the Watery Lane district of Sutton.

The water levels in houses in Moss Nook and Parr were reported to have reached their kitchen ceilings. Peasley Cross Lane was flooded to a depth of five feet with the road, as the Lancashire Evening Post put it:

...turned into a swirling river for a distance of more than a quarter of a mile....the thunder was unceasing, and it was impossible to see more than a few yards in any direction, so dense was the rain. Vivid lightning lit up the town, which was overhung by exceptionally heavy clouds, and the thunder rolled again and again in a terrifying fashion, shaking the houses and frightening the people.

Flooding at Peasley Cross Bridge

The St Helens Reporter described the flooding as "phenomenal". Water got into the gas pipes and Sutton was plunged into darkness for the remainder of the evening and cut off from the rest of St Helens. Cars and buses became trapped on the flooded roads and their passengers had to wade waist-deep through the water in order to escape. The trams that were stuck on the Sutton side of the flood were abandoned, with their drivers and conductors having to walk miles out of their way to get home. That was until a wooden trestle bridge could be erected over the flood.

And at the sanatorium / fever hospital in Peasley Cross, a combination of lightning and flooding caused problems. Over 30 yards of the institution's surrounding wall was levelled by the lightning strike and a nearby brook burst its banks. The water poured into the grounds of the sanatorium creating a lake and entered its admin blocks. The floodwater took some time to recede and by the following day it was still four feet high at Peasley Cross Bridge and much deeper in other parts of the road.

Another dramatic storm struck the town on December 2nd 1920, as described by the St Helens Reporter:

> Thursday night was one on which prayers for the safety of those at sea would have been most appropriately offered up. On land the storm, which endured from Thursday evening until Friday, ravished the house tops and all structures with the least inclination to flimsiness. It drove the inhabitants from the streets, and when the rain came beating on the window with a terrific clatter, there was no little apprehension for as to one's safety indoors. They were unfortunate people who had to roam the streets on Thursday and Friday nights.

Also unfortunate were eight members of the Bostock family from Liverpool Road – and their lodger called Mr Parsons. They were sat in their kitchen just about to have their tea when a 15-ft tall chimneystack came crashing down. Actually they were very fortunate folk as the chimney just missed them with only one person slightly injured – although it took several hours to remove all the bricks and plaster.

Walter Marshall's new garage that was being built in Corporation Street to house his eight new charabancs also took a battering. Other damage was done to a wall in Windle Street and a large stretch of fencing round Sutton Conservative Club's bowling green was blown down.

And finally, on September 8th 1922, the St Helens Reporter wrote:

> A thunderstorm of exceptional severity broke over St. Helens shortly after three o'clock on Friday afternoon and lasted for

an hour and a half. Whilst at its height the lightning was of the most vivid description, and the thunder crashed overhead in shocking fashion. The rain poured down in torrential amount, and at times large hailstones pelted down mercilessly. The drains were unable to carry off the water, which overflowed in channels, and the roadways had the resemblance of rivers.

The only serious flooding was again at Peasley Cross bridge where the road was completely blocked by water. The unfortunate folk that lived in the appropriately named Watery Lane in Sutton always suffered at times of heavy rain and they endured the usual flooding.

Flooded Watery Lane in Sutton

The children in the town's schools should have been let out at 4 o'clock but due to the intensity of the thunderstorm were kept in until five. The Reporter commented that during the storm their "minds were kept occupied as pleasantly as possible". And so were their feet, as in some instances dancing took place.

d) SWARMS OF BEES IN ST HELENS

Heavy rain descending from the skies can, of course, be an unpleasant experience for those in its firing line without an umbrella. But unlike a swarm of bees, rain does not possess much of a sting. For many years during the 20th century there was only one man to call if a swarm of bees suddenly appeared out of the St Helens' skies. And that was farmer Harry Almond from Eccleston.

It didn't matter if worried residents contacted the council or the police – they'd simply ask Harry at his Burrows Lane dairy farm to deal with the emergency. And Harry did not kill or otherwise dispose of the unwanted bees. Often he would take them home to add to his own burgeoning bee collection.

According to various newspaper accounts, the residents in Harry's hives expanded from 200,000 in 1955 to around 640,000 in 1970. But busy bees need a holiday (apparently!) and so every summer Harry would pack his mini-menagerie into a specially designed trailer and drive off to north Wales. That was so the Eccleston bee-man could enjoy a week's break while his bees feasted on heather to boost their honey yield.

Harry began his unusual hobby around 1930 and five years later made the pages of the Liverpool Echo. Their report of August 24th 1935 described how Alf Hodgetts of Park Road in St Helens had suffered a "unique if painful experience" when Harry's hive of bees had swarmed upon his head.

Alf had been on his way to watch a practice cricket match and as he walked past Harry Almond's farm had stopped to study the bees that were clustering around their queen. As Alf started to leave, the bees swarmed around his head, as he explained to the Echo:

> "I felt something on my head and said to a boy standing near 'I think there is a bee on my head, will you brush it off?' The boy looked amazed and said 'A bee? There's a swarm on.' I did not know what to do, but Mr. Almond told me to walk away from the farm and as I did so the bees left me and returned to the hive. I was stung in several places and Mr. Almond took out the stings with a knife."

I'm not sure what sounds worse. Being stung by bees or have Harry use his knife on your head! When the Eccleston bee expert was called out to deal with unwanted swarms he appeared to use little, if indeed any, protective clothing.

Instead Harry relied on puffs of smoke that he believed calmed the swarm and prevented them transmitting danger signals to each other. At least in his very early days, Harry also used a cloth dipped in carbolic acid, although that method has long been discontinued by beekeepers.

Holiday For Stings

Taking 200,000 Bees To Wales

Farmer Harry Almond, of Eccleston, near St. Helens, and his 200,000 bees will be having their usual holiday this year among the heather near Mold, in North Wales.

Early in August the farmer will load his bee-hives on a lorry and make the annual trek to new feeding grounds. This year he hopes that this refresher will bump up the honey yield from his apiary to a ton, a target last attained in 1949. The heat wave is all in favour of the bees, says Mr. Almond, a member of the Liverpool branch of the Lancashire Beekeepers' Association and regarded as a

Wednesday, July 22, 1970 3

Man takes his bees on holiday

Mr. Harry Almond, aged 75, of Church Lane, Eccleston, St. Helens, is getting ready to take his bees on their annual holiday.

While most people are busy packing their suitcases Mr. Almond is packing his hives — all eight of them, with 80,000 bees in each.

Mr Almond will be transporting his honey-making pets by car and special trailer to North Wales. He will be staying at Llandegla and will

BEES WERE IN UNLIKELY PLACES

An Expert To Move Them

MANY CALLS

Bees as well as the weather have interrupted the hay harvest this week of farmer Harry Almond, of Eccleston, near St. Helens.

Emergency telephone calls have been reaching his home

Various Liverpool Echo reports on Harry Almond

The newspapers were fascinated by Harry's annual holiday with his huge bee collection and the Liverpool Echo covered the story on at least three occasions. This is what they wrote on July 15th 1955, under the headline *"Holiday For Stings – Taking 200,000 Bees To Wales":*

> Farmer Harry Almond, of Eccleston, near St. Helens, and his 200,000 bees will be having their usual holiday this year among the heather near Mold, in North Wales. Early in August the farmer will load his bee-hives on a lorry and make the annual trek to new feeding grounds. This year he hopes that this refresher will bump up the honey yield from his apiary to a ton, a target last attained in 1949. The heat wave is all in favour of the bees, says Mr. Almond, a

member of the Liverpool branch of the Lancashire Beekeepers' Association and regarded as a foremost authority on beekeeping.

During the bad weather of last summer, which almost decimated the bee population of Lancashire, Mr. Almond, by careful feeding, maintained his stock. This week he has added to his bee collection by taking in swarms which were reported on the wall of a banana store in Shaw Street and in buildings in Glover Street, St. Helens. Whenever there are appeals from the public about bees the police call him in. Armed with skep smoker, and carbolic cloth, Mr. Almond turns out at any hour to collect a cast which he rounds up within the hour and transfers to the cottage garden which overlooks Eccleston Mere. This bee reserve is surrounded by acres of wild white clover. Beekeeping is Mr. Almond's principal hobby and he makes it pay.

In July 1956 the Echo reported that Harry had been receiving emergency telephone calls of bee infestations every day that week. Swarms had been removed from a garden gate post at Blackbrook, the door of a house in Phythian Street, garden hedges at Portico and a street in Sutton Manor.

"Householders always seem a little panic-stricken when they tell me about a swarm", said Harry. Then four years later under the headline *"Naturally, They Sent For Harry"*, the St Helens Newspaper of July 9th 1960 described more actions of the brave beeman of Eccleston:

Bees, thousands of them, migrated in two dense swarms on Thursday afternoon. It appeared midsummer madness to the casual onlooker – but to the bees it was obviously a serious business. Swarm number one, comprising some 25,000 caused consternation and not a little amusement when they descended in Pocket Nook Gas Works – on the rear number plate of a grey saloon car belonging to Mr. Bert Oulton, a gas-fitter, 8, Ash Avenue, Newton-le-Willows. This resulted in Mr. Harry Almond, beekeeper for 40 years, Springfield Farm, Eccleston, being called in. The rear number plate of the car was literally dripping with insects, inches deep. The car was moved from the main thoroughfare of the gas works to the car park for safety.

Mr. Almond, dressed in green top and matching corduroys, was as cool as ice in contrast to the large gallery of bemused spectators, and simply scooped the bees with his hands into a box, a temporary hive occasionally dosing them with smoke. He said: "They have probably swarmed because their hive was congested." It was a prime swarm, including one queen. He estimated there were 25,000 bees – 5,000 to the pound. Swarm number two landed in a low privet hedge at the side of a bowling green in Recreation Park. They also came under the control of Mr. Almond. It is believed a third swarm landed in a telephone kiosk near the Fingerpost public house during the week.

By 1970 the 75-year-old had retired from his dairy farm and was living in Church Lane in Eccleston. However, Harry had still retained his beehives, which had expanded considerably. The Echo on July 22nd 1970 described how he then possessed eight hives with 80,000 bees in each and would soon be taking the lot on their annual Welsh holiday. Harry passed away in 1983.

e) THE ST HELENS EARTHQUAKE

Unusual manifestations don't necessary have to come out of the skies, of course. Ground-based ones can be pretty scary too. In St Helens subsidence – that has been mainly caused by mining activity – has regularly occurred over the years. Usually the deterioration in buildings' alignment and the appearance of sinkholes has been a slow process over time. But when other factors were keyed in – such as heavy traffic on roads – dramatic collapses sometimes occurred.

On the morning of August 7th 1920 a large sinkhole measuring a dozen feet deep and several yards long and wide suddenly appeared on a stretch of Liverpool Road, near its junction with Glover Street. The St Helens Reporter wrote:

> Had the fall occurred as a tramcar was passing, the vehicle would almost have vanished from sight, as the hole was nearly deep enough to hold it.

Then on May 30th 1961 two Parr schoolboys called Geoffrey Waring and Mark Burke were returning home after playing cowboys. They were about to jump from a pile of sand on to the surface of the filled-in Ashtons Green Colliery shaft when the ground on which they would have landed suddenly gave way leaving a gaping 50-feet deep hole. The boys' escape from death was described at the time as miraculous.

And on November 20th 1970 the Reporter described how a huge hole that had appeared on a Parr housing estate was being blamed on the 1926 miners' strike. The sudden earth movement took place on a lawn yards from houses in Cotswold Grove and created a hole measuring 10 ft deep and 5 ft wide. St Helens Corporation officials felt the most likely cause was a surface mining shaft giving way. A Town Hall spokesman said: "Many people dug for coal in the area during the miners' strike in 1926. Timber pit props probably rotted and caved in."

But earthquakes are without doubt the most dramatic and scary of the lot. Fortunately, the quakes that we experience in this country are very minor, with the biggest occurring in 1931. That is dubbed the Dogger Bank earthquake and it had a magnitude of 6.1 on the Richter scale. The tremor began at around 1:30 am on June 7th with its epicentre at Dogger Bank, sixty miles off the Yorkshire coast. The effects were felt throughout the country with the worst damage occurring in eastern England.

In St Helens the quake was believed to have brought down a garage in Hardshaw Street but the main concern had been fear, as the St Helens Reporter described:

> The earth tremor was undoubtedly felt, and singularly enough, was more severe in some parts of the town than in others. Dentons Green seems to have been fairly rattled, and though no damage is reported, many stories are told of shaking beds, rattling pictures, and vessels that were shaken. Then from York-street through Kirkland and Peter-streets the shock seems to have travelled with some intensity and away out at Thatto Heath it is learned that the 'quake caused considerable alarm by reason of houses being rocked, and pictures thrown from their hangings.
>
> Tremors of the earthquake caused alarm in Kurtz Ward at the St. Helens Hospital. Mr. H. Latham, 112, Peasley Cross-lane, who has been a patient in Kurtz Ward for some weeks, declared that the building shook and there was a rumbling sound which lasted from ten to fifteen seconds. "It was like heavy traffic going past the hospital," he said. The patients were awakened in their beds shaking, and a number of them called out in alarm, bringing Nurse Cookson, who was in charge of the ward, hurrying to them to see what was the matter. The fact that this ward alone of both the hospitals felt the shock is probably accounted for by the presence of a seam of coal which runs some way below the surface directly beneath the ward. This seam would be likely to conduct the tremors more readily.

St Helens Dogs That Have Made The News

*"We know he is not much good;
he is only a mongrel, but we love him!"*

Over the years St Helens dogs have made the news for all kinds of reasons – some good, other less so. This chapter is devoted to a wide range of doggy activities that made the pages of the local newspapers and I begin with a couple of comical canine tales.

THE HOLIDAY ADVENTURE OF BOW-WOW P.C. 9

On Whit Bank Holiday Monday of 1917 a Liverpool police dog with the name of Bow-Wow P.C. 9 decided to get into the holiday spirit and make his own excursion to St Helens. The Airedale terrier's adventure began after the dog had recognised a former member of the Liverpool constabulary who was stationed with his army regiment in Knowsley Park. Bow-Wow P.C. 9 followed the staff-sergeant to his camp but was ejected and so hopped onto a passing tram that was making its way to St Helens.

The canine traveller took a seat next to the driver, who after reading the lettering on the dog's collar passed his four-legged passenger onto St Helens police who contacted their colleagues in Liverpool. This is part of the Liverpool Echo's report into the activities of the canine truant:

> One of the Airedale terriers retained by the Liverpool City Police for auxiliary duty in searching out park pests, night larkers, &c., caught the Bank Holiday spirit on Monday, and vanished. When the dog – Bow-Wow, P.C.9 – failed to answer to the roll-call, inquiries were made, and eventually a telephone bell was rung by the St. Helens Police, who

announced that the missing "officer" had been handed over to their care by a driver of the South Lancashire Tramways Company....On the St. Helens report, the dog was brought back to the city, and by strict attention to duty is covering up his delinquency. Indeed, Bow-Wow P.C. 9 seems in a fair way to be awarded an extra "Liver" on his collar plate.

THE DOG THAT REFUSED TO GET OFF A TRAM!

It sounds like Bow-Wow P.C. 9 went quietly when asked to leave the tram on which he had briefly stowed away. But the St Helens Reporter of April 17th 1925 told of a dog that liked a double-decker tram so much that he stubbornly refused to vacate it. The comical story was told under the headlines *"Tramway Hold-Up – The Dog Which Wouldn't Get Off – St Helens Officialdom Defied":*

This is the true tale of a St. Helens dog which had so deep an affection for a tram-car that it refused to get off. It happened on Easter Tuesday, when, with its mistress, it boarded a Denton's Green car bound for the [St Helens] Junction. Its mistress dismounted at the Sefton Arms stop, forgetting her dog, which was left to the unfettered choice of staying on top of the car. Why, is not known, but the theory which gains general credence is that the lady was so mystified at finding all the shops closed, that the profundity of her predicament drove all thought of the dog out of her head. Master dog, however, was a particularly confident specimen of his tribe.

He remained behind as contented as you please, and when the car continued its journey was not a bit nonplussed. When, later, the conductor spied him he sniffed disdainfully – and the man with the punch continued his important functions down below. In due course the car reached the Town Hall-square, and when an inspector was informed he was rightly indignant. He would soon put that dog about its business! In language suitable to the occasion, and with the aid of a mysterious system of semaphoring especially designed by the department for the Removal of Stubborn Dogs Which Refuse to Understand Plain English, he made known his intention. The dog simply stayed put. A moment later he tasted the inspector's thumb, for which there is no suitable lotion detailed in the Guide Book for Perplexed Inspectors. Shedding his officialdom, the inspector did what every citizen in a quandary does. He called a policeman. If anything – loyal to the traditions and habits of its tribe – the dog thought less of that officer than he did of the inspector. His defiance was indisputable. It also possessed elements of danger. The P.C. knew the value of discretion. He washed his hands of the whole affair.

Meanwhile, things were getting serious. Traffic could not be held up indefinitely. So the word was given that the car, with the dog its solitary passenger, was to be taken to the [tram] shed, which was done accordingly. In the privacy of their own secret domain, the higher officials of the tramways department tried some very special methods to eject the unwelcome passenger – short, one presumes, of enlisting the aid of a live wire. Result, nil; and a growing savageness on the part of the dog, which was obviously getting tired of its unsought importance in the tramway scheme of things. A brain-wave on the part of an unnamed hero of the service developed a new line of attack. Why not find the owner's name from the dog's collar? How it was done is not revealed; but it was successfully accomplished.

A messenger was hurriedly sent to the address revealed on the collar. He did not own the dog, but his sister did. All the same, he was sure the dog knew him as an old and trusty family friend. Which, as events turned out, he did. Without so much as turning a hair, he commanded the dog to take its proper place in St. Helens and to come off that car. It did so, and the wagging of its tail seemed to indicate that nothing would have pleased it better than to have done so earlier on, if only it had been properly approached. Tramway officials will tell you, if you ask them, they have no theories to offer on How to Eject Unwelcome Dogs From Tramcars; but they are very emphatically of opinion that if someone with personal knowledge of this particular dog's demonstrably stubborn ways had not come to their rescue, the whole staff would have been gnawed to death, and the entire service indefinitely suspended.

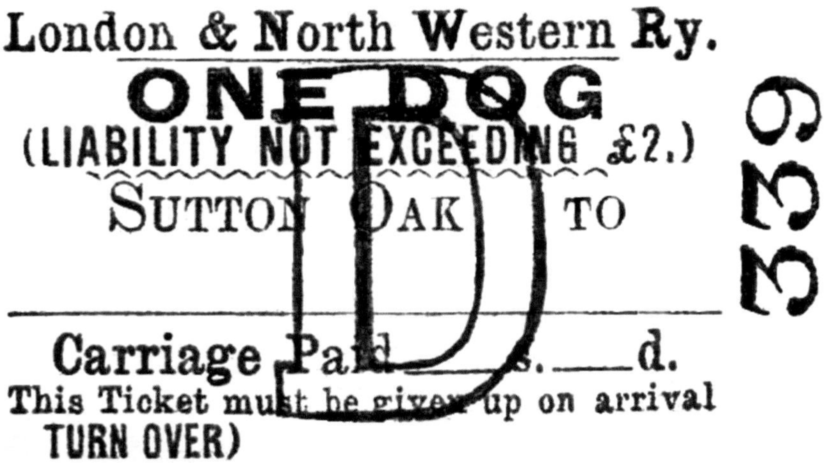

I can't say whether tram tickets for dogs were required – But you certainly needed a ticket to take your dog on a train.

THE MAN WHO PLACED HIMSELF UNDER THE PROTECTION OF A DOG

In Prescot Petty Sessions on May 3rd 1870, William Parr from Rainhill faced three charges of drunkenness. He pleaded not guilty to all charges, although the St Helens Newspaper said Parr did not appear to have been sober in the courtroom. PC Cook explained that the defendant had a habit of taking refuge by a dog kennel at Broach Villa on Warrington Road in Rainhill, "where no policeman dare touch him". Parr was familiar with a big dog at that house and would lie down in the open yard whenever the police were chasing him. The officer said: "It is his custom, when he got drunk, to place himself under the protection of the dog."

That did not please the dog's owner, William Johnson, who told the court that on the evening of Easter Sunday when people were coming out of church, William Parr had staggered onto his premises in a state of intoxication. Johnson added that the man had previously worked for him and so the dog knew Parr well. The Prescot Reporter's account of the hearing described how Parr had complained to the Bench of police persecution. They wrote:

> They had chased him some time ago to that degree that he had to fly out of this country into Yorkshire! Prescot was the town in which he was bred and born, and he had brought up a family of ten children here, and he wanted to live amongst them, but the police would not let him. He hoped their worships would not allow this, for he had always conducted himself rightly, and never injured anybody. The Chairman (looking at the charge book that had been handed up to him). Then it is a mistake that you were fined a few months ago for assault? – Defendant made no answer but scratched his head. The Chairman (continuing): And there are eight other charges recorded against you; but it will, no doubt, be a mistake altogether. You will be fined 5s. and costs in each of the three cases, altogether amounting to 31s. 6d.

THE DOG THAT SPOILED THE DRAPER'S CHRISTMAS DISPLAY

On Christmas Eve of 1906, the Liverpool Echo wrote about a dog having fun in what appeared to have been the draper's shop in

Bridge Street that belonged to Samuel Stansfield. Unfortunately, the animal's antics did not have a happy ending:

> A dirty mongrel dog rolling about the cottonwood, knocking down toys and Christmas decorations in the windows of a large drapery establishment, created great amusement and caused a crowd to assemble at the top of Bridge-street, St. Helens, this morning. The dog had entered the shop probably with the idea of securing some of the fancy rabbits that were on view. It bounded up and down and began to bark, and before it could be secured did considerable damage and quite spoiled the Christmas display. When secured the dog was handed over to Police-constable 80 (Evans), who conveyed it to the abattoir, to pay the penalty of its misdeeds.

THE MONGREL WITH NO LOVE FOR POSTMEN

The St Helens magistrates often despatched dogs that had bitten people to the Corporation abattoir to be gassed to death. That was in spite of what could be harrowing appeals for clemency from their owners. But on November 13th 1939 under the headline *"But No Love For Postmen"*, the Liverpool Evening Express described a dog from Normans Lane in Sutton that had won a reprieve:

> "We know he is not much good; he is only a mongrel, but we love him," said Mrs. Agnes Tickle, Norman's-lane, St. Helens, answering a summons at St Helens Police Court today, for not keeping a dog under proper control. Evidence was given that the dog had bitten a couple of postmen, but not seriously. Mrs. Tickle, in evidence, said the dog seemed to have no dislike to anyone but postmen. It played with children. The Chairman of the Bench (Mr. A. Rudd): "We will give you another chance to keep it under proper control." A postman's witness fee of 2s. 6d. was allowed.

THE PARR DOG THAT SAW OFF BOGUS GASMEN

A dog called Lady that had battled bogus gasmen in a most unladylike way was pictured in the Liverpool Echo on March 19th 1971 with this description of her heroics:

Vera Griffiths and Lady pictured in the Liverpool Echo on March 19th 1971

> Lady, a two-year-old mongrel under sentence of death, has earned a reprieve and the love of a St. Helens family after saving their mother from would-be intruders. The future looked bleak for the "unwanted hound" until she astonished everyone by attacking two tricksters who tried to force their way into Mrs. Griffiths' home in Brookway Lane, Parr. Mother of four, Mrs Vera Griffiths, had been considering having the family pet put to sleep, but after her heroic deed, Lady – shortly expecting her third litter of pups – is getting VIP treatment. Last night, as Lady chewed her way through a piece of best steak, 51-year-old Mrs. Griffiths explained what had happened:
>
> "A knock came at the back door and when I answered two well-dressed men asked if my husband was at home. They said they were from the gas board, but I immediately became suspicious as one of them was wearing gloves and was crunching his knuckles. The other man wedged his foot in the door and I became anxious. Lady must have sensed danger

> and leapt at the man, gripping his hand. Then she jumped at the other man and tore away at his trousers. The first man must have received a nasty gash because as they fled there was a trail of blood. We had talked about getting her put down, because it is such a nuisance when other dogs pester her. Today I wouldn't part with her for the world."

DAISY THE KIMMICKS CAVE DWELLER

The St Helens Reporter on April 27th 1968 carried a report on an abandoned dog called Daisy, which was living with her pups down a hole in the ground – "just like a rabbit", as the newspaper put it. In fact the white and brown mongrel was living in what was described as a mini-cave on the Kimmicks chemical waste heap off Borough Road. Edna Hillan had been helping to feed Daisy and her litter and told the Reporter:

> "The hole is very deep, and it's just impossible to reach inside...It looks as though her owners brought her to the area by car when they found she was having pups, and dropped her off. The local kiddies love her, anyway."

THE DOG STUCK IN A GRID

Do you remember that scene in Dad's Army when Pike got his head stuck in park railings and Captain Mainwaring chose to remove him (and the railings) to their HQ? Well, on June 20th 1969 the St Helens Reporter described a canine equivalent when a dog got its head stuck in a grid in Parr:

> When St. Helens firemen answered an emergency call to Fleet Lane, Parr, on Tuesday, they were faced with two hours of carefully manoeuvring to free a dog which had trapped its head in a sunken iron gas grid. The dog – a mongrel terrier – was carried, grid and all, back to the fire station after firemen were unable to free him and were

forced to dig up the grid. A fire brigade spokesman said: “We had to be very careful. We kept pulling the skin on the dog's head back a bit at a time and managed to wriggle him free.”

THE CALLOUS CULLING OF DOGS IN ST HELENS

In June 1969 Senior Inspector Alfred Drew of the St Helens and Wigan branch of the RSPCA made this disturbing statement to the Liverpool Echo:

> "It's quite common for people to ask us to put their dogs down because they are going on holiday. Or they come in with some lame excuse. The figures for the number of cases of dogs and cats put to sleep shoot up with a hell of a thump at holiday times. We have no option really. We know what would happen if we refused. They will have it done some way or other, and the animal may suffer."

Then at the start of January 1970, Inspector Drew complained to the St Helens Reporter about the increasing number of dogs that he had to destroy after Christmas. He told the paper that he was expecting to have to put down up to seventy Christmas pets at his Westfield Street clinic during the following few weeks, adding:

> "People often bring old pets to make room for young ones they are getting for Christmas. Then they return in a few weeks to have the new one destroyed."

Then on April 7th 1972 the Reporter ran a hard-hitting editorial on its front page calling St Helens a "topsy-turvy town". That was because its people raised huge amounts for charity every year – but also condemned 300 dogs annually to death. "Why don't we give a damn about dogs?", asked the paper's editor.

A separate front-page article in the Reporter by Eric Leatherbarrow described how the canine "death row" in St Helens was doing "brisk business", after dogs had been found guilty of the crime of being unwanted. Death row was the seven-day period from being handed into the police before the dogs were gassed to death. The week-long stay of execution was in the hope that the animals would either be claimed by their owner or found new homes. St Helens police handled a dozen strays every week and only half were saved from being put down in what the Reporter called the "gas chamber".

Dogs on "death row" as pictured in the St Helens Reporter

Pat Colgan was now the RSPCA inspector in charge of the St Helens district and he told the paper that St Helens had the worst record for stray dogs that he had encountered in his seventeen years of service:

> "I have worked in seven other places from Birmingham to Birkenhead but I have never seen a town like St. Helens for stray dogs. I wouldn't say people are cruel. They are just indifferent. So many want to get rid of dogs once they pass the puppy stage. They don't want the responsibility so they just turn them out. Other owners don't put a collar on their dog but they allow it to wander."

SCRUFFY THE REUNITED TERRIER

A far happier tale was told in the St Helens Reporter on December 31st 1971 when a terrier called Cindy *(aka Scruffy)* was rescued after being discovered in distress in Thatto Heath:

> Scruffy the terrier, might not be the prettiest lady on four paws – but this week she high-tailed her way into a family of top dogs. Now Scruffy, who's about a year old, has found a home-

from-home with Cathleen Forshaw. Cathleen, 23, and her husband Peter, spotted the wire-haired terrier, alone and lost – sitting in the middle of a busy main road. They took her home to join their own four dogs in Ilfracombe Road, St. Helens. Scruffy soon settled in with collies Cilla, Sherry and Vogue and alsatian Duke. "We were driving along Elephant Lane, Thatto Heath when we spotted Scruffy sitting down in the middle of the road," said Cathleen.

"Traffic was flying past her, just missing the poor thing by inches. We knocked on the doors of houses nearby, but nobody knew who she belonged to, and she had no collar on. We called her Scruffy because she was in such a dirty state when we found her. She's very friendly and gets along very well with our own dogs. But she whimpers when she hears a car – as if she is expecting someone to arrive in one. If nobody claims her, we'll definitely keep her."

However, it only took a few hours from the story's publication before the white terrier's rightful owner turned up to claim her. He was James Bottell of Harlow Close in Sutton Heath who told the Forshaws that Scruffy's real name was Cindy and she had been missing from her home for ten days after managing to slip out of their back door unnoticed.

Scruffy aka Cindy

Mr Bottell said his young son had been very upset over Christmas because of the dog's disappearance and Cathleen said that when the family had arrived at her home in Ilfracombe Road to claim Cindy, the terrier had been "all over them".

A man and his dog in Mill Brow in Sutton

PATSY THE MIRACLE CHIHUAHUA

The St Helens Reporter on March 27th 1970 told the miraculous story of Patsy the Chihuahua. The little dog had been missing from her Windle home for a fortnight during what was described as severe Arctic weather. Eventually Tom Anderton found the 3-year-old exhausted animal trembling in a ditch near the Bottle and Glass Inn in Rainford.

The gamekeeper on Lord Derby's estate at Knowsley almost shot Patsy thinking she was an injured rabbit. Realising his mistake, Tom took the dog to his home where his wife Sylvia and three young children brushed the mud off the little dog's coat and warmed her in front of the fire. Two days later the family discovered that Patsy's real owner was Ellen Owen of Blindfoot Road. However, Mrs Owen decided that her Chihuahua could stay with the family. Sylvia Anderton told the paper:

> The children are really thrilled with her. When Tom brought her in, she was in a really shocking condition – covered in mud, and really terrified. She refused to eat a thing until the

weekend. We never expected her to live the night. My youngest daughter, Beverly, couldn't sleep at all. She is only four, and she kept coming downstairs trying to feed Patsy with chocolate buttons. It seems impossible that such a little dog could have lived in the open through the terrible weather we've had.

A PUP GETS A CHANCE TO LIVE

With so much open water in St Helens, many dogs died by drowning – either by accident or the design of their owner. The fire service had their hands full rescuing such dogs – but, sadly, most were never claimed and had to be put down. Under the headline *"A Pup Gets The Chance To Live..."*, the St Helens Reporter of April 13th 1973 told of a happier outcome for one rescued dog:

> Men from St. Helens fire brigade this week saved a puppy from death by drowning – then from the threat of death. The firemen went into action when weeping children told them a terrified puppy was floating on rubbish in the polluted Sankey Brook. Leading fireman Eric Holland supervised the operations as fireman John O'Connell swarmed down a ladder secured to the bank to rescue the dog. Then another fireman, Ray Cotterill, of Newton Road, Parr offered the mongrel, called Major, a permanent home. Said Ray, 20: "I'd just returned from a fire call when I saw the pup, and I took to him straight away. I felt sorry for him. The last dog we rescued had been put down. I didn't want that to happen to Major." Eric Holland said: "We sometimes get tired rescuing these dogs from the brook, knowing they are going to get put down." And rescuer John O'Connell, 24, commented, "The dog was terrified but he let me help him. We took him to the station, gave him something to drink and washed him down. We were all made up when one of the lads decided to keep him."

THE FANTASTIC DISTEMPER DEATH TOLL

In the 1960s it was still common for dogs to be allowed by their owners to roam the streets of St Helens during the day. As well as causing many traffic accidents, the canines would congregate with others and, unless vaccinated, would often spread distemper. The contagious disease usually proved fatal and about 1,300 dogs died from distemper each year in St Helens.

Under the headline *"Dog Deaths Toll 'Fantastic'"*, the St Helens Newspaper of April 14th 1964 published this front-page article describing the problem:

> More than 25 dogs a week are dying needlessly in St. Helens and, unless something is done quickly, the town will have the worst record in England for dog deaths. This fantastic death roll can, and should be, stopped, a local veterinary surgeon told the Newspaper. In the last 18 months, 2,000 dogs are estimated to have died from distemper alone. The tragedy is that most of the deaths could have been avoided. The veterinary surgeon said that many heartbreaks could have been prevented for the cost of a couple of weeks' dog food. "There is an appalling ignorance among dog owners who have the idea distemper is akin to the common cold in humans, and can be cured. There is virtually no cure for this dreadful, quick-spreading disease. The only way owners can protect their pets is by vaccination which gives the animals an almost 100% protection against this most common dog disease." He added: "If babies died in St. Helens at the same rate as dogs in these last 18 months, it would be a national scandal. People just don't seem to realise that they are leaving their dogs open to a killer disease if they allow them into the streets without being vaccinated. Dogs in the town are

allowed to roam around in packs and, therefore, are much more prone to pick up the disease."

THE BOY BOOKIES AT THE DOG TRACK

The inaugural meeting at the greyhound racecourse in Park Road in St Helens was held on November 5th 1932, with the first winner being a dog called Zelah. The animal was named after a place in the Bible – but that did not assuage local clergy who strongly objected to the existence of the track.

A year later it appeared their worst fears were being realised when on November 28th 1933 an article describing a court case was published in the Liverpool Echo. The piece began with a quote from magistrate William Gentry:

BOY BOOKMAKERS AT GREYHOUND TRACK.

"HORRIBLE" STATE OF AFFAIRS AT ST. HELENS.

A boy of 15 was ordered to pay a fine of 20 shillings at the juvenile court at St Helens yesterday for loitering for the purpose of betting outside the St. Helens greyhound racing track.

It was revealed in evidence that between 150 and 200 people—men, women and children—gathered outside the track nightly around boy bookmakers and boy clerks. and children carried on betting on a large scale.

Nottingham Journal November 29th 1933

> "It is one of the biggest, blackest blots on the fair name of this town, and this greyhound racing business, particularly among the children and little toddlers, is doing more to bring people to the gutter and intensify the already existing poverty and suffering than everything else of which we have knowledge." So said the chairman of the St. Helens Juvenile Court (Mr. Gentry), this morning, in dealing with a fifteen-years-old "bookie," who was charged with taking bets on Monday evening, November 13. Constable Davies said he saw this lad acting as clerk to a man who was taking bets on the railway embankment alongside the greyhound track at Park-road, St. Helens. There was a crowd of from 200 to 250 people clustering on the embankment, a good

proportion of which were women and children. The bookmakers and some of the children had flashlamps, which they were working. They could see the races and tell from the colour of the dogs which had won. It was difficult for him to get near when in uniform, but on this night he went in plain clothes. There was a great turmoil and rushing about, and he could hear the young boys asking one another how much they had won at the conclusion of each race.

St Helens Newspaper advert from 1937

The Chairman. – What ages were they? [Constable Davies:] – From nine to fifteen years. I saw one boy writing on a programme with the help of a flashlamp and he told me that he had a record of the times each dog took for the race, and when asked his age he said he was nine. The Chairman. – So this defendant was encouraging the kiddies? [Constable Davies:] – Yes, he was acting as clerk and I caught him, but could not get hold of the adult.

Superintendent Cust said this was a great nuisance. There was no doubt that the bookmaking went on as much outside the course as inside, and it was done by children of all ages. He asked the magistrates to assist in putting a stop to this state of affairs. The Chairman said it was particularly sad to

> find children mixed up with this scandalous, anti-social state of things. They fined defendant 20s, as he had been before the court on two previous occasions. They considered they were treating him very leniently.

THE FEROCIOUS PUP

As stated some dog owners were quite happy to allow their pets to roam the streets of St Helens, only returning home for their meals and to sleep. In St Helens Police Court on June 12th 1925, it was stated that Michael Nolan of Rigby Street had told a constable that his animal was perfectly entitled to wander about:

> My dog will not hurt anyone if it is left alone. I have a licence for it and it has as much right to go about the footpaths as any of the people.

He was in court for "allowing a ferocious dog to be at large, and with not keeping it under proper control." Michael Nolan claimed his animal was far from ferocious, insisting it was a harmless 11-month-old pup. But a couple of lads begged to differ. 15-year-old Charles Yates of Rigby Street told the court that he had been visiting a pal when Nolan's dog bit him on his leg.

Eric Minshall lived at the Running Horses Hotel and corroborated Charles' account. The 12-year-old also complained of the same dog biting him at Easter as he was playing with a ball. The dog's owner insisted that the boys must have "done something wrong to it" for his animal to bite them. The magistrates knew that lads did sometimes torment dogs and decided to dismiss the case upon payment of costs but advised Michael Nolan to keep his pup under proper control in future.

Memories Of The Old Days

"We enjoyed Christmas immensely under the circumstances of workers getting wages you could just exist on. Everyone seemed in the same boat. The poor helped the poor."

The "old days" is, of course, a very subjective term relative to an individual's time of life. During the first half of the 20th century, the old days were, to many people, the Victorian times when life was very different. Then in the second half of the century, the old days referenced the first or second world war and for some people periods of unemployment and poverty.

Sometimes when a worker retired from their job after decades of service or reached a landmark age, they would reminisce about their old days to the St Helens' newspapers. And so this chapter is devoted to a number of examples of such recollections:

a) William Davidson – Blacksmith For The Trams

The horse-drawn omnibus service between St Helens and Prescot

William Davidson had been born in Montrose in Scotland in 1865. When the young man came to reside in St Helens in the late 1880s, the trams comprised passenger carriages hauled by horses. The service operated by the St Helens & District Tramways

Company had only begun in 1881 but within eight years the decision was taken to replace horsepower with "Puffing Billy". That was the nickname that some gave to the steam tram, which used a separate engine to haul the passenger conveyance.

The steam-powered "Puffing Billy" replaced the horse-drawn bus

"Puffing Billy", like the horse-drawn trams, was short-lived and in 1899 electrical power replaced steam. Their convoluted overhead traction wiring caused some curiosity and one miner was reported as saying: "Well, I've seed mony a tram pulled by 'orses and steam-engines, but I never seed one driven by a ______ fishing-rod afore."

The electric trams replaced steam in St Helens

Then in 1914 the first motor bus service started running and in 1927 trolleybuses began appearing on the St Helens' streets. The career of William Davidson transcended all these innovations in modes of transport and under the headline *"Trams Blacksmith Retires – Mr. Davidson Looks Back – 'The Good Old Days'"*, the St Helens Reporter of January 13th 1931 published this article:

"If some of the young bucks of to-day were to see a tramcar pulled by horses along Church-street, they would either have a fit or sign the pledge." Thus declared William Davidson, blacksmith, of Harris-street to a Reporter representative the other day. Mr. Davidson, who is in his sixty-sixth year, recently retired from his position as blacksmith to the St. Helens Tramways Department, a post that he held for more than forty-three years. "It is a far cry," he said, "to the days when the horse drawn tramcars used to carry passengers. In days gone by, a young fellow, who did his courting, say, at Prescot, journeyed slowly and painfully along, the journey taking almost an hour. Sometimes when the tram carried a big load of passengers, a spare horse would be trotted from 'The Feathers Hotel,' at the foot of Croppers Hill, and the animal would help to pull the load to the top of the brow. It [Croppers Hill] was known as 'Combshop Brow' in those days. Nowadays, the young bucks take out their motor bikes, and they're at their destination, before you can say, 'Jack Robinson'."

Mr. Davidson said when first he came to St Helens a stable of more than ninety horses was kept at the tram sheds, and it only cost about 3s. 6d. a week each to keep them – a great difference from what it costs to keep a horse these days. "You will often hear folks talk to-day," he went on, "of the good old days. They were good old days in many ways, and in some ways they were bad. People who travel in the modern luxurious trolley buses and motor buses, perhaps never give a thought to the days of the old horse trams or the snorting old steam trams, and the discomforts of travelling in them. Yet the cost of living in the old days was much easier. I got 32s. a week when first I came to St. Helens – and that was considered rather a princely wage in those days. A fellow could have a jolly good night out on a couple of bob. It only cost a few coppers for a first class seat at a theatre, and for a couple of shillings I have seen the late Wilson Barrett, one of the greatest actors of his day, play two or three times a week in such shows as 'The Silver King' and 'Romeo and Juliet'." Mr. Davidson has seen every form of transport in St. Helens from the old horse drawn car to the modern trolley bus. "Before I die," he added, "perhaps I may see St. Helens served by a fleet of airplanes and the road transport scrapped – but I am afraid I shall have to wait a good few years yet for that."

b) Police Inspector William Jackson

Inspector William Jackson

The retirement of a long-standing police officer sometimes led to an article being published in the St Helens' press describing their crime-fighting experiences. The 1911 census lists Inspector William Jackson as living in Sutton Road in St Helens with his wife Emma and four children. It was a hard life being a bobby but at least you could retire in middle age with a reasonable pension. Inspector Jackson retired in 1916 at the age of fifty and was awarded a pension of £109 10s per year. On February 4th 1916 the St Helens Newspaper published this profile of Jackson's career:

After twenty-nine years of meritorious service in the Borough Police Force, Inspector William Jackson retired on

Wednesday last. Possessing a rich fund of anecdote and narrative, Inspector Jackson related to a "Newspaper" representative many stories of the fierce fights between the police and Greenbank ruffians, of the stirring happenings during the great coal strikes of a decade ago, and of numerous mysterious cases investigated and the offenders prosecuted. A native of Westmoreland, he came to St. Helens to join the Borough Police Force on its inception in 1887, and his subsequent rise to superior rank was rapid. He relates how fierce conflicts commenced when the raw policemen, many of whom had not been served with their uniforms, commenced upon their unaccustomed duties. The exact date of this event was June 30th, 1887, and on that day the county policemen surrendered their task of preserving peace and order in the town to the St. Helens Borough Police Force, under the command of Chief Constable Wood.

Among the rougher element in the town the event was hailed with exceeding joy, and it was evident that the police were in for some stubborn fights. Inspector – then Police-constable Jackson – sallied forth from the Town Hall on the second day, with the pleasant anticipation of having to face the "music." Needless to say his anticipation was realised to the full. When patrolling the Greenbank district with Police-constable Hurst (later Police-sergeant Hurst), they were informed that a fight was in progress not far away. Hastening there they took the peace-breaker into custody, and simultaneously the wrath of the eager populace was let loose upon them.

The police did not hold their prisoner long, because Hurst was completely knocked out by some burly fellow, and Police-constable Jackson also sustained several injuries.

Despite the unwelcome attentions of the hostile mob he succeeded in removing Hurst from the scene of action. The ice being then broken the neighbourhood simply seethed with excitement, and altogether fifteen arrests were made that day. At night, when the weary policeman returned to the Town Hall, Chief Constable Wood said to him, "Go home Jackson, you have had enough for one day." Eventually, in April, 1893, he attained the rank of sergeant, so that in five years nine months service he had risen from constable to sergeant, and had gained the constable's merit badge.

Then he was sent to Sutton, and was there in the year of the great coal strike [1893], which commenced in July and lasted until November. The fact that many men persisted in working caused a lot of trouble, and matters became very serious on the 17th of October. At 12-30 on that memorable day Sergeant Jackson was on duty at Ashtons Green Colliery, with a few men. Thousands of people thronged the roads there, and the police were absolutely helpless. A message to the Town Hall brought relief in the shape of Chief Constable Wood with 30 men, and it was deemed advisable to bring up the men who were in the pit, before the night came on. The mob, however, was determined not to move until it had seen something. All the men arrived safely from below the ground, and then the game started.

A fusillade of stones came from an elevated waste bank, and the sight was one which will live long in the memories of those who participated in it. Several men went down in the first vicious attack, but the police commenced a return journey right on to the colliery premises. The fighting now raged more hotly than ever, and Sergeant Jackson was knocked down and severely injured in the back. Owing to the serious nature of his wounds he was detained in hospital, and for the following three months his duties knew him not. In connection with this strike he received the warm encomiums of persons in high authority.

In 1900 a case happened which occasioned tremendous interest locally. Two young children were drowned in a reservoir whilst in [the] charge of their mother, who told a strange but quite plausible story. It appeared that she was walking past the reservoir, which was unfenced, and the banks of which sloped downwards, carrying one child in her arms, and the other was toddling alongside. Some time later all three were found in the water, but the two children had succumbed. The mother told a very coherent story at the time. She deposed to Sergeant Jackson that she was walking along when the elder child slipped down the bank into the water. Placing her baby on the grass the mother jumped into the water to rescue the unfortunate youngster, and the devoted younger child followed also. The inquest was held at the Locomotive Inn after an adjournment, and the prisoner commenced to make a statement. Suddenly, she made a dramatic confession that she had murdered her two youngsters by drowning them. Sergeant Jackson at once took her into custody and conveyed her to the Town Hall, where it was afterwards found that she was insane, and she is insane to-day.

[Nb. The woman was Sarah Walton from Sutton Moss and the tragedy occurred at the reservoir of the Sutton Rolling Mill. It was eventually decided that the mother of ten had not drowned her daughters but had been "under a hallucination" when she'd confessed at the inquest due to severe mental stress. Sarah still spent sixteen days in custody, mainly prison.]

Fourteen or fifteen years ago party feeling ran high in municipal elections, and the police had to exercise

> considerable tact in dealing with the excited population. The subject of our sketch was on duty at no fewer than six General Elections, and he also played no unimportant part in the quelling of the Orange riots which were an annual occurrence in those days. Reverting to a subject which is very dear to him, Inspector Jackson expatiated on the improvements which have taken place in Sutton of late years. A tram service had been inaugurated and a new library and police station built. Street brawling had become a thing of the past, and as a working population he thought the people of Sutton would compare with any community in Lancashire. In 1905 Sergeant Jackson became Inspector Jackson, a position which he has occupied honourably and well for over ten years.

c) Police Inspector James Curran

James Curran was born in 1870 in Horwich near Bolton and came to St Helens as a boy when his father was made head gamekeeper to Richard Pennington of Muncaster Hall in Rainford. James later joined the police and like William Jackson experienced much violence in the Greenbank district of St Helens, sandwiched between Liverpool Road and Canal Street, as well as in other rough parts of the town. On January 2nd 1925 the St Helens Reporter published this account of the inspector's career under the headline *"Inspector Curran – Retirement From St. Helens Police Force – Stirring Experiences In A Varied Life":*

> In the early days of his career, as a constable in St. Helens, he witnessed some stirring "shindies" in the Greenbank, Pocket Nook and Gerard's Bridge districts. At that time, these districts were well-known as very lawless places, and the ability to "scrap" a little was a very useful accomplishment to any policeman whose duties carried him into these spots. As a policeman walked down the streets of

those neighbourhoods it was no uncommon experience to receive a sudden present of a "punch on the nose," and this was not the worst feature of the inhabitants' infringements of the law. All these districts were infested with thieves, and cases of looting and shop-breaking were by no means few. On one occasion a van and a number of shops were raided, and a considerable amount of property was stolen. This was about the time [1905] when the present Chief [Chief Constable Ellerington] took over his duties and he immediately set about to reform Greenbank. He issued warrants to search a great many houses in the district for stolen property and the inhabitants did not get much rest. All the property was eventually recovered, the thieves arrested, and punished. Comparatively speaking, these districts are now meek and mild localities, due beyond doubt to the rigorous methods of Chief Constable Ellerington.

One of the many hundreds of cases, in which Insp. Curran has figured was a well-known case that occurred some years ago in Parr, when he arrested a man and woman who were subsequently tried and acquitted at the Liverpool Assizes on a charge of poisoning a child whom the woman had insured for a large amount. On another occasion about five years ago he arrested single-handed one of the most notorious coiners and criminals in England, Charles Knight Beaumont. He was a very dangerous and violent man, wanted all over the country, and was known to carry firearms. When Insp. Curran arrested him he found a large number of counterfeit half-crowns in his possession.

d) Centenarian Mary Hill

When Mary Hill died in the geriatric ward of St Helens Hospital in December 1967 at the age of 109, it was reported that she had been the oldest person in Britain. Four years earlier, Mary had been interviewed by the St Helens Newspaper, which on August 20th 1963 published this article:

Parents today are not strict enough with their children, says Miss Mary Maude Hill, 47, Kiln Lane, Dentons Green, who celebrated her 105th birthday yesterday. "Young people are allowed too much freedom. Far more than we had and this is a bad thing," she commented. Miss Hill thinks this is because parents are not interested enough to take time and trouble with their children. Miss Hill's 105th birthday began with a wonderful surprise – a telegram from the Queen. She last received one on her 100th birthday. The telegram read:

"The Queen is much interested to hear that you are celebrating your 105th birthday and sends you warm congratulations and good wishes on this memorable occasion."

Miss Hill

Miss Mary dies at 109

Believed to be the oldest person in Britain, Miss Mary Hill died in St. Helens Hospital to-day aged 109.

She had been a patient in the geriatric ward since last July.

Miss Hill, who formerly lived in Kiln Lane, St. Helens with her niece, Mrs.

Liverpool Echo
December 13th 1967

Although Miss Hill's pale blue eyes are now practically sightless, she still dresses herself. As she says, she is in the dark all the time now, but every morning, sitting on the end of her bed, she brushes and fixes her silvery hair herself. What does she think of the modern beehive hair-do?

"Much easier to manage than ours was," said Miss Hill, recalling the elaborate hairstyles, dressed with fresh flowers, that she and her friend had to go to dances and parties. Miss Hill is shocked at the way in which today's young women can go dancing unescorted. "I never went in a dance hall in my life," she added. "Parties and dances were always held in the homes of friends or at school." Receiving a telegram from the Queen reminded Miss Hill of an incident when she was 21. An attempt was made on Queen Victoria's life and she and her sister Alice sent a message expressing their concern at the incident. They received a letter bearing Queen Victoria's seal, which Miss Hill still has. Sitting in the armchair in the front room of No. 47, Miss Hill, a slight but lively lady, chuckled as she said a few words on today's short skirts, "I think they're ugly," she said emphatically. "And the shorter they go the uglier they are."

e) Ice Skating Champion William Hughes

Big freeze brought back memories

'Old timer' would like a partner to go skating

Ice leaves most people cold. But this week's big freeze has brought many happy memories for 81-years-old Mr. William Hughes, 183, West End Road, Haydock. Gazing through the window of his home, he recalls the days when he was famous in the district as a skater.

"I wouldn't mind having a go even now, if I could find some old fellow to come with me," said this grand old man who can remember the time 80 years ago when chestnuts were roasted on the frozen Carr Mill Dam.

"In those days it was a common sight to see horses and carts on the ice" he said.

Mr. Hughes started work in the mines when he was 12. "I started skating when I was nine," he said, and added as an afterthought, and was supping ale too.

St Helens Reporter January 25th 1958

For hundreds of years ice skating contests took place at Carr Mill – attracting, at times, many thousands of spectators. On January 25th 1958 the St Helens Reporter profiled William Hughes as he reflected on his days as a champion ice skater on Carr Mill Dam. The report was published at the end of a week in which snow had fallen quite heavily in Lancashire, with over a foot lying on Saints' ground in Knowsley Road. So Mr Hughes – pictured with his wife Margaret – was wallowing in nostalgia and wishing he could get back on the ice, as the Reporter described:

> Ice leaves most people cold. But this week's big freeze has brought many happy memories for 81-years-old Mr. William Hughes, 183, West End Road, Haydock. Gazing through the window of his home, he recalls the days when he was famous in the district as a skater. "I wouldn't mind having a go even now, if I could find some old fellow to come with me," said this grand old man who can remember the time fifty years ago when chestnuts were roasted on the frozen Carr Mill Dam. "In those days it was a common sight to see horses and carts on the ice", he said.
>
> Mr. Hughes started work in the mines when he was 12. "I started skating when I was nine," he said, and added, as an afterthought, "and was supping ale too." In his youth, Mr. Hughes was the target of young ladies in the district who wished to learn how to skate. "I really liked skating and racing over any distance from 100 yards to a quarter of a mile, although my best distance was 200 yards," he said. "In 1906 I raced against Tom Colquitt of Fingerpost, who was very well-known. The race was over a 180 yards on Carr Mill Dam and he won a very close verdict. In a 200 yards match against Bill

Tom Colquitt

Highcock, of Parr, I won easily after giving him a five yards start. He beat me over 100 yards so a return match over 200 yards was arranged. There was an agreement that if either of us refused to take the ice on the day of the match we would forfeit £25. There had been a thaw and the ice was six inches underwater. I jumped on to the ice and Highcock followed me. We were the only ones who went on the ice that day and I managed to win easily but at the finish I was like a drowned rat."

Forty-one years ago Mr. Hughes almost lost his life after falling through the ice while practising on Blackbrook Canal. "I can't swim but I managed to struggle back to the hole in the ice and was rescued by other skaters. But I had to have 17 stitches in a head wound," he said. "I don't know how he is still living," remarked Mr. Hughes' 78-years-old wife, Margaret, who watched her husband race on countless occasions. "He could do anything on ice and other skaters used to stop and watch him," said Mrs. Hughes.

Mr. Hughes' racing days came to an end after a bad fall on Carr Mill Dam. Revealing the incident Mr. Hughes said, "I was 41 and my opponent, Jack Highcock, of Parr, was only 22. It was a 200 yards race and I was winning by about 13 yards, when about 15 yards from the tape, I slipped and somersaulted several times. That ended my racing days."

With pride, Mr. Hughes examined the silver-plated size 6 skates he used in most of his races. "They are 60 to 80 years old and I bought them from Joseph Bates, of Leigh. He was an all-England champion – over any distance – he wasn't particular." There was a far-away look in Mr. Hughes' eye as, looking at the snow through the window, he said to his wife, "I wonder if it will hold."

f) Arthur Jones' Memories of Christmas

On December 13th 1974 Arthur Jones had a letter published in the St Helens Reporter describing his life as a child at the beginning of the 20th century. The "luxuries" that his family enjoyed in their Peasley Cross home at Christmastime would certainly be considered trivial today – but nonetheless they were very special to them then. Arthur's remarkable letter was published under the headline *"Christmas Luxury Years Ago":*

> Christmas Day was a day of luxury for us; we had a large family and had to prepare for this special festival weeks before. It was a period of the "patch and mend" days and sock-darning. The churches played a very important part along with the day and Sunday schools in the social and spiritual side of the Christmas season. I was one of the many lucky children. In my day I had ½d a week to spend, which I used to take to Mr. Kinnan's sweetshop at the corner of Cleveland Street and Marshalls Cross Road. Mr. Kinnan, a very kind man, would mark it on a card each week for 24 weeks, until it mounted up to one shilling. Then, on Christmas Eve, I would go and collect my large box of sweets and chocolates ready for Christmas Day. That was my Christmas present, solved by my own thinking. We had to stand on our own feet in those days. Some children were luckier than I was – they had a penny a week, especially if they belonged to a small family.
>
> I went to Robins Lane council school. We always broke up at midday on Christmas Eve and came home with a large orange, books etc. supplied by Beechams and oracles and books advertising their wares. We used to light these oracles and a spark would travel round and turn a design out. I never see them these days; they are out of date. They used to tell me that saltpetre was added to the paper in

manufacture. I attended Sunday school regularly and we always had a motto, which had various texts printed on it from the Bible. We would hang these up in the bedroom. On Christmas Eve we would all go to bed early and on a cold night, my father would wrap the warm oven shelves in cloth and place them in the bed to keep us warm.

Then we would go through the motions of hanging our stockings on the bedrail, hoping Father Christmas would come down the chimney. He was not very generous to us because he had such a lot of houses to go to in Peasley Cross. We would wake up on Christmas morning, crawl in the dark to the bottom of the bed and shout with joy when we found an apple, orange and some nuts. If we were lucky there was also a small toy valued at one penny. We would go to sleep again, only to be awakened by bands playing at the crossroads. Despite the weather, they always turned out, including the concertina band.

We did all our own decorations – holly from the hedgerows – and, as we could not afford a Christmas tree, we used to use a gorse bush. It was a bit prickly, but served the purpose and we made our own games in the house, never bored at any time. A great friend of ours would come on Christmas night and recite some poems. We had an old harmonium we played; my father gave £1 for it. Christmas dinner went very well. We would have a couple of imported Australian rabbits – frozen in those days – costing 6d. each at the butcher's. As we lived behind the butcher's shop in Peasley Cross, we would thaw the rabbits out for him in front of the fire on a large clothes maiden.

We enjoyed Christmas immensely under the circumstances of workers getting wages you could just exist on. Everyone seemed in the same boat. The poor helped the poor and all the people of Peasley Cross were a magnificent community. Any descendants of those people now spread out in the world should be proud of them and the sacrifices they endured to survive stands out in my memory. Lest we forget. We all looked forward to Christmas for that bit of extra food.

g) Dolly and Cecil Wood's Homemade Remedies

Pictured here are Dolly and Cecil Wood as they appeared in the St Helens Reporter on July 17th 1965. The couple were celebrating their golden wedding anniversary and in the accompanying report described how they had used traditional homemade remedies to keep their children fit and healthy:

"Oh we hardly ever had the doctor to our children" said 'Dolly' Wood, 95, Furness Avenue. And then she explained why: "For chest trouble the kiddies wore shirts of brown paper coated with goosegrease. For a cough they consumed a stewed-in-the-oven concoction of linseed, thick spanish and lemon juice." A tickle in the throat? – Honey and paragoric drops was the remedy. Dogfat for aches and (dare I go on) a sprinkling of mustard on treacle for the bronchials. But the "warder-off-in-chief" was dished out to the six Wood children every Saturday morning. They lined up before Dad for their senna pods in water, which had been placed in the oven the night before by Mother. "The children were fit all right," said Mr. Woods. He was 72 on Tuesday, and he and his wife celebrated a half-century of marriage on Wednesday. The couple reminisced this week at their neat home on the Windle Hall Estate.

Cecil Wood was born on Friday the 13th. "I wanted to get married on the same date," he said, "but my wife wouldn't have it. So I had to wait 24 hours. Anyhow," he chuckled, "this way I'm getting two lots of cards." The couple were married at Lowe House Church by Fr. Reginald Riley. Mrs. Wood ("Mary Agnes they christened me, but everyone calls me Dolly") was born in St. Helens at St. Anne's Cottage, Laurel Road. All his working life – 52 years of it – Mr. Wood was a plumber, and for 25 years was secretary to St. Helens Plumbers' Society. They have 16 grandchildren and one great-grandchild. Their success recipe for a 50 year course of happiness: "Tolerance," they chorused. "Back down, and let the other person be right."

h) T. A. Owen

Thomas Alfred Owen was born in 1899 and brought up in Elephant Lane in Thatto Heath. He rose to become the secretary of the T. & T. Vicars engineering works by Earlestown Station and also wrote many articles for the St Helens Reporter. These were under the pseudonym of "Satiricus" – when Mr Owen was contributing to features on current affairs – and as "Recorder" when writing about rugby league. In later years he occasionally wrote articles on the history of St Helens as T. A. Owen. In a two-part piece published on April 24th and May 8th 1970, Mr Owen lamented the loss of many colourful characters from St Helens:

> In the course of my lifetime so much of the colour and excitement has gone from the streets and from human contacts. Take food. At one time, a baker like Harry Parr in Thatto Heath used his ovens to bake domestic bread. Women mixed the dough and used the tins supplied, and their children took the family bake to Parr's, receiving a tally which they later used to collect the baked loaves. He charged, I think, 1d. per loaf. Bread was bread in those

days. "Lightcake" sellers used to go from door to door with trays suspended from their necks. The goods were laid out in snow-white linen – lightcakes, oatcakes and muffins. The sellers announced themselves by the tinkling of a silver bell. Gaunt men trudged along the streets, carrying long poles, split at the top and shouting a most melancholy cry, "Line-Perops," meaning props to hold up a line of washing. A smart, natty chap, answering to the name of "Oyster Tom," visited all the pubs at weekends, with a basket filled with oysters, and complete with salt, pepper, lemons and vinegar. Oysters were 1d. each.

Another smart little man was Tommy Mather, complete with a hair-line moustache and a brisk line of patter with which he regaled pub hunters, via a talking doll. Tommy Mather made it his business to know all the local scandals and adventures, and for many, many years made a good living out of teasing the population and making them howl at each other's discomfiture through his "talking doll." One splendid thing about pubs – there were some bad things too, because of excessive drinking – was that when the men got to the singing stage, they were just as likely to sing hymns of the livelier sort and even anthems, often most harmoniously.

Female gypsies went from door to door, often with quite large caskets on their heads, selling pegs and lace and telling fortunes. And I vividly remember a tribe of gypsies settling for a day or two on Thatto Heath's great heath, called the "Mushroom Field", alas now sadly diminished and tamed. They toured the neighbourhood in batches and laid siege to all houses either selling things or collecting scrap. They had a herd of donkeys – at least 50 beasts – which they drove down Elephant Lane and all adjacent streets. They were selling grown animals at 10s. and part-grown for as little as 6d. One day I saw a horse and cart piled up with large bowls for kitchen sink washing up. The salesman was singing his offer: "Fine pan mugs, large pan mugs, good pan mugs today, who'll buy my fine pan mugs, two shillings to pay." It was a lovely sing-song tune, with a sad cadence to it. It brought me to tears.

Chief Constable Ellerington was a giant of a man, more than six-feet-tall and built proportionately. For a Royal visit Ellerington had himself rigged out in a most magnificent uniform – to which the Labour members of the council vociferously objected. They sought to refuse to pay the £40 or £50 bill. He sat in an open car looking for all the world like a cross between an Admiral of the Fleet and a Field Marshal. I heard one awestruck bystander shout, quite loudly: "By gum! He looks like a proper bloody Prussian." And in some ways, Prussian he was.

Fridays and Saturdays could be a rough place in St. Helens. When Ellerington came he increased the size of the force, and (so the tale went) he said he would be able to suspend a gold watch from a spar in the centre of Greenbank (a district where the police when they patrolled it all went in squads) and find it still there the following day. True or not, it was characteristic and could have happened, for he masterminded the magistrates into severer sentences and he put the fear of God into known criminals. A hard disciplinarian, he was respected, but not loved.

Who remembers Johnny Dempsey? Is Billy the everlasting, unchanging newsboy still crying his wares in that wailing, almost unintelligible voice of his? Does anybody still remember "Rag Mary," who trailed a large barrow for years, all over town and suburbs? She had the one unchanging, high-pitched bellow of a cry: "Rag-bone, chalk or rubbing stone and brick-dust." She accepted jam jars, rags, and odd pieces of domestic ornament or kitchenware and gave yellow sticks of sugar toffee to the children, in exchange. A tall, gaunt woman with trailing skirts and many woollen jumpers she was tireless and ageless. There were many such and I still see the last remaining rag-bone man occasionally. A sturdy fellow, by no means subservient, his outfit lacks the charisma of rag-Mary.

Now Johnny Dempsey lived by his wits. He had quite a brain and a ready wit. He was not above taunting and insulting Town Councillors in the street and on their way to the Town Hall. They would laugh and grind their teeth doing it. One of his sources of income came from the sale of cough candy, at 1d. per small packet, to theatre and lecture queues. Yes! We had long queues for the theatre in those ever to be lamented days when grand plays and fine actors delighted audiences who had far finer perceptions and took far greater intelligent interest, than the moronic pop fanatics of today. Films were well made and well acted. We cheerfully queued half an hour to get in. And, as such, we were ready-made clients for Johnny Dempsey who really forced you to spend a penny on his aromatic confections, especially as he always threw in free, a step dance and a snatch of comic song – sometimes a quip about prospects with the girls.

Long after his passing, while yet queues were still the rule, a very solemn, well-dressed, and rather handsome man continued for quite a few years to walk slowly along the queue. He never spoke. He was never aggressive, even when attacked or insulted. His wife (presumably), usually came with him to carry a kind of framed placard on which he had carefully printed a message. These were of the "Beware the day of Wrath" type, or "Jesus saves Sinners." He let you read his message and so passed slowly down the queue. A most sad, most dignified, most strange man. I hope he found peace. He had earned respect, if he made no converts. He never solicited money. Virtue, in his case, was its own ample reward. They said he'd been a captain in the late war.

As for Billy the newsboy, he hailed from Peasley Cross district. He had some severe impediment in his speech and he seemed always to be shall we say, inadequately covered up, his bare chest often showing through his open-at-the-neck shirt; and his shoes hardly stout or waterproof to look at. Yet in hail, rain or snow, Winter and Summer alike, Billy cried his evening papers, often until past the closing of the pubs and the emptying of last houses of the theatres and lecture palaces. I should add that Billy was by no means unintelligent and could make a lovely retort now and then. The story goes (I can't vouch for it), that a smart-Alec said to Billy, "No use offering me an evening newspaper. I've heard and seen it all. I've got a telly." "Aye," said Billy, "but tha' can't use th' telly in th' W.C. afterwards".

Another possibly well remembered character was our last sandwich-board man. His name was Jones. He had a brother – so I was told – holding a foreman's job at one of the local works, but sandwich-board Jones was not one of your solid work-a-day types. Far from it. For one thing, he was a part-time artist's model, and art students at the Gamble Institute have (in an earlier generation) portrayed, or modelled him in many guises – usually as a prophet. Caravaggio would have loved him as a "subject" for Jonesey had the face of an Angel. Local shopkeepers hired him to patrol the streets with a board front and back advertising some "special offer". He was on the portly side, and shabbily attired in old cutaway coats; but he usually contrived to have a top hat, somewhat battered on his noble head.

I last saw him, many years ago, made something of a fool of – to my bitter resentment – at a big Rugby League match at St. Helens Football ground. They had dressed him in Red and White bands – the team colours – even to his faithful top hat, and they had him capering about the field, as a pre-match entertainment doing silly little prancing dances and kicking the ball about. I should add that he did, many times up there, receive "a bob or two", and a splendid tea of dear old Lionel Swift's excellent meat pies, and ham sandwiches. After all, I knew an ex-bare fist fighter of some distinction in Thatto Heath, who would stand in front of the pub and cheerfully invite you to give your hardest thump in the jaw or the midriff, if you also gave him the price of a pint. In short poverty cannot afford tender feelings.

i) The Residents of Atlas Court

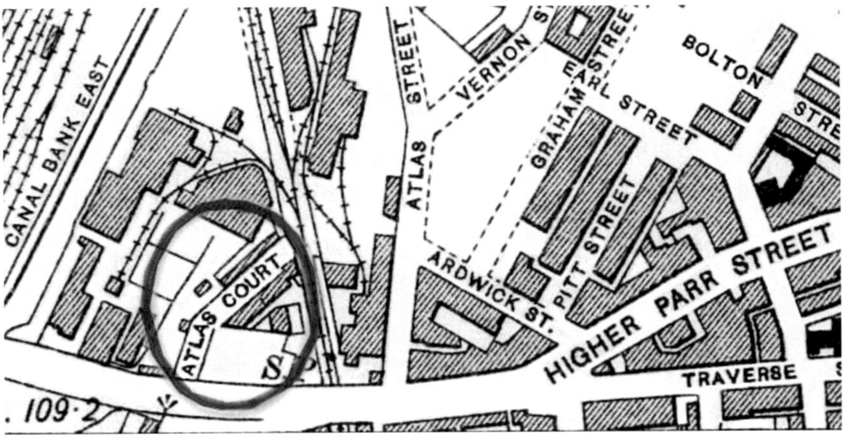

This map from 1906 shows the location of the short street in Parr known as Atlas Court. It was a tiny cul-de-sac of a community boxed in by railway lines but which over the years generated countless characters and memories. First appearing in the censuses in 1881 listing 17 households, Atlas Court by the 1960s was only hosting a dozen homes.

During the '60s and '70s, the St Helens Reporter published many articles about the conflicting sides to redevelopment. Scores of streets in the town were then being scheduled for demolition as part of slum clearance plans. However, many longstanding tenants were happy in their old homes and did not consider them slums.

This view looks towards the rear of little Atlas Court

Such folk had many memories of living in a community where everyone knew each other and often popped in and out of each other's houses. They knew that life would never be the same in their new place of abode – even if the replacement house was modern with much better facilities. The cheap rent in their old house was also a consideration for those on low incomes – as it would shoot up in their posh new property. When in 1961 the St Helens Reporter wrote about the doomed Atlas Court, it was one of the first articles that examined residents' conflicting feelings and some interesting memories of the past were also shared. The piece was published on May 13th under the headline *"Old World Part Of St. Helens – The Happy Dwellers Around Atlas Court":*

> Traffic clanged monotonously by overhead. Shunted railway wagons clanked and rattled, and a lorry backed slowly up the cobbled roadway. Atlas Court, nestling below one of St. Helens busiest thoroughfares, a little to the East of the local shunting yards, has remained undisturbed for over a century. Shortly this survival of a bye-gone decade will pass into oblivion, as it will be reduced to a mound of dust and rubble beneath the blows of the workman's hammer. Time, which wrote such transformation all around, has now ordained its fate. Atlas Court is a "Tom Thumb" picture of domestic Lancashire life in the last century. Many memorials still remain in numerous towns. But St Helens is soon to lose one of the most picturesque relics.
>
> Slum clearance these days is generally understood to mean old houses. Outwardly, the small, cramped dwellings in Atlas Court qualify. Within are some of the cosiest homes found anywhere. When a Reporter staffman strolled into the cul-de-sac on Wednesday, it presented a scene depicted many times already on screen and in books. Dropping down from the highway, was five flights of old stone steps, and one has to pass beneath the bridge across which the world rushes by. Only then are you in the "Court." Submerged and separate from the life surging all around, this quiet little backwater has marked time. Children still play in the gutter and in the alley which links Atlas Court with Back Atlas Court. A dozen houses all told, but a community of its own.
>
> "We raised big families in this street," said an old man reclining in his armchair by the fire. Potato peelings hissed

on top of the glowing coals – an old Lancashire habit. John Drury (aged 67) has known no other habitation – except during the first World War – for 53 years. His sprightly little wife, Mary, 12 months his junior, has shared most of that time with him. They were unanimous on one point. "We are very happy here. This is just nice for us. The rent is only 6s. a week. If we get into a new house it will mean 30s. Our income is only £4 16s." The couple had seven children, but only four are living. "We would prefer to stay in Atlas Court," they said. On Monday they celebrated 45 years of married life in the same house with its two small bedrooms.

The greatest disturbance in Atlas Court came during the last war. The day it was bombed will long be remembered. Suddenly the lazy afternoon exploded in a great rumble and a cloud of dust. When the first shock had died away, people started taking stock. Smarting eyes gazed apprehensively out of doorways and windows. Fear gave way to laughter – the harsh type that stems more from relief than humour. The old brick wall opposite the houses had yielded, with advancing years and collapsed into the roadway.

Old William Power – 83 next month – can rake up some other memories. He used to help to harness an extra horse to take the old tram up Blackbrook Brow. That is going back some! He has lived at number 42 for more than 30 years. "You were not sure of your life when you first came down here," he said. The derelict old pub at the end of the Court had housed some unruly lodgers. "They would be fighting from morning till night," he remarked. William is quite a character. He is a veteran of the Boer War, and did his bit in the first world war as well. He served as a despatch carrier in the South Lancashire Regiment. Of Atlas Court, he said:

"In the old days people had large families. Although each house had only two bedrooms. But they were happy days."

On Wednesday a number of youngsters were pottering about. These younger residents in the Court would be glad to move house into the more spacious modern homes. For the kind of habitation in Atlas Court is outdated, to say the least. But cheeks will be streaked with a tear or two when the time comes. The older ones feel that a large amount of history is rooted in the old cobbles and cramped, factory-type houses.

j) Memories of Margaret Houghton (& Hudson Binney)

EIGHTY YEARS OF LOCAL HISTORY.

MISS HOUGHTON'S REMINISCENCES.

St Helens Newspaper May 23rd 1924

Margaret Houghton was born in 1841 in Church Street in St Helens, the sole child of Ann and William. Over the years her father's occupation was described in different censuses as a labourer, carter and finally as a coal dealer. The family also lived in Market Street and Tontine Street and by 1924 Margaret – who never married – was a resident of Hamer Street. On May 23rd and 30th of that year, the St Helens Newspaper related Margaret's memories with the octogenarian described as having:

> ...amazingly clear recollections of what St. Helens was like in her girlhood...Miss Houghton has lived throughout the most interesting period of the history of St. Helens. She has seen it as a little country village, just beginning to spread its tentacles into the surrounding countryside, but still

> comprising little more than the old Chapel-lane [Church Street], with Toll Bar, Dentons Green, Peasley Cross, Hardshaw, Newtown, merely the names for pastoral districts, whose beauty has vanished for ever. She has seen the coming of works and factories, the rapid growth of the population, the expansion of St. Helens until it has burst its borough boundaries, and she lives to-day in the era of the motor-car, the aeroplane, the wireless, the cinema, and all the scientific wonders of the age. From the stagecoach to the aeroplane – what a giant stride!

Margaret Houghton had been born in one of eight cottages in a portion of Church Street. She described it as a very pleasant spot, with the houses surrounded by red, white and black currant bushes. On the corner of Hardshaw Street and Church Street a Miss Cross ran a school for young ladies and Miss Houghton recalled how through a little iron gate the youngsters had "tripped daintily in their frills and poky bonnets to learn the three 'R's".

The mention of a Miss Cross *(the 1851 census suggests sisters Anne and Mary Cross ran the school together)* led to Hudson Binney from Rainhill – a retired accountant and glassworks manager – writing this letter to the paper:

> "Upwards of fifty years ago a Miss Cross – probably the Miss Cross of the reminiscences – told the present writer that she at one time lived in Hardshaw-street, and in the season had an abundance of roses in her garden. She said, also, she had a distinct recollection of Louis Napoleon, afterwards Emperor of the French, frequently passing on horseback unattended, when he was the guest of a noble house in the neighbourhood."

Louis-Napoleon Bonaparte was born in 1808 and would likely have been trotting through St Helens during the 1840s. Indeed, there is a record of Sir John Gerard entertaining Bonaparte at the Sefton

Arms in 1846 after the pair had been hunting in the district. That was after the Parisian nobleman had moved to London after escaping from a French prison where he had been serving a life sentence. Two years later as Napoleon III he became France's first president and in 1852 he was made Emperor.

Louis-Napoleon

Louis Napoleon was known to stay at the Gerard family home, Garswood Hall, and a bedroom inside the mansion was for many decades afterwards still referred to as the "Emperor's Room". The Newspaper said it was hard to imagine an emperor riding from Garswood into St Helens along Hardshaw Street – but they loved the idea of flowers growing in the centre of the industrial town:

> ...but how much more intimate is the mere mention of the forgotten and faded floral charms of Hardshaw-street. So to our reconstructed picture of St. Helens we must add to Miss Houghton's verdant currant bushes in Church-street, Mr. Binney's perfumed roses in Hardshaw-street.

Baldwin Street workhouse

In the second part of Miss Houghton's reminiscences – again recounted in the third person – the 83-year-old told the Newspaper how she distinctly recalled inspecting the old workhouse where the Co-operative Stores would later be built. That became Baldwin Street but it was then in the neighbourhood of Moorflat and bordered by cottages, each having its own front garden.

During the 19th century there were a number of very small breweries in St Helens that were situated within people's homes. Some houses also had their own wells that these microbreweries might have used as their water supply. But as piped water became more widespread, many of these wells became redundant and Miss Houghton vividly recalled a dramatic incident in Tontine Street in which a back kitchen brewery had seemingly vanished.

The owner had returned home and had just finished washing himself when the whole of his little beer plant – including the slopstone *(stone sink or slab)* and pantry – disappeared into the ground. It subsequently transpired that there had once been a large well under the house, which had not been capped off once it became disused.

Margaret Houghton also remembered the original market in St Helens, which was situated at the corner of Church Street and Market Street and known as Market Place. A drinking fountain subsequently marked the spot, with the Newspaper writing:

> The old Market Place was a busy place in Miss Houghton's youth. Then it was the Market Place in actual fact, and a great business was done in greengrocery which was brought in from the surrounding countryside. Now the only thing that reminds us of the fact that there was once a market in the "market place" is the occasional presence of the old ladies who – or who did until a short time ago – sit at the foot of the fountain selling shrimps and periwinkles.

Nearby was an old-fashioned shop run by a tailor named Bankes that was accessed by climbing a dozen steps. Later Miss Houghton lived in Market Street in one of two old cottages that were sunk below the level of the road. There she lived for 26 years and on the other side of the street was the post office. The Newspaper wrote:

> Those were good-old-fashioned winters in those days, and many a snowball fight did the post office messenger boys have in Market-street, and even carried their warfare into the rooms of the cottages opposite.

k) Beatrice McGhie

On May 12th 1899 a massive explosion at the Kurtz Alkali Works killed at least 5 men. Beatrice McGhie of Wynne Road in St Helens told the St Helens Reporter on May 19th 1962 that she had vivid recollections of the blast, with the 82-year-old writing:

> The first indication that something was wrong came when policemen were heard blowing whistles and telling people to open doors and windows and turn the gas off at the main. They were expecting an explosion at a chemical works. I was then living at 85, Corporation Street, quite near the fire station. We always ran across to the station when the fire bell rang to see the horses turn out and watch firemen's wives bring their coats and helmets. I had only been there a minute or two, when the explosion occurred. The Town Hall building rocked and we were thrown against the wall. The horses nearly panicked and the firemen had to hold on to the reins. Then I realised my father was working at a chemical works making chlorate. I ran all the way to the Globe Chemical Works over the Hardshaw fields to see if he was all right. My sister and two young brothers ran with hundreds more to Carr Mill and stayed there most of the day. The shock seemed to catch every other shop on one side of Church Street. All the scent bottles and other displays in a chemist's were shattered in the middle of the road.

Two images of the 1899 Kurtz disaster

The Petrol Shampoo At A St Helens Hairdressing Salon

"The next thing that happened was a great gust of flame came leaping from her hair, burning her head horribly."

Lockhart's was a popular hairdressing salon in St Helens for more than fifty years. Herbert Lockhart had founded the family firm in 1919 and he soon developed a busy salon *(or "saloon")* at 14 George Street. But the business needed to overcome a dreadful incident in December 1924 in which a client received life-changing injuries. That was after petrol had been used as a shampoo on the young woman's hair and the damages that Mr Lockhart was ordered to pay as compensation drove him into bankruptcy.

The application of refined petrol as a dry shampoo on the hair used to be quite common – both in hairdressing salons and at home. At an inquest hearing in London in October 1909 it was stated that thousands of women gave themselves petrol shampoos in their own homes. That was after two women had been killed and a third badly injured following a gas explosion inside a salon.

The owner of the hairdresser's told the inquest that they sometimes used petrol to wash hair because it dried fast and gave a nice finish. Several such shampoos were given at his establishment each day, although the man stated that they were only carried out when requested by customers. To that the Coroner replied: "If you are asked to do a foolish thing there is no reason for you to do it."

Then the hair dryer and curling tongs that salons employed incorporated a gas burner. So it took little imagination to deduce what would happen if a naked flame came into contact with the petrol and the gas. The inquest heard that often a special room was used when such shampoos were given to lessen the danger but that some women smoked while having their hair done. The

Coroner asked the salon owner whether he knew of any form of dry shampoo that was safe. To that he replied: "I know of none".

Then in December 1909 at a meeting of a Parliamentary committee hearing on petroleum, the Coroner for Westminster and South-West London was quoted as saying in evidence:

> "Petrol is largely used for shampooing by hair-dressers; the danger of using it is generally known, but safeguards are not complete, and probably in practice never could be; the petrol vapour is highly inflammable and causes instantly large flames; when once a person is attacked by these burning vapours there is a very great probability of fatal injuries; the pressure put on hairdressers by ladies to use petrol is so great, the profit of using it is so much larger, the time occupied so much less, that nothing short of prohibition will prevent its use; if used there seems to be no practical way of avoiding risk to life."

TO BOB OR NOT TO BOB

It's understandable that Herbert Lockhart did not initially choose ladies' hairdressing as a career – as it was unlikely to have been encouraged as a manly pursuit. Born in Dentons Green in St Helens in 1892 to glass blower father Robert and mother Harriet, Herbert was listed in the 1911 census as an apprentice moulder in industry. However, eight years later he opened his own hairdressing salon at 14 George Street, after briefly being in partnership with his brother. On April 18th 1924 Herbert had a letter published in the St Helens Reporter in response to a short piece in a previous edition about bobbed women's hair. The letter was published under the headline *"To Bob Or Not To Bob":*

> Sir – Would you please try to find space in your most excellent paper for an answer to the question, "When will the 'bobbed' craze go out?" which you recently printed. In the

first place, it has long ceased to be a craze, and is now more a necessity for ladies suffering from nerves, headaches, etc., who have found such a benefit from 'bobbed' hair that they never wish for it long again. There are a few who have not yet taken the plunge, but no doubt they will come to the scratch in the end. Shingle is a craze at present, but it does not suit everybody. Those whom it does suit I strongly advise them to have it done. Some papers say that shingling causes grey hair, but it is not true, that I can prove. As regards long hair being "a woman's crowning glory," I would like to ask what benefit is gained by that lump at the back? You cannot mention any. On the other hand, 'bobbed' hair is beneficial to the health, which is a thing to be studied before the pride of long hair. As regards 'bobbed' hair being "the ugliest of fashions," I am afraid that requires a lot of proof, for in my opinion, and in most people's, it is the most sensible. I did no fewer than 150 last week. – **H. LOCKHART**.

Adverts in the St Helens Reporter from September 1924 and February 1925

Towards the end of the year it was decided to open new premises in Hardshaw Street to help cope with the demand. Everything was looking good for Herbert but his world changed at 8pm on December 5th 1924. That was when Doris Halsall from Dilloway Street in St Helens paid a visit to his George Street salon. The 22-year-old with what was later described as a "beautiful head of wavy hair", asked Mr Lockhart for a dry shampoo. Some petrol was placed on her head but a naked gas jet was nearby and the result was described as a "rapid burst of flame" over Doris's head. She was severely burnt and for ten days her life was in danger and Doris had to spend six months recovering in Providence Hospital.

Pain management was, of course, very limited then compared to today and Doris was said to have been in so much agony that at times she had pleaded with her doctors to let her die. And in order to sleep at night morphine needed to be administered to the young woman. But in spite of the fire the new salon in Hardshaw Street was opened as planned three days later.

On June 24th 1925 Doris sued Herbert Lockhart at Liverpool Assizes claiming damages for her suffering and what was claimed as permanent injuries. A single woman now aged 23, Doris lived with her parents and had been employed by the Automatic Telephone Company in Liverpool where she was paid 39 shillings a week. Doris's counsel, Howard Jones, explained to the court how his client had received her injuries at Mr Lockhart's salon. He described how she had been taken into a small cubicle where the styling took place and photographs of the shop and cubicles were shown to the jury. Mr Jones said to them:

> "You will see these cubicles consist of quite a short space on either side of the wash bowl, where there is a chair and the partition is a curtain. It is only a tiny room. To the right of the washstand there is a gas ring, which apparently is used for the purpose of heating curling tongs for waving the hair. The defendant attended to her on this date, and put some powder on her hair, and left her for a moment to attend to

something else. When he came back she was still sitting in the chair and he told her to hold a towel with her hands in front of her face, and asked her to stoop over the wash bowl. The next thing that happened was a great gust of flame came leaping from her hair, burning her head horribly. Apparently, in the agitation of the moment – incredible though it might seem – petrol was spilled on the floor, and the flames came rushing round her legs with such effect that they left permanent scars. All the hair was burnt off her head and there is a deformity behind her ear.

"Mercifully, the towel which she held in front of her saved her face from being burnt. Her left hand was badly scorched, and as a result of the burns on the leg the muscles were constricted, and she was rendered a little lame. She would bear the marks of her disablement to her grave. Incredible as it might appear, the defendant seems to have sprinkled petrol on the lady's hair in the confined space of a tiny room within an arm's length of a naked burning gas jet.

"I think the defendant had done so without knowledge of the consequences, otherwise there would be more than negligence involved. I can only imagine that defendant had forgotten that the gas jet was lit. Anyone dealing with a highly inflammable thing like petrol should take the utmost precaution to see that no naked lights were near. As a result of the accident the plaintiff suffered intense pain, which was made all the worse because she did not entirely lose consciousness at the time."

The jury also heard that the young woman had rushed out of the salon after the explosion and Herbert Lockhart had chased after her and bravely thrown her down to extinguish the flames. As a result he had been badly burnt and also needed hospital treatment at Providence. Mr Jones claimed that the hairdresser had said he would pay for Doris to be treated in a private ward but then rescinded his offer once her family had consulted a solicitor.

In giving her own testimony to the court, the young woman described how there had been a "constant roar of flame" all around her. However, she denied having told Herbert that she had previously had her hair treated with petrol at another salon, which had made it look glossy. In fact Doris insisted she was unaware that petrol was ever used on hair but did admit leaving it to Mr Lockhart to decide what to use. A specialist in skin diseases told the hearing that he could not imagine Miss Halsall ever getting over the shock of what she had experienced.

THE REPORTER, FRIDAY JUNE 26, 1925.

GIRL'S HAIR ON FIRE.

SEQUEL TO ST. HELENS SALOON INCIDENT.

DAMAGES CLAIMED AT ASSIZES.

£533 AWARDED FOR BURNS AND SHOCK.

John Singleton was the defence barrister and he told the court that Mr Lockhart had never before used petrol as a shampoo and kept none on his premises. He insisted the young woman had asked his client for a petrol shampoo and the defendant had consequently had to send out for some. That fundamental dispute over whether the petrol shampoo was requested or not was never resolved. However, it was later revealed that legal advice had been given to the litigants, which stated that admitting asking for a petrol shampoo would have weakened the young woman's case.

Mr Lockhart's version of how the accident occurred was that Doris Halsall had jerked her head backwards while the shampoo was being applied and that movement had caused some petrol to spill.

An explosion immediately took place but he insisted that he did not know how or why it had happened. When he had looked at the gas jet just before making the application, Lockhart said he had thought it was out.

Doris's counsel appealed to the jury to consider the effect of his client's injuries on her matrimonial prospects, adding, "We cannot ignore that aspect, even in 1925". They responded with an award of £533 damages, plus £184 costs. £717 was a huge amount that is equivalent to around £60,000 in today's money. Herbert Lockhart did not possess such cash or public liability insurance and later he offered Doris £200 to settle her claim but his offer was rejected.

LOCKHART BANKRUPTCY

"YOU WANT TO MAKE YOURSELF OUT A PERFECT FOOL?"

OFFICIAL RECEIVER'S DISBELIEF

St Helens Newspaper August 21st 1925

Two month's later on August 18th 1925 Herbert appeared in Liverpool Bankruptcy Court declaring liabilities of £806 with assets of £46. After receiving the rejection of his £200 offer to Miss Halsall, he said he had paid off all his trade creditors. The £806 that was outstanding was the compensation money owed to Doris, plus the court costs and cash that some relatives had lent him.

Those appearing before bankruptcy courts for what was known as a "public examination" tended to be given a grilling and the Official Receiver gave Herbert Lockhart a particularly hard time. However, the interrogation wasn't so much about the circumstances of the accident but the financial arrangements concerning his new premises in Hardshaw Street. These were being rented for £80 per year with £200 having supposedly been needed for decoration and fittings with the cash borrowed from Herbert's sister-in-law. The Official Receiver remarked:

> "I must comment upon the lack of common sense you displayed in spending £200 or £300 in fitting up a place of which you had only an annual tenancy. No man who is not a fool would spend that money. And now you suggest it was a weekly tenancy?"

Upon Herbert claiming that his landlord could turn him out at a week's notice, the Official Receiver accused Mr Lockhart of trying to make himself out to be a "perfect fool", adding:

> "To suggest that you spent £200 or £300 in fitting up and decorating a place you took on a weekly tenancy is a story you will have to get someone else to believe, we won't."

It was common, if not the norm, for persons undergoing bankruptcy proceedings to attempt to disguise some of their assets or to transfer their ownership to family members – hence the Official Receiver's third degree approach. Mr Lockhart claimed during his interrogation that he owned none of the furniture in his house. He insisted that it all belonged to his wife and his sister-in-law, with the latter also holding the mortgage on his home.

Mr Lockhart's solicitor might have also recommended transferring the ownership of his business to his wife, Alice, in order to provide extra protection. I cannot be completely certain of such an arrangement but during the summer of 1925 in the light of the bankruptcy hearing, the George Street premises *(and possibly those in Hardshaw Street)* were closed for some time.

Then in early September advertisements began to appear in the St Helens' newspapers stating that the business would shortly be reopening under the name of A. Lockhart but they stressed that the hairdressing establishment would be operating under the same management.

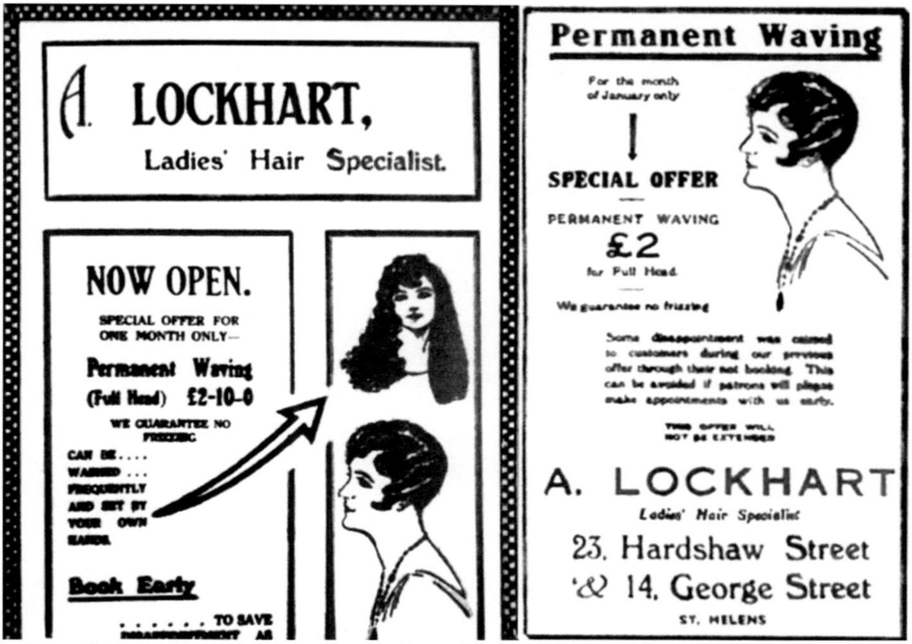

Two St Helens Reporter adverts from September (left) and December 1925

On October 14th 1927 Herbert Lockhart returned to Liverpool Bankruptcy Court, where he was discharged as a bankrupt. Assets of £359 had eventually been declared but his liabilities were now assessed at almost £1,000. As a result only 4 shillings 7d in the pound was being paid to his creditors, meaning Doris would have been better off if she had accepted the offer of £200.

"This bankruptcy is a case of pure misfortune," commented Judge Thomas as Herbert's solicitor stated that there had been no "rash or hazardous speculation". By that he meant no financial mismanagement that had led to the insolvency – but Doris Halsall, of course, was the one who had suffered a far greater misfortune with her life-changing injuries. It was also mentioned at the hearing that Lockhart was at present managing an unspecified business but hoping to recommence on his own account soon and "remove the stigma from his name". That would, of course, have been the stigma of being a bankrupt.

The burning incident was essentially part of the culture of waiting for accidents to happen before safety procedures were brought in. That laxity existed for much of the 20th century and few buildings in St Helens were constructed or extended without construction workers suffering injuries, if not death.

For example, three men *(and possibly four)* died and others were badly injured in a spate of accidents during the building of Pilkington's Glass HQ in Prescot Road. In 1959 two St Helens steeplejacks fell 150ft to their deaths while taking down a chimney after rejecting an offer to be connected to safety lines.

In 1972 a three-year-old girl died at Barton's Carpets after a 6-foot-high roll of lino weighing one cwt that had been stacked on display collapsed upon her. As a result the Duke Street firm installed brackets and chains to prevent a recurrence. And it was well known that the authorities routinely refused to install safety measures – such as pedestrian crossings and traffic lights – on dangerous roads unless deaths had occurred.

The Lockharts overcame what occurred and ran a successful hairdressing business for decades. But you can be certain that they never used petrol again as a shampoo. Health and safety regulations can sometimes be scoffed at for curtailing freedoms but they have a purpose built on lessons learnt from the past. As to Doris Halsall – who suffered so much – she appears to have married in 1930 and hopefully had a very happy life.

St Helens Reporter March 6th 1970

The Gorgeous Carnivals And Pageants Of The Past

"Morning and afternoon great crowds gathered in Victoria Square to witness the ceremonies, and when the vast procession converged on Victoria Square from all parts of the town, the drab old square was filled with life and colour."

INTRODUCTION

The inter-war years were hard times for many St Helens' folk. But that didn't stop people from having fun; and there seems to have been no greater pleasure than participating in the pageants, processions and parades that were held. Months of hard work went into making costumes for the children and preparing and decorating floats and lorries. In Charles Forman's book 'Industrial Town - Self-portrait of St Helens in the 1920s', an unnamed female organiser of such parades said: *"Those were the happiest days of the time. Nothing was too much for the women."*

Although walking days and the odd carnival still take place today, they seem a pale imitation of those of the past when the participants possessed so little. And music always played a very important part of the celebrations with St Helens notable for its brass bands and during the inter-war years numerous jazz bands were also formed to add to the fun. However, children remained the main focus, as can be seen from the following reports.

THE RAILWAY QUEEN AND THE FAIRY QUEEN

The first National Railway Queen was selected in 1925. These were girls aged between 14 and 17 that were daughters of railway workers and their role was to act as ambassadors for the industry. The chosen girl would visit towns in Britain and abroad promoting "international brotherhood and peace" and in 1930 Molly Brown from Preston served as the Railway Queen having been selected out of 4,000 candidates.

When she came to St Helens in July of that year, Molly was treated as if she was a real monarch! She had been invited to appear at a Labour Party gala in which she would crown a Fairy Queen. But Molly also received a civic reception at St Helens Town Hall; laid a wreath at the nearby war memorial and to a huge crowd in Victoria Square she delivered a speech on international peace. Not bad for a girl of around fifteen!

The day began when Molly arrived at Shaw Street station, which was described as "beflagged", with crimson carpet laid on the platform. Local railwaymen provided a guard of honour and four girls acted as trainbearers to carry the queen's long dress.

Molly Brown pictured in Barnsley

The St Helens Reporter of July 11th 1930 stated these had been Joyce Clitheroe, May Dagham, Olive Jones and Gwennie Jones and said they had on "pretty frocks of shell pink silk, with wreaths of silver leaves on their heads." A dozen maids of honour were also in attendance, wearing dresses of petunia silk and on their heads were wreaths of gold leaves and each girl carried a posy.

The Reporter described a "general murmur of admiration" as the young Railway Queen stepped on the red carpet in her silk dress with long train. Molly and her sixteen young helpers were then led off in a short procession to the Town Hall. There the mayor and other leading folk of the town greeted her. Even the St Helens Chief Constable was present, along with the Town Clerk and Molly delivered a short speech on the importance of world peace.

After lunch it was back to Victoria Square for the second half of her itinerary involving the Labour pageant. Molly's main task would be to crown the Fairy Queen, who was Mary Burns from Parr. The ceremony was due to take place in the field in Bishop Road and a quite remarkable procession was set to depart the Square for Dentons Green led by brass bands. This is how the Reporter described the scene:

> Morning and afternoon great crowds gathered in Victoria Square to witness the ceremonies, and when the vast procession converged on Victoria Square from all parts of the town, the drab old square was filled with life and colour.... Bounteous sunshine favoured the event. It was the brightest day that has yet graced the annual event. And while the thermometer soared, tar melted in the streets and men, sweltering in their surfeit of clothing, mopped the perspiration from their brows with handkerchiefs. The only cool persons in the assembly were the girls dressed in their flimsy frocks. The trees in Victoria-square looked refreshingly cool, while a hanging basket of foliage and flowers added an extra touch of colour to the entrance of the assembly hall. The approach to the Town Hall was a riot of colour. Fairies, butterflies, bees, elves and dwarfs were grouped together on the steps. And, as the procession streamed through the square, it became a living garden. There were bluebell girls, snowdrops, daffodils and violets, shamrock and roses.
>
> Queen Victoria blinked down in astonishment from her pedestal. The procession was held up at the Town Hall owing to the belated arrival of one of the wards who had to make the journey from an outlying district of the town. The interval of waiting, however, was pleasantly filled in by little Miss Iris Houghton, a school-girl who gave an exhibition of classical dancing. She was attired in a beautiful fairy dress

of shimmering white and as she gaily pirouetted on the steps and pavement she became the cynosure of 10,000 pairs of eyes. She was not nervous and she responded to encore after encore bestowed upon her by a delighted crowd.

To the strains of the British Legion Band the Railway Queen now proceeded from the Hardshaw-street exit of the Town Hall out to the square, accompanied by her court, and she entered her car stationed near the Town Hall steps. Close by was the flower decked car belonging to the Fairy Queen. This car was fashioned in the form of a huge swan whose wings and body were composed of thousands of tiny flowers. The Fairy Queen, Miss Mary Burns, of Mather-avenue, Parr, looked a regal figure in her dress of white soft satin trimmed with lace, and train of similar material lined with white tinsel. A halo of tinsel formed her head-dress edged with pink roses. Her crown was of silver trimmed with pearls and she carried a bouquet of roses. Her shoes were of silver brocade. In attendance was the crown-bearer, Miss Hilda Pennington of O'Keeffe-road, dressed as a bee with a black and gold body with wings of golden gauze, and two butterflies, Miss Elsie Appleton and Miss Connie Atherton. There were also a large number of maids-of-honour dressed as green fairies carrying wands and wearing crowns, and a number of fairies dressed in white Tarleton and wearing white gauze wings and carrying silver wands. Brownies, elves and pixies followed.

However, the little Fairy Queen had a big problem. The designer of the flower-decked swan that was being carried on a lorry had seemingly forgotten to design a door to allow its rider to access it and Mary was left stranded. I always thought fairies could fly – but apparently not! And so as the little girl could neither soar into position nor climb the steep sides of the bird, Mary was stymied. But a kind chap called Jack Houghton came to her rescue. He picked up the Fairy Queen and carried her onto the swan. The St Helens Reporter then described the make-up of the long parade:

> Thatto Heath led the procession, the Nutgrove Prize Band discoursing bright and breezy music. A big troupe of blue bells swayed in the breeze, the leader of these girls being Miss May Burrows. Then followed a number of Scotch Highlanders, who executed a merry "fling." These were under the leadership of Mrs. Middlehurst. Then came a cluster of gipsy girls, wearing the St. Helens Recs.' colours of red, yellow and black, followed by a swarthy band of Red Indians, who brandished tomahawks, and executed all sorts of weird dances in the square, causing a mounted policeman's horse to shy and rear at the unaccustomed sight and sound.
>
> There were many interesting exhibits in the Thatto Heath section of the procession, which included a youngster dressed as a petrol pump. Parr and Hardshaw made a brave show. They had with them Parr St. Peter's Girls' Fife Band, girls all dressed in natty navy blue uniforms, with slouch hats and red cockades and cross-belts of khaki and white, and they tootled their section of the procession gaily along on its way to the field. There were clusters of snowdrops and daffodils, and Miss Rachel Johnson lent a pretty touch to the picture. She was dressed as the embodiment of "Peace," in a white dress, with olive leaves around her head.
>
> A huge lorry draped in purple, and carrying groups of girls attired as violets, was one of the principal tableaux in the North and South Eccleston portion of the procession. They had also a big banner depicting a colliery headgear and the gates leading to the colliery yard. A girl wearing a sash inscribed "Labour," held aloft in her hand a key. They had

also a smart jazz band and Morris dancers. Heading the Central Ward group were two figures "Erin" and "Robert Emmett." The leaves of the shamrock were depicted by a large group of children dressed in green, and a band of jazz instrumentalists formed part of the ensemble. North and South Windle chose the English rose as their emblem. These children dressed in pink and red formed a most artistic addition to the procession, and they were accompanied by a jazz band.

Spectators lined the route to Bishop-road and, as the tableaux passed by, they were enthusiastically applauded. On reaching the field staged for the coronation ceremony the various tableaux ranged themselves around the platform and the meadow, and the Queens took up their positions on a tastefully decorated platform. Cameramen and film photographers got busy. Mr. James Sexton [the St Helens MP] solemnly handed the crown to the Railway Queen, who crowned the Fairy Queen, and the band played appropriate selections. Concerts followed, and in addition to the sideshows, dancing was enjoyed until dusk to the strains of the British Legion Band.

Sutton Oak May Queen Parade in 1925

ST HELENS' HOSPITALS 1937 CARNIVAL

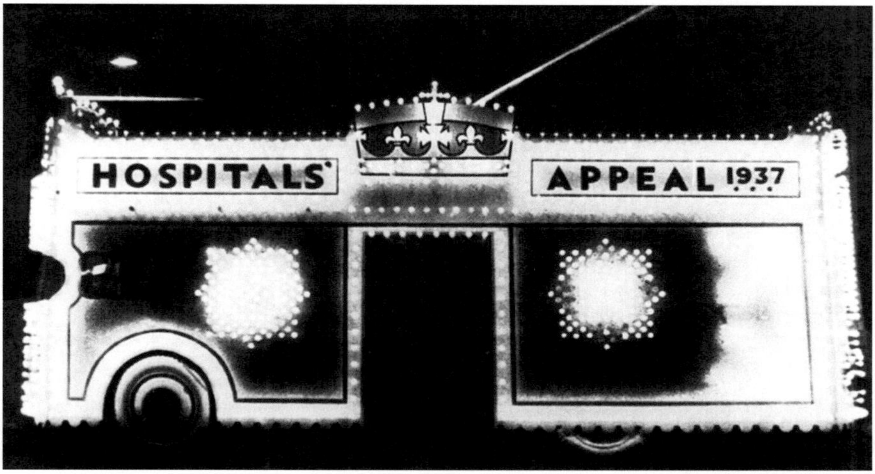

This is a photograph of the special trolleybus that the St Helens Transport Department created for the 1937 Hospitals Carnival. The annual fundraising event had begun in 1934 with its purpose of raising cash for both Providence and St Helens hospitals. However, the 1937 carnival was the penultimate one – as the war and the creation of the NHS brought an end to the annual festivity.

Months of preparation went into creating the extraordinary floats and tableaux that formed part of the mile-long parade, which ended in what we know as Queens Park where "revelries" took place. And the float that St Helens Corporation's Electricity Department made to sell electric cooking was the most extraordinary of the lot! This is how the St Helens Reporter vividly described the affair on June 22nd 1937 under their headlines of *"Brilliance of the Carnival Cavalcade – Gorgeous Tableaux and Novel Characters":*

> Radiant beauty rubbed shoulders with the bizarre and grotesque in the mile-long procession of the Mayor's Hospitals Carnival of 1937, and Saturday last saw the culmination of months of preparation in the wonderful cavalcade which lent brilliant colour to the principal

thoroughfares and the later revelries at Queen's Recreation Ground. The Carnival, now, in its fourth year, is established, and last Saturday's affair, which aims at bringing in £1,000 to aid the hospitals, was well ahead of its predecessors from the spectacular point of view, and – which is of vital importance – is confidently expected to show the greatest financial returns yet achieved. A brilliant sun, occasionally obscured by cloud, and tempered by a cool breeze, gave promise of favourable weather conditions, and as the procession moved off on its long trail to the Recreation Ground, many thousands thronged Victoria Square, and the streets on the route, to admire and applaud the many beautiful tableaux, and the attractive troupes of dancers who occasionally gave displays in the streets.

There were lorry loads of colour and beauty; there were characters on foot that drew boundless admiration, or evoked laughter by their comicality, and, though few in number, there were magnificent horses that were the pride of their owners and riders. All these combined to make unforgettable scenes of life and colour such as are rarely to be witnessed in St. Helens, and they made memorable the Carnival of 1937. At Queen's Recreation Ground a huge crowd awaited the arrival of the procession, and when the festivities began, there was a host of attractions by way of dancing displays, aerial gymnastics, concerts, and innumerable sideshows, and from early afternoon till late in the evening there was something doing to obtain the interest and to delight the eyes of thousands of visitors.

The work of marshalling the procession in the streets adjacent to the Town Hall was carried through smoothly, and after a charming little Queen had received her crown at the hands of the Mayoress, the cavalcade was ready to move.

The two hospitals were well to the fore in providing magnificent tableaux. "St. George and the Dragon" was the subject chosen to represent St. Helens Hospital. On a lorry, richly adorned in red and white, stood a valiant St. George (Nurse Yeomans) in full armour of chain mail and helm of steel emblazoned with the cross of St. George. The same emblem decorated the shield. A stout lance completed the ensemble, and at "St. George's" feet lay the "dragon" (Miss Hilda Ronson), whose recumbent position in "dragon's" skin, must have been uncomfortable during the long ride.

Providence Hospital chose Grace Darling for the subject of their tableau and on a tumbling paper mache sea Northumbria's heroine towed her craft – a boat from Taylor Park – named for the occasion "H. M. Providence." Grace Darling was impersonated by Margaret Fildes, and her father was Frank Cunliffe. Ringed round the tableau were eight little sailor boys in suits of white and blue and peaked caps. The Corporation Public Health Department was represented by a beautiful group representing Maternity and Child Welfare. The whole deck of a motor lorry was draped in Royal blue satin, and seated on a silver chair was the figure of Motherhood (Mrs. Barton). She was resplendently attired in a cloak and headdress of silver satin, and she nursed her own baby, a bright little seven months boy, who beamed as the crowd applauded his appearance.

Miss Olive L. Johnson, of the Greenfield School of Dancing, provided two outstanding displays, "Golden Opportunity," and "Chinese Carnival." On a lorry dressed in Royal purple and gold, rose a tall column in gold. This was surmounted by a crown of violets. At this central column stood Thelma Briggs, a lovely figure in classical dress of green velvet. She held a golden pipe which symbolised the heralding of "golden opportunity." Other children similarly dressed and holding golden hoops or goblets were gracefully posed.

For the first time a church was represented in the procession – St. Andrew's Mission – and their tableau represented "The World's Breakfast Table". At a table sat a small family, and they were surrounded by the representatives of many nations. A very uncomfortable looking figure dressed in tropical khaki kit and pith peeped out from a fearsome cannibals' cooking pot. Around him danced three men in leopard skins, with spears and shield, and a fourth nonchalantly stirred the contents of a soup-pan on an electric stove! It was the Electricity Department's effective demonstration of the fact that "there are many ways of cooking, but the electricity way is best."

BRILLIANCE OF THE CARNIVAL CAVALCADE

GORGEOUS TABLEAUX AND NOVEL CHARACTERS

REVELS AT QUEEN'S RECREATION GROUND

HOPES OF REALISING £1,000

RADIANT beauty rubbed shoulders with the bizarre nd grotesque in the mile-long procession of the Mayor's Hospitals Carnival

The St Helens Reporter vividly described the event on June 22nd 1937

A WEEKEND OF FROLICS IN 1930

There was, of course, one essential ingredient that helped to make any carnival a success – sunshine, and lots of it! On July 18th 1930 the St Helens Reporter devoted a whole page to describe in vivid detail the previous Saturday's range of events in the town that had benefitted from excellent weather.

The paper's reports appeared under the headline of: *"St. Helens Revels in the Sunshine – A Week-End of Frolics – Fetes, Queen-Makings and Burlesque Football"*. The Highfield that is mentioned was the Thatto Heath home of solicitor Henry Oppenheim and Mrs Lansdale Hammill, who is also referenced, was the wife of a chartered accountant from Eccleston Park. This is an edited version of the reports, which began with this introduction:

> Following a glut of carnivals and queen-makings a week ago, St. Helens again took a day off, on Saturday, when fetes were held in many parts of the town, and the music of brass bands could be heard coming from all directions. At the Rose Queen carnival at Highfield where fairies and elves played hide and seek among the rhododendron bushes, the Queen, Miss Stella Caine, was enthroned with much pomp and circumstance. Eccleston also lived up to its reputation, and a glittering procession of knights, Queens and Elizabethan ladies toured its leafy lanes, the carnival winding up with a comic football match. Sutton National schools held high revels at the Sherdley Hall grounds, where an exhibition of folk-dancing was given by the children.

THATTO HEATH ROSE QUEEN CARNIVAL

> The beautiful grounds at "Highfield," Scholes-lane, the home of Mr. H. S. Oppenheim, were placed at the disposal of the Thatto Heath branch of the Women's Unionist Association for their Rose Queen carnival on Saturday. The Loyalty

League children of the branch wore the costumes that had been made for them for their winter production, "What's Become of the Fairies?" The crowning of Miss Stella Caine, the Rose Queen-elect, was a delightful ceremony, and was performed by Mrs. Lansdale Hammill.

Along a passage in the rhododendrons behind the tall shrub came first children dressed in green and brown, hopping and jumping like frogs and rabbits. The sight of one of the rabbits pausing in her dance to dab her nose vigorously with a hanky was a little too much for some of the audience. Then followed the dance of the disappointed fairies. Why they were disappointed, I don't know but the programme said they were. The disappointed fairies were dressed in grey material on which was a black cob-web pattern. They looked really nice and danced even better. The Morris dancers were rather more cheerful though, and in brown and green costumes they flitted about the lawn in their graceful dance.

The actual entry of the queen was very prettily staged. Little Stella Caine was dressed as a pink rose, her skirt was of pink rose petals, and her train of green ruffle was trimmed with rosebuds. The crown, which Mrs. Lansdale Hammill finally placed on her head, was of pink rosebuds, as was the bouquet she carried. The train bearer, Jean Richie, represented a rose-bud, and she was wearing a green bodice and rose leaf skirt. The crown-bearer, Margaret Millington, was a butterfly, in a full dress of yellow organdie with a tight yellow cap of the same material, and yellow wings. Little Bessie Varley, as Cupid, in pink, scattered rose leaves in the Queen's path.

Throughout the performance by the children the Loyalty League Jazz Band acted as accompanists. In the grounds adjoining the house there were sideshows which did a remarkably thriving trade, refreshments were served on the lawn, fortunes were told at the gypsy encampment in the field, a putting green did good business, a barrel organ wandered about the grounds in charge of gaily dressed and foreign-looking damsels, and in the evening a further entertainment was given by the children. Gramophone records were also played through the amplifier on the lawn.

THE SUTTON PARISH FETE

The procession held in connection with the Sutton parish fete attained record dimensions, and the streets of the district wore an unwonted festive appearance with ribbons and colours flying, and a brass band playing merry airs. The gay column assembled at the Sutton National Schools on Saturday afternoon before proceeding through the various streets to the Sherdley Hall grounds for the fete and sports. The weather was glorious and the usual spectacular sight provided by the different hues of dresses transformed Ellamsbridge-road into a fairyland.

The Clock Face Colliery Band took part in the Sutton Parish Fete

Prompt at 2 o'clock the Clock Face Colliery Band took their place at the head of the procession, which very quickly formed behind them. With the beat of the drum and a shrill note on the cornet, the happy band of children and adults, numbering some 1,200, started on their way to the field via Ellamsbridge-road, Peckers Hill-road, Robins-lane and Marshalls Cross-road. The girls presented a charming appearance in their beautiful dresses, which were enhanced by the gay colours and the flowers most of them carried.

The Women's Fellowship, under Mrs. Kain, the Young People's Guild, the girls of the Sunday and day schools, led by Miss Roscoe and Sutton Manor Colliery band, and the boys of the Sunday and day schools, under Mr. Kenwright and Mr. Plews [Sutton National headmaster], the chief marshal, brought the huge procession to a close with the exception of a number of lorries carrying the younger children, who were really enjoying themselves and making others en route feel happy with them. When the grounds were reached, the announcement that tea was ready was received with loud cheers, and for at least half-an-hour the happy youngsters took part in what they considered the best part of the programme. They were spoken to by the Vicar (Rev. W. E. Colegrove) and everyone feeling much better and in a fitter condition for the sports. No sooner were the sports over than country dances commenced. These were indeed very picturesque with almost 100 dancers in all.

THE ECCLESTON CARNIVAL

A fancy dress parade, a comic football match, a display of classical dancing, with two Queens walking in a glittering procession, were features of the Eccleston carnival. Bright sunshine on this occasion transformed the procession into a glittering carnival, and the pretty dresses of the children were shown to the best advantage. The procession assembled at the Post Office, and although the tour was shortened in comparison with previous years, it was nevertheless longer than in June, and on this occasion the Queens and Courtiers were able to use open carriages. Led by the Thatto Heath Prize Band, the procession consisted of Bakers Boys, Clowns, Costers [street sellers], jam creations, human petrol pumps and all sorts of varieties all making up a charming and enterprising turn-out.

The ex-Queen (Miss Connie Anderton) who with her retinue, came first was charmingly attired in a gown of pink celanese satin underlined with pink satin and trimmed with diamante. She carried a bouquet of blush pink roses, her crown being of diamante and roses. Miss Peggy Foote, the Queen Elect looked winsome in a dress of Delustral satin and lace trimmed with a diamante buckle. Her train was underlined with blue silk and edged with swansdown, her bouquet being of pink roses. The Queen's attendants wore blue, and following the retinue were quite a number of children of the Sunday school dressed in white and carrying flowers. On arrival at the crowning enclosure where a specially erected platform had been placed, the "Royal" procession slowly took up its position and more than three hundred people gave hearty greetings to the children.

Canon Child in an address which was interspersed with flashes of humour, declared the fete open, and added that he felt quite at home at Eccleston. The crowning ceremony was then carried out, a panatrope [type of record player] providing the incidental music, and the "Wedding of the Painted Doll" was featured. Following this there were Maypole dancing, and competitions, but chief amongst the latter was the comic football match, in which Hutt, Hall and Hardgrave, the Saints' New Zealanders, took a principal part. The game, which lasted about twenty minutes, was a perfect scream, and nothing quite so funny has been seen for some time in connection with a church function.

New Zealand Saints stars Louis Hutt (left) and Roy Hardgrave

Roy Hardgrave was attired in the rig-out of a Troubadour cum bullfighter; Trevor Hall, a cook, complete with rolling pin; and Lou Hutt in the minor part of a civilian. The latter was the referee, and used one of those hideous Fan whistles, in which one blast gives you half an octave, with a few consecutive thirds and diminutive fourths thrown in. It was alleged that Dr Marriot [Vicar of Christ Church, Eccleston] should kick-off, but when he did so, it was found that the hilarious Roy was holding on to the ball from behind, and when the Vicar kicked, the leather flew the opposite way. A stout boy wearing Alf Ellaby's jersey, scored a few gift tries, but he was eclipsed when Hardgrave shot under the ropes, skittled a few onlookers, and hurled himself over at the corner for a perfect try, which Referee Hutt said was nothing more or less than an outrage, his decision being that it was a forward pass.

Knocks-on, fouls, players leaving the field to inspect flowers in the wood near by were frequent, and the game concluded with a budding Eccleston lad attired as an 18th century old woman being carried off the field, preceded by a clerical-looking individual and the players acting as mourners. Near the ropes the "injured lady" was shot over amongst the crowd and told to go and have a cooler at the "pop" stall.

THE 500 FANCY DRESSES AT PARR

On August 20th 1946 the St Helens Reporter described how Fred Percival of Nutgrove Road had won £3,021 *(about £170,000 in 2024 money)* on Littlewoods pools – but had "nowt" to spend it on. That was because of post-war shortages and seaside resorts like Blackpool being packed out through lack of accommodation. The paper added:

> With nothing to buy worth having, and nowhere to go worth going (all the pleasant places are full), War Savings seem to be the only resource even for those not naturally of a "saving turn". Perhaps in happier days that £3,000 odd will buy something worth having. Or will it?

But you didn't need lots of money to have fun in 1946. The outbreak of war had led to a suspension of carnivals in St Helens but once peace was restored they returned as victory parades, with the walkers having an extra celebratory spring in their step. Although materials were in short supply, the "make do and mend" attitude that had taken root in the 1930s and been expanded during the war, came to the fore in the years of post-war austerity. That was exemplified in Parr when on August 17th 1946 their 2nd Victory Carnival took place. The mile-long procession was organised by the residents of Waring Avenue, Inman Avenue, Reynolds Avenue and part of Fleet Lane and the St Helens Newspaper subsequently wrote:

> Never has such a galaxy of colours been seen by the hundreds of spectators. There were nearly 500 men, women and children, all in fancy dress taking part in the parade. The residents had seven weeks in which to make the costumes, and flour bags, wall paper, blackout curtains, table cloths and everything imaginable were expertly made into the most exquisite fancy dresses.

The St Helens Reporter in their account said:

> The event was so colourful and cheerful that it made one wonder at the "miracles" some mothers must have performed to turn their children out in such dresses and costumes in this coupon age.

VICTORY QUEEN CROWNED IN RAIN

A torrential downpour sent the Mayor Coun. Mrs. M. A. Shard), the Victory Queen (Miss Rene Jolly), of Fleet Lane, with her retinue, and the Parr Public Band, scurrying for shelter at the crowning of the Fleet Lane and district Victory Queen, on

Miss N Smith won the girls 16 to 18 80 yards race and the boys 16 to 18 100 yards race was won by Mr J Lavin.

MYSTERY MAN CAUGHT

The mystery man, Mr P Haley was caught by Mrs. Hurst. During

St Helens Reporter August 20th 1946

The Parr Public Prize Band headed the procession and twenty-six Morris dancers followed in their wake, dressed in white silk frocks with red sashes and each bearing streamers. They danced all the way from the starting point in Sexton Avenue to Fingerpost where the parade turned round. One of the most spectacular outfits was worn by a man called Simpson and represented victory. The costume depicted a knight resplendent in armour and carrying a victory banner. The St Helens Newspaper added:

> Another spectacular performance was given by the boys' bazooka band [the Reporter called them the "toy soldiers kazoo band"] which was led and trained by Mr. Roden. The boys were all dressed in red, green and gold shirts, black trousers with magnificent hats of silver green. En route to the Fingerpost, these boys gave a "wooden soldier" display and the applause was well appreciated by young and old. Many other such tableaux and costumes were well portrayed and the work which was put into some of these had to be seen to be believed. Little Red Riding Hood, Little Boy Blue, cow girls, cow-boys, Indians, pierots, jockeys, warriors, in fact, every kind and type of costume under the sun was made to make the carnival a complete success.

Despite a heavy downpour of rain the Mayor of St Helens, Cllr. Margaret Shard, crowned the Victory Queen, who was Rene Jolly of Fleet Lane and her young attendants were Rita Storey, Patricia Pickersgill and Ann Storey. The aforementioned Mr Roden was one of the chief organisers of the carnival and he told the St Helens Newspaper that he alone had used three hundred dyes in the costumes he'd made – and there had been countless other designers at work:

> "The people who helped to make this carnival a success would fill the 'Newspaper.' I would like to take this opportunity of expressing my sincere thanks to one and everyone of you. The mothers, fathers and many of the children have not been out for over seven weeks. We have worked night and day but it was worth it."

Following the procession sports and dancing took place in a field at Tickle's Farm in Parr. That lasted until 9pm when all the participants began making their way home. The Newspaper said:

> ...in their minds a memory of a carnival which surpassed in originality all other carnivals ever held in the Parr district.

A May Queen crowning in St Helens

"Dear Sir" – A Collection Of Curious Correspondence Part 3

In 'The Hidden History of St Helens' volumes 2 and 3, I transcribed a number of letters that had mainly been published in the town's newspapers during the late 19th century. This chapter is devoted to a third batch of correspondence but all of these missives were mailed to local papers during the early 20th century. Usually signed with a pseudonym, they can provide more insights into the social life of St Helens than the newspapers' own reports from that time.

THE SACKING OF MARRIED WOMEN WORKERS

Women to Lose Jobs on Marriage

Council's Policy Causes Alarm

Career or Home?

SHOULD married women work in wage-earning jobs? The question came into focus, last week when, at the meeting of the Town Council, Coun. W. Marshall raised a

St Helens Reporter April 8th 1938

In 1928 St Helens Corporation decided to clear up confusion in its terms of service by stipulating that all of their female employees must leave their jobs within two months of getting married. That requirement was not new but the rule had been inconsistently applied within council departments. Ten years later the Town Council decided to extend that notice period to three months.

The question of whether married women with husbands in work should be in employment themselves was then a highly controversial one. And it has to be said that many women felt such a rule was appropriate. The main argument in favour was that running a home and raising a family was a full-time position in itself. But a correspondent writing to the St Helens Reporter – who adopted the pen name "Indignant Mother" – felt the forced resignations were wrong and her angry letter on the subject was published in the paper on April 8th 1938:

> In the *REPORTER* last Friday I read of the decision of the Town Council to confirm, among other conditions of Corporation service, that if a female official marries she must automatically sacrifice her position under the Corporation, and leave three months after marrying. I ask, as the mother of a girl who is now being trained, at considerable expense for a commercial career, which training also may fit itself for an appointment under the Corporation, is this condition of service just and right? If such a girl desires to continue in her career after marriage, and increase her earning capacity, it provides others with work to care on her household. Is it fair to deprive her of continuing in her chosen profession?
>
> The Corporation is supposed to be the ideal employer, and why should they thus act like tyrants in so arbitrarily dictating the course of the private lives of their female employees? I think it is a monstrous decision, and one that ought to be removed at the earliest possible moment. If this principle is followed to its logical conclusion, other employers of female workers may adopt this policy, and if it were carried out in a general state, it would loose a flood of unemployment that would mean misery in many homes. Again, if this principle is lost, would it be equally just for lady doctors to cease to practice once they had taken the marriage vows? The same applies to every other profession in which women are now consolidating the gains they have painfully won after generations of struggle. – **INDIGNANT MOTHER**

GIRLS AND COMPETITIVE SPORT

Discrimination also used to be openly practised against females in St Helens‘ schools. In 1916 it was revealed that Cowley Girls

School banned women from St Helens from teaching there and they were also expected to resign upon getting married. The St Helens Education Committee subsequently passed a resolution not to enforce both rules due to the shortage of male teachers during the war. Girls studying at Cowley also had fewer facilities than boys – something that was reflected in the school fees. In 1918 these were £3 1s 4d and £2 13 shillings per term for boys and girls, respectively. On June 19th 1925 this letter was published in the St Helens Reporter wondering why schoolgirls were also missing out on competitive sports:

> Sir, – I have witnessed several inter-school cricket matches, and learn that these are part of a local competition for a shield. I commend the teachers and others engaged in fostering such sports in the boys' schools. Nothing, however, seems to be done in the girls' schools, yet our tennis courts prove that the ladies are also keen sports. Is there no competition for our girls? Cannot the girls' schools cultivate healthy rivalry in, say, net-ball, tennis or rounders? – **INTERESTED. St. Helens**

A DISTRAUGHT WIRELESS LISTENER!

Home life in St Helens tended to be rather quiet in the past with the residents' talking to each other (and sometimes shouting!) being the main sounds. Even those few houses with pianos or gramophones inside would only play them every now and then. But the advent of the wireless coupled to an amplified loudspeaker changed all that. Being able to play the radio throughout the day must have been a boon to many women undertaking the drudgery of housework. But, it seems, not everybody appreciated the noise. On May 13th 1930 the St Helens Reporter published this letter from a correspondent that adopted the pen name "Distraught":

> If you had a “Questions and Answers” department, I should ask your specialist what ought to be done when you have a neighbour whose wireless is in constant operation – doing

overtime every day. In these days of tissue paper walls, when even whispered conversations are overhead, the constant grinding of a wireless is an intolerable nuisance. What can I do? If it were a case of cats, dogs, pigeons, poultry, I could get a Town Hall Committee to discuss it for hours. This is worse. A little can be borne, but served up all the time it is too much of a good thing. Perhaps someone will tell how they have dealt with the difficulty? – **DISTRAUGHT**

THE POLITICAL POSTERS

The political allegiance of the St Helens Reporter was very much tied to the Conservative Party, with the St Helens Newspaper initially supportive of the Liberals. But as that party's star dimmed in the town, the Newspaper transferred their affections to the new Labour Party. Elections could be brutal affairs with much negative campaigning, as shown in this cartoon published in the St Helens Reporter on January 7th 1910. Tom Glover had become St Helens' first Labour MP in 1906 and the illustration accused him of reneging on an alleged promise to reduce food prices. But much of the election campaigning also took place through posters that were stuck on many hoardings and walls in the town.

At normal times these were reserved for promoting local shops, food brands and the acts performing at the theatres. But at election time when it was usually a two-horse race, such posters were replaced by dramatic imagery advertising the merits of one candidate over the other. On January 28th 1910 the Reporter published this letter lampooning the derogatory imagery within such posters and welcoming the post-election return to normality:

> Sir, The hordes of peregrinating political propagandists have departed from our midst to inflict upon other constituencies their indisputable logic, their forensic eloquence, and their irritating cocksureness that their own particular party alone possessed the monopoly of truth and patriotism. No longer are our hoardings a veritable nightmare, for gone are the writhing serpents and the tentacled monsters of a pre-something-or-other period, resurrected to warn us of our impending fate should we assist the return of Mr. What's-his name's party or vote for Mr. Thing-umy-bob. Gone – let us hope for ever – are the agonising features of those battalions of imploring women, of starving men and destitute children, that beset us at every corner. Gone are all those, more or less, works of "art" that "adorned" our streets and lanes; the caricatures of prosperous complacent foreigners, the caricatures of John Bull, maimed and fettered, and of John Bull striving heroically with this, or that, prejudicial interest. No longer haunted by the sight of the fair Britannia in the strangling clutch of some ruthless, relentless and remorseless-less, we breathe again.
>
> For weeks our daily journey to the office, or to the shop, was timidly undertaken. Furtive glances from side to side were occasionally ventured upon, fearful lest some fresh horror should assail our already sufficiently offended sight; fearful lest some fresh horror should further bewilder our disordered mind by raising fresh issues that carried in their train untold possibilities of pictorial treatment and reply. What a rainbow of promise was that prosaic invitation to try so-and-so's lung tonic – or was it rubber heels? – which we saw with delight was pasted over the legs of a demented female who with

outstretched arms had been piteously appealing to us for weeks. And now the deluge is over. How we welcome with delight even that black-hearted villain of the melo-drama. How we bask in the sunshine of pills and potents, of extracts and unguents and caramels that beam upon us again. And can we not feel the warmth of the smiles of those ladies whose comely features and attractive figures at this time of pantomime have been temporarily obscured, but, happily for our sanity, reign supreme once more. – Yours, etc., **A RELIEVED WORKER, St. Helens**

THE INDIGNITY OF THE DOLE

Little consideration used to be given to people's dignity when in dire straits. On New Year's Eve 1923 hundreds of unemployed people were forced to queue in the rain in public view for long periods as they waited to file into the Assembly Room of the Town Hall to receive a basic food parcel. On March 27th 1925 this letter appeared in the St Helens Reporter about a similar experience at the Employment Exchange in Church Street:

Sir, – Will you kindly grant me a little space to make a plea for the honest but unemployed men who are forced by circumstances to use the Labour Exchange, the men who really want work, not the dole. Last Friday, 20th inst., men went inside the Exchange, signed on, and had to come out again to queue up on the footpath, and return in single file, to receive their benefit. I most earnestly appeal to the officials who made this arrangement to consider the feelings of many of these men, honest, respectable citizens, who would gladly take work if it were offered to them. They do not want the dole. They want employment. It is degrading to any man to be made a public exhibition of, and a little thought would save them from that degradation. It was raining on the Friday in question, and the archway, where the men usually parade, was quite convenient, and not an open public thoroughfare. It is a misery enough for these honest men to be tramping around seeking work, without dragging them through the gutter, or holding them up to public exhibition. All our officials are not callous. All our unemployed are not idle loafers. Give them a little consideration, and save many respectable men a pang of misery. Roll on the day when we shall all attend the funeral of the dole, and the resurrection of employment; the closing of Labour Exchanges, and the opening of workshops. – **IN SYMPATHY, St. Helens**

The grim-looking St Helens Employment Exchange

POOR BUT PROUD

Six years later an individual adopting the pseudonym "Poor But Proud" stated in the Reporter of April 10th 1931 how he was a "victim of trade depression" on reduced circumstances. The correspondent described how he had attended the St Helens Labour Exchange, not to claim the dole but to obtain health and insurance cards that the centre also issued. However, he said he had been shocked by his treatment. "Poor But Proud" did accept that in his almost one-hour wait to be seen, the sole assistant had been "rattled" by claimants incapable of answering the simplest of questions. But his politeness, he stated, was met with rudeness:

> My complaint, sir, is that I was treated with unnecessary and unjustifiable discourtesy, and my plea is for a little more of the milk of human kindness in the relationship between Authority and the unfortunate beggars who have to humble themselves before Authority's servants. While I admit I am not entitled to one little bit more special treatment than any of the hundreds of the other unfortunates who have to go to the Labour Exchange, I do insist that I am entitled to be treated as a human being who knows his manners...I do not like being talked to as if I were a pig; a slight change in the inflection of the voice would make all the difference, plus a less challenging expression of the face, and an endeavour to say "Thank you" when something is handed over, instead of it being snatched from one as if it were a packet of germs from an infected person. For almost the first time in my life I have had personal experience of the "incivility of some civil servants"; hence this protest. – **POOR BUT PROUD**

OVERWORKED MP

James Sexton MP

It only took a few months from when James Sexton was elected the Labour MP for St Helens that he was complaining of overwork. These days, of course, members of parliament have a team that supports them on constituency business and they can use email to reply to correspondents. But in 1919 Sexton did not even have a secretary to deal with his letters and he had to pay for stamps for all of his replies – unless a stamped addressed envelope had been provided for him to use. On June 6th Sexton had this letter published in the St Helens Newspaper explaining his difficulties:

> House of Commons, June 3rd, 1919. To the Editor of the St. Helens Newspaper. Sir, – Will you allow me, through your columns, to advise my numerous correspondents that it is physically, mentally and financially impossible to keep pace with all the communications I receive from the constituency. My average daily post bag amounts to fifty letters, exclusive of, say, twenty others on [trade] Union business, and I am on committee for three days of the week from 11 a.m. until 6 p.m. Three halfpence [for a stamp] may appear a small matter to the person who sends a letter, but when it means from 3s. to 5s. a day to answer them, it becomes a very serious item. I am doing my best under the circumstances, but my correspondents must not be surprised at any delay. – Yours, etc., **JAS. SEXTON**.

THE ROUGHS AND LOAFERS ON BENCHES

These days the euphemism "kick it in the long grass" is often employed when something is considered worthy of being ignored. In the past at St Helens Council meetings, the saying "let it lie on the table" was routinely used when it was decided that no action should be taken over some issue.

However, on July 18th 1906 when the council's Parks Committee discussed a letter they had received from their Chief Constable, Councillor Hatton had a more blunt recommendation of what should be done, saying: "I move that the letter be put on the fire". St Helens' top policemen, Arthur Ellerington, wanted the council to stop installing seats in public spaces as, he claimed, "loafers" sat on them and spat on women's dresses. This is what he wrote:

> I am continually receiving complaints from persons of the great annoyance caused by roughs and loafers who

habitually use the seats supplied by the corporation in various parts of the borough. When passing along females complain bitterly of insulting remarks being made to them, and in many instances these loafers expectorate tobacco juice, &c., immediately in front of them, not caring whether the juice strikes on their dresses or not. These dirty, unmanly practices are generally performed amid laughter from the others; and an inspection of the seats in front of the Town Hall will confirm this. Loafers may be seen finding relief from vermin, &c., by rubbing their backs against the backs of the seats. It is very rare that one sees a respectable person taking a rest on them; while after closing hour the seats, may be seen fully occupied by persons peacefully sleeping off the effects of drink until ousted by the police. I find it difficult, with my limited force, to keep abreast with the complaints, and reports of robberies, &c., and I should be extremely obliged by your doing all you can to discourage any more seats being placed on the streets.

WOMEN POLICE OFFICERS

Arthur Ellerington was also firmly against the appointment of female police officers. When the annual conference of the Chief Constables Association was held in London on May 31st 1918, Lady Nott Bower told the police bosses that more women should be recruited to their forces to deal with cases involving children and girls. But Ellerington was unimpressed. He told the conference that women police patrols were an "expensive luxury" and added that from what he'd seen while being in London, the female police seemed to "do nothing but gossip and obstruct the footpath". Ellerington's opposition meant it took until 1942 before St Helens had its first WPC.

Arthur Ellerington

In 1914, under the headlines *"Are St. Helens Girls "Freaks" and Flirts? – A Serious Indictment – The Danger of Street-Walking"*, the St Helens Reporter's letters column had discussed the question of young females being in moral danger and it was suggested that policewomen should be employed in St Helens to supervise them. On July 3rd 1914 this irate response was published in the paper:

> Sir, – As a confirmed opponent of officialdom, I view with alarm the suggestion made by a writer in the "Reporter" last week that a police woman is needed in St. Helens to save our girls from the dangers which face them. Whatever degree of truth there may be in his general charge that girls have too much liberty, and so forth, I think an emphatic protest ought to be made against his suggestion that additional police supervision is necessary – petticoat police government, in fact. ...But the bare idea of a police constable in petticoats is simply unbearable, and I sincerely hope she will never come here to harass the girls of St. Helens. – **J. S. St. Helens**

STANDING FOR THE NATIONAL ANTHEM

The playing of the National Anthem in cinemas at the end of each evening's programme ceased during the 1970s. Some patrons stood respectfully while the music played – but for others it was their cue to dash for the exits. The rush of bodies was depicted in an episode of the TV show 'Dad's Army' and the practice was criticised in a letter published in the St Helens Reporter on November 28th 1930. Then the anthem was known as "the King" and the letter was published under the headline *"'Pig-Headed' St. Helens People – Put On Hats And Coats When 'King' is Played":*

> A lot can be said for the general good character of citizens of St. Helens, but in one respect at least they are very far from coming up to scratch; at least, a great majority of them are. I refer to the habit of 95 per cent. of the picture-goers of

this town of immediately springing up from their seats after the performance and proceeding to struggle into their coats, cram their hats on, and walk out during the playing of "God Save the King." It is positively disgusting! It is very rare that St. Helens people have the chance of showing any outward sign of loyalty to the King, and the one chance they do get they very coolly and pig-headedly throw away. I am afraid visitors to this town, observing such a state of affairs, leave with a doubtful opinion of the good manners of St. Helens. What's more people of this type not only do not show any loyalty to their King and country, but they do not allow anybody else to do so. Anybody attempting to do so gets roughly elbowed out of the way by the crowds moving towards the exits. Surely these men who have not time to keep still during the playing of the National Anthem can at least refrain from putting their hats on. – **LAPOLYA**

GHOULS IN PETTICOATS

Everybody should have a hobby, of course. But I don't think constantly attending funerals is a recommended one! On October 14th 1927 this letter was published in the St Helens Reporter:

The Borough Cemetery has many and varied attractions, and they draw people whose motives are as varied. Among them are the hordes of women whose behaviour at funerals, and whose actions at other times, calls for more than mere protest. At almost every funeral, be it that of a public personage or of one in lowlier rank, the service at the graveside is witnessed by these women, and the solemnity of the occasion has an accompaniment in the noisy chatter of the spectators. Immediately the service is ended, and even while some of the mourners linger about the grave, there is a rush of these females. Without ceremony, and without the slightest pretence at decorum, they begin their inspection. Wreaths are seized and the cards examined.

They are tossed here and there by these ghouls in petticoats, and their value is appraised and crudely commented upon. Even the coffin, as yet uncovered by the kindly earth, is judged as to whether it is creditable to them who had to provide it. There is a jostling and a jesting among them that is sickening to anybody with a sense of the fitness of things, and the Parks and Cemetery Committee might consider means of maintaining some sort of order and decency at funerals in the future. – **MOURNER**

SLAVES IN INDUSTRIAL SCHOOLS

Industrial schools were created to deal with juvenile delinquency and to teach youngsters a trade and were for wayward kids yet to commit a serious crime. The schools were harsh places, centred on strict discipline and magistrates would commit young children to such institutions for several years. For example, in September 1920 ten-year-old James Friar of Pennington Square, off Elephant Lane, was despatched to an industrial school in Liverpool for six years after entering a house in Heath Street and stealing a watch.

Arthur Johnson was no fan of industrial schools and on April 17th 1925 he had this critical letter published in the St Helens Reporter:

Sir, – It has always been the boast of the average Britisher that this is the freest country in the world. The liberty of the subject, we have often been told, is the true corner-stone of all our freedom, which has been won from tyrant powers through centuries of struggle. In the face of such Chauvinism, one views with alarm the decision of the St. Helens Magistrates (Juvenile Court) to send a poor lad, guilty of committing a trivial offence, to an industrial school.

Notwithstanding the appeal of the Education Committee, supported by the school attendance officer, and last, but not least, the natural solicitation of a fond and affectionate father for the boy to be given another chance, the Bench consigned the unfortunate little chap to the care of an adamant officialdom and a life of slavery. Children of both sexes are sent to such institutions with the idea that they will receive training which will enable them to become useful citizens. They look forward with anticipation to being restored to their parents on reaching the age of adolescence, only to realise bitterly as the years pass by that their hopes are doomed to disappointment. In many instances, the effect of the training, which is to convert them into creditable citizens appears to be to turn them into slaves of the State, officially classed as half witted.

I, for one, vehemently protest against such a tyrannical travesty of justice, and strongly object to any child being forcibly estranged from its parents in order to satiate the muddy mentality of any police inspector. This boy is not a hopeless and irretrievable criminal, even if he has yielded to temptation, and stolen a bit of sheet lead. After his term of incarceration, he will return home a hardened, anti-social, brutalised man. To the unknown Neros who ornamented the Bench on this particular occasion, I would say: This is your doing! Have you no children of your own? Do you never feel a pang of regret, a trace of compassion, a gleam of pity? – **A. JOHNSON, 84, Church-street, St. Helens.**

The Goings On In The Gamble's Central Library

"In St. Helens Free Library sleepers have become so numerous that the committee yesterday decided that policemen should be called in to eject persistent offenders."

INTRODUCTION – Of all the places in St Helens where members of the public congregated, one would not have thought that Central Library would have proved one of the most troublesome. Talking by patrons that rose above the level of a whisper and which led to them being shushed by librarians was, perhaps, the height of unruly activity that might be expected.

But all sorts of folk, not just bookworms, used to make a beeline for the rooms in the Gamble Institute. These included vagrants who came in out of the cold, gamblers, and even what some might call the dirty old men who liked to leer at the females studying and working in the library. And this chapter is devoted to a number of examples – but first some background.

The first public library in St Helens opened inside the first town hall in New Market Place in 1855. It was run by the Mechanics Institute and anyone who lived in the four St Helens townships – Eccleston, Windle, Parr and Sutton – could borrow any of their 2,500 volumes, initially for just a penny a week.

There were few borrowers and after the St Helens Free Lending Library had reopened in 1872 after a fire at the Town Hall had led to its closure, it was reported that there had only been 138 borrowers over three months. And these had taken out just 691 titles between them. However, the library's opening hours were only 7 to 8pm on three evenings a week and those wishing to borrow books needed to bring in a "certificate from a respectable householder" to confirm their identity.

Some workplaces and even churches did also have their own libraries. Pilkington's workers had their own Recreation Club, which contained a library, with newspapers available in a reading room. So did the Union Plate Glass Works at Pocket Nook. And since 1855 Lowe House Church ran a "circulating library", which by the 1870s had 1,700 volumes. But their lending library in a large room in the church tower was not provided free, although it only cost a penny a week to take out a book.

When the second Town Hall was opened in 1876 and then the Gamble Institute was created twenty years later, the free libraries and reading rooms within them were seen as important tools to improve the education and knowledge of local people. These, and the various branch libraries that opened soon became very popular, sometimes arguably, too popular!

a) THE BOOKIES IN THE BOOK LIBRARY

This photograph shows how books used to be issued inside Central Library, with the browsing of books by library members not permitted until 1925. Until then only the staff had access to the book collection, which were issued to members through the windows on the right of the picture. These books could either be taken home or studied in the library's reading room.

Inside the main reading room in Central Library

It was in the reading room in 1920 that a couple of elderly bookies set up operations, as described by the St Helens Reporter of March 19th of that year:

> In consequence of complaints of certain illegal practices taking place in the Reading Room of the Central Library, PC's Shepherd and Reynolds kept observation there for three days and what they found was conveyed to the magistrates at the St Helens Police Court on Thursday. The Mayor (Mr. J. R. Turner) presided. The prisoners were Peter Woods, of Watery-lane, and Robert Burns, Salisbury-street lodging house, and they were charged with using the public library for the purpose of making and receiving bets on three different occasions. Mr. E. Townson said that evidence would be brought to show the prisoners frequented the

Library on three separate occasions, and used the room as a place to carry on their business. They used racing papers to pick up the business. The Mayor hoped Mr. Townson did not suppose that they got the racing papers in the Library. Racing and betting news was all blocked out, as is known. Mr. Townson said that that was not his meaning. Continuing, he said, that the prisoners received betting slips and money from various people. The maximum fine that could be imposed in such cases was £5, and in view of the fact that betting was very rife in the borough, he asked the Bench to impose a heavy penalty.

P.C. Shepherd said that on Saturday last, about 11.10 a.m., he along with P.C. Reynolds took up a position in the Gamble Institute overlooking the general reading room. The two prisoners were then sitting at a table along with another man and they were reading a paper. Burns made out three betting slips and handed them to Woods. At 12 noon Woods received seven slips, and money, from different men in the room and at 12.10 Burns went round the paper desks and was seen to hand him slips and money.

At 1.40 Woods went out and witness followed him and saw a boy about 14 years of age ride up on a bicycle and Woods handed something to him. The boy immediately rode off. At 1.45 Burns commenced to take money out of his pockets and to count it on the table. That day Woods received seven slips and Burns ten slips. On Tuesday Burns took six slips and money, and Woods also took six slips. On Wednesday Burns received six slips and money, while Woods received five slips and money. P.C. Reynolds corroborated the evidence. Prisoners, who were both elderly men, were fined £3 in each of the three cases, £9 cash in all.

b) ROWDYISM IN CENTRAL LIBRARY

The requirement for almost total silence in the library is underscored by the comments that were made by a member of the St Helens Free Libraries Committee in August 1898. A Mr Slater wondered whether anything could be done to reduce the irritating sound of people walking round the reading room, as he said the noise was proving to be distracting for those studying books. It was decided to make enquiries with other libraries to see what they did to combat the annoyance.

"Rowdyism At The Central Library – Attendant Slapped", was the headline to an article in the St Helens Reporter on December 12th 1930. The piece described how a recent meeting of the council's Libraries Committee had discussed the need to hire a uniformed male attendant to keep order in their reading room – although the problem in the main seemed little more than people talking. This is what the Chief Librarian, Herbert Edwards, was reported as having told the committee members:

ROWDYISM

AT THE

CENTRAL LIBRARY

ATTENDANT SLAPPED

UNIFORMED ATTENDANT WANTED

The question of providing a uniformed male attendant to keep order in the reading room at the Gamble Institute was raised at a meeting of the Libraries Committee on Wednesday.

"The matter was brought up a year ago," said Mr. H. H. Edwards (Chief Librarian) "It was decided that a

St Helens Reporter Dec 12th 1930

> "The matter was brought up a year ago. It was decided that a policeman should call-in occasionally on his beat, instead of a regular attendant being engaged. It has proved unsuccessful. On Sunday night the young ladies who were in charge reported that they could not control the place. I have watched the policeman come in and walk round the reading stands. The people stopped talking as soon as they saw his uniform, but hardly had he got outside the door than they were at it again. On Monday night I told the men about talking. I cannot help it. I have put the assistants in charge,

> but it is absolutely necessary that a man should be there to keep the men under control. Recently it has been necessary to have an assistant in the corridor to turn children back. Every seat in the reference library has been occupied. Some nights the place has been in terrible disorder. I do not think it right that a girl should have to try to control the place. The other night when my deputy was asking a number of youths to be quiet he received a slap in the face with a rope that one of them was carrying."

The Chief Librarian proposed hiring what we might call a security officer to work in the library during the winter months. The committee decided to request the provision of such an attendant at a salary of £60. Clarence Crossland was subsequently hired and on January 13th 1933 Michael Gilhooley appeared in St Helens Police Court charged with assaulting the library attendant and behaving disorderly. The 35-year-old Crossland explained to the Bench how he had asked Gilhooley to cease talking.

He said the labourer from Hatton Street, near Prescot Road, had initially ignored him and carried on speaking to some other men. And so Crossland told him that if he did not stop talking he would have to ask him to leave. "And who is going to put me out?", Gilhooley demanded to know. "I am", replied the attendant and he placed his hand on the man's shoulder. Gilhooley immediately punched Crossland twice to the head and as the attendant fell to the floor, he was kicked and lost consciousness. Gilhooley – who had 38 previous convictions – did not turn up to the hearing and in absentia was sentenced to two months hard labour.

c) THE LURKERS, LEERERS AND SNORERS IN THE LIBRARY!

In 1897 Alfred Lancaster bore the title of Borough Librarian and he told a conference in London that the atmosphere in the old library in St Helens Town Hall used to send readers to sleep. He said it had been one of his daily duties to walk round the reading room and wake up drowsy readers – but he said the new library at the Gamble benefited from a constant supply of fresh air and sleepy readers were now rare. But eleven years later it was reported that some men actually went into the reading room to doze. The Manchester Evening News on April 15th 1908 wrote:

> In St. Helens Free Library sleepers have become so numerous that the committee yesterday decided that policemen should be called in to eject persistent offenders. The prospect of half a dozen noisy ejectments in the course of an hour or so – for newly-awakened slumberers are sometimes disposed to be troublesome – is not very pleasant for the quiet and studious section of library habitues.

The St Helens Reporter preferred to call the sleepers "loafers", although accepted others did sometimes inadvertently nod off. The paper explained that the Borough Librarian had even been to see the Chief Constable of St Helens to discuss the problem and they quoted the comments of Cllr. Foote at the committee meeting who said Cental Library had a nickname:

> "They call it the “day doss house”. That is the name amongst loafers; and they say, “I am going to the day doss house for a snooze”."

It was decided that library staff should be more active in ejecting habitual sleepers and if they failed to leave as requested, a constable should be summoned. Fast-forward seven decades and the subject was back on the agenda, as the St Helens Reporter of September 11th 1970 described. That was under their headline *"Dozers' Rude Awakening At The Library",* alongside a picture of a supposedly sleeping Frank Gladwin:

> Sleepyhead Frank Gladwin has been caught napping by St. Helens councillors. Frank, 47, a gentleman of the road for 10

years is among scores of drifters hit by a new rule approved by St. Helens Libraries Committee. They have decided to close down the Central Library newspaper room at 7 p.m. instead of 8 p.m., because it's being used as a drowsers' den. Chief Librarian, Mr. Herbert Caistor, told the committee:

> "This room is not being used in the evening except as a shelter for a few down-and-outs. Library staff work on a rota system, so that there is always someone on duty when the room is open. But there are women members of the staff who are scared of going into the room because of the tramps." And the committee's chairman, the Mayor, Councillor Eric Kerr, commented: “I have been in there in the mornings and found some of these people fast asleep.” Last word from Frank, 47, a “roadman“ who uses the room regularly: “I go in the library to read the papers, and now and again I have a sleep. I don't disturb anybody though. If they had shut the room earlier in the summer, it wouldn't have mattered because the weather is fine. But in winter it's important that it is open because it gives us somewhere to go.“ The rest of the Central Library already closes at 7 p.m.

In August 1973 members of the St Helens Libraries Committee were told that some of the old men that lurked in Central Library's reading room were not doing much reading – or sleeping. Instead they were leering at the women that were inside, causing them to feel uncomfortable and leave. Cllr Bill Shepherd told the committee: "The men don't seem to be looking at the papers – they just stare at the women." Cllr Shepherd later told the Reporter:

> "This is a social problem. These men are often from hostels – they have nothing to do. But they will have to stop using the reading room. It's a nice bright room, but it should be for reading. One particular lady had gone in to see the Times Educational Supplement. She complained to me when she

saw what was happening. The men just stared at her and she left because she was embarrassed."

And the Chief Librarian, Geoffrey Senior, added this:

> "People tend to go into this room – and not read. People like to sit in it. Now, this is becoming a problem. Up to now there has been no supervision, but we will ask people to leave and make way for others who want to use the room. We will be keeping our eyes open."

d) TEENAGERS CLOGGING UP THE LIBRARY

Herbert Caistor served as Chief Librarian for St Helens for 23 years before retiring in 1972. On November 29th 1957 the Liverpool Echo wrote how Mr Caistor believed that television was driving children to books – rather than the other way round:

> A sharp increase in the number of children's book issues by St. Helens public library is puzzling officials. Mr. H. C. Caistor, the town's chief librarian, says the increase has gathered momentum during the last two years in the face of a decrease in the adult issues. The trend, he says, has become even more apparent since the opening of the new Moss Bank Library in September. "We at first estimated about 2,000 children's books with 3,000 adult fiction and 1,000 adult non-fiction for the library," he said. "Since then we must have put in another 700 or 800 children's books," he added. But the newness of the library is not the whole answer to this pleasant problem. The demand for children's books at the St. Helens Central Library also shows a sharp upward trend. Mr. Caistor put forward a theory that television, which has been mainly responsible for the decline in adult issues, has helped to stimulate young readers. "Viewing is largely a passive occupation, and after so much

of it I think many children become bored and are eager to do other things like reading," he said. "With my own 11-years-old son I find that reading often takes the place of passive viewing. Children can be even more selective with their programmes than grown-ups."

e) FIGHTING FOR BOOKS IN THE LIBRARY

On June 8th 1955 the St Helens Libraries Committee discussed a complaint from a female reader alleging that other women using Central Library monopolised the shelves and swooped on batches of new books as assistants carried them in. This was the letter that the unnamed woman sent to Chief Librarian Herbert Caistor that was read out at the meeting:

"As a ratepayer of the town, I feel entitled to complain about the selfish and unseemly behaviour of certain women who use the central library. These people have apparently unlimited time to waste, and spend it in the library waiting for more light novels to come in. They are in the library no matter what time of the day I come in – I have seen them at all times. I know for a fact that some of them come twice a day, and sometimes more often, until they get what they want. When your assistants place the books in the racks, these women follow them about and impede them in their work. Ask the assistants and they will tell you this is correct. They also stand in front of the racks to keep other people off until they have made their choice.

"When your assistants place the books in the racks, these women swoop like hawks and some take three or four books though some have only one ticket. Then they peruse part of these books, even sitting down at the table to do so, and when they have made their final choice they cry to their friends and pass the other books on to them. The net result is that ordinary people cannot get any of these books. Recently, one woman nearly took a book I had selected out of my hands because she had been 'waiting' for it. This has gone on for months and I have been forced to join a private library to get some up-to-date light reading. This is supposed to be a free library and all ratepayers should have equal chances of all books not on the reserved list. The human nature of these people being what it is, I don't suppose you can do anything about it."

Herbert Caistor told the meeting that it was true that assistants had to sometimes fight their way to the shelves with new books and that fighting for them did take place between members of the public. The committee decided to leave the behaviour in the library up to the Chief Librarian.

Clearly some of the volumes were not booked out to borrowers in the usual way. Four years later Mr Caistor reported how a stocktake had revealed that 1,000 novels had gone missing from Central Library. He said he believed they'd been taken out under coats, in shopping bags "or by sheer nerve".

ST. HELENS PUBLIC LIBRARIES.

BORROWER'S TICKET EXPIRES 28·5·1937

No. 10327 (— (12) 28.5.32

Name Isaac Smith

Address 139 Chamberlain St

Class school

Isaac Smith's library card (aka borrower's ticket) – the son of a tram driver was aged twelve when he took it out

f) VANDALISM IN CENTRAL LIBRARY

On January 9th 1899 three boys named Thomas Thompson (14) from Bold Street, John McCormick (15) of Wright Street and Alfred Houltram (15) of Phythian Street appeared in St Helens Police Court charged with doing wilful damage to books in the boys reading room of St Helens Free Library. I wonder if there was a similar room for girls? Anyhow, it had only been a bit of horseplay in which the lads had thrown books at each other and caused minor damage to them.

But a prosecution was seen as worthwhile for the deterrent effect it might have on others. In fact Chief Constable James Wood told the court that boys in the library had recently committed a great deal of damage to books and they wanted to make an example of these lads. The Chairman of the Bench said as it was the first such case that had come before them they would only impose a fine of 2s 6d each. But he warned the threesome that they and their friends must behave themselves in future when in the library and if they returned to court they would be dealt with more severely.

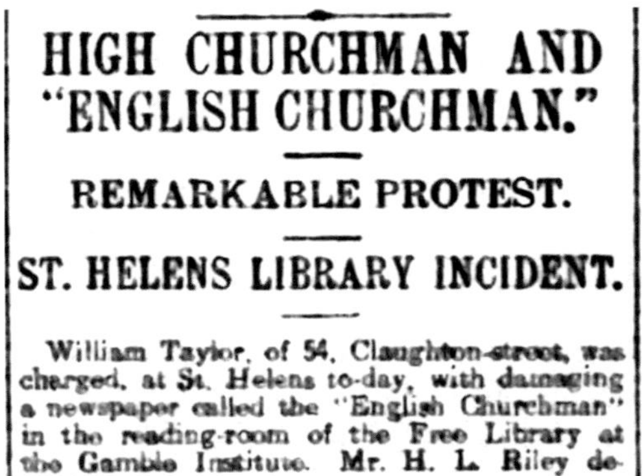

HIGH CHURCHMAN AND "ENGLISH CHURCHMAN."

REMARKABLE PROTEST.

ST. HELENS LIBRARY INCIDENT.

William Taylor, of 54, Claughton-street, was charged, at St. Helens to-day, with damaging a newspaper called the "English Churchman" in the reading-room of the Free Library at the Gamble Institute. Mr. H. L. Riley defended.

Chief Constable Wood said that for several

Liverpool Echo June 10th 1904

On June 10th 1904 an unusual form of vandalism in Central Library was related in St Helens Police Court. That was when William Taylor of Claughton Street was charged with damaging a newspaper called the English Churchman. For a number of months, newspapers and periodicals in the reading room had been deliberately torn and so a detective went undercover to locate the culprit. Subsequently DC Staveley spotted Taylor pick up a copy of the English Churchman, place the newspaper under a table and tear it to pieces. After being arrested, Taylor said: "I am a High Churchman. I am sorry for what

I have done, and if you will look over it, I will never let it occur again." Taylor was the son of a clergyman and a member of the High Church party and thought the English Churchman was not a fit publication to be in a library. The Chairman of the Bench decided to dismiss the case upon payment of 20 shillings costs but warned Taylor he must keep his promise not to repeat his foolish action.

Then on October 2nd 1928 when George Ashall of Hardshaw Street appeared in St Helens Police Court to face a charge of assaulting a 10-year-old boy, his excuse was that a "riot" had been taking place in the boys' reading room. He said that as he passed the door, a book flew past his head and he had "sprung into the room to box the boys' ears" but accidentally caught one lad on his eye. Ashall was fined 20 shillings or 14 days in prison.

g) LIBRARY STORIES IN BRIEF

And to conclude this chapter here are a few library stories from the 1960s and '70s:

~ Here's a headscratcher. What cost 1d in St Helens in 1879 and still only cost a penny in 1968? The answer is the library fine for the late return of books. That had been a penny a week *(or part of a week)* since when Benjamin Disraeli was prime minister. However, the pennies did mount up. In fact the fines for overdue books brought in over £1,000 per year, which helped to offset the cost of running the library service. But in 1968 St Helens Libraries Committee decided to double the adult fines to twopence.

~ A gramophone record library was opened at Central Library in 1962. Within its first fortnight the new library had 167 members with operatic and orchestral works proving the most popular. Ten years later an article in the St Helens Reporter revealed that the Gamble Institute held a stock of 3,000 records, which 1,100 people borrowed each year. Music scores and books were now going to be grouped with the records in a new dedicated music room in the library in what had previously been a space for periodicals. The gramophone library at Central Library was renamed the Beecham Music Library in 1975 and it closed in 1986.

~ When St Helens Libraries Committee met in September 1970 they decided to invest in an "electric copying machine" for use by the public in Central Library. And what an expensive beast it was! The machine cost £356 – the equivalent of about £6,000 in today's money. That did not impress Councillor Bill Shepherd, who said: "I am not convinced of the need to spend £356." To that Cllr. Jim Hand responded: "For too long this committee has been cheese-paring. Let's have a top class machine". Although Cllr. Hand did feel it would be better for the copier to be kept behind the counter for the staff to run off copies for customers at a shilling a time.

~ The Reporter on June 29th 1973 revealed that St Helens magistrates had recently fined a woman £18 for failing to return six library books. That's the equivalent of over £300 in today's money! And at the same court hearing a husband and wife were fined £12 for not returning their borrowed books. Chief Librarian Geoffrey Senior told the Reporter: "We want these books back – that's our main aim. We don't lose a lot, but we get a fair number of people who don't return books without constant reminding." These days there are no fines for the late return of library books.

Coronation Street Stars' Visits To St Helens During The Early 1960s

"Miss Carson drew gasps of admiration from the crowd as she prepared to declare the show officially open. Her remark, "I have left my hairnet in Coronation Street," brought a roar of laughter from the onlookers."

INTRODUCTION – It did not take long after the first episode of Coronation Street was broadcast on ITV on December 9th 1960 for the actors to realise their lives would never be the same. When Jennifer Moss popped into a shoe shop in Golborne a little more than two years later, the St Helens Reporter wrote that her presence had "nearly caused a riot". Jennifer – who played Lucille Hewitt – was looking to buy some knee-length boots from her friend who managed the store. But she had to make a quick exit once word of her presence got round. The St Helens Reporter said:

> The shop was besieged by a huge crowd of youngsters and children all hoping to get a glimpse of her. A local constable had to be called in order to get her through the crowd and into her car, which she had parked at the side of the shop.

Apparently the Coronation Street actors were not paid particularly well considering the massive audiences that their show reached. But their incomes were boosted by personal appearances and the St Helens district received the Corrie stars on many occasions during the early 1960s. This chapter is devoted to newspaper reports of some of these.

a) LYNNE CAROL (aka Martha Longhurst)

Do you remember Martha Longhurst in Coronation Street? Along with Ena Sharples and Minnie Caldwell, Martha was one of the trio of milk stout suppers who put the world to rights each Monday and Wednesday evening in the snug of the Rover's Return. Lynne Carol played Martha Longhurst from 1960 until the character's dramatic heart attack in the Rover's four years later and she visited St Helens in 1962 to open an exhibition.

The image shown above was part of Oxley's advertisement that the department store had published in the St Helens Reporter on Saturday September 15th 1962. Another part of the full-page advert read:

Oxley's department store

> **"WAIT TILL I TELL ENA"**, says Lynne Carol (Martha Longhurst) of 'Coronation Street' fame. "She won't half be surprised when I tell her! I'm opening Oxleys marvellous Ideal Home

Exhibition this morning at 9 o'clock. It's on the third floor – and it's really wonderful!... See you there."

The Reporter was then published on Saturdays and Oxley's must have assumed that St Helens folk read their papers very early in order to have seen their ad and dashed to their department store on the corner of Barrow Street and Claughton Street for 9am!

b) VIOLET CARSON (aka Ena Sharples)

I don't think Ena Sharples would have been all that impressed with Martha's opening of an exhibition at Oxley's, as her real-life persona, Violet Carson, had been in the district herself only days before opening a much bigger event. The occasion was the Billinge and Winstanley Horticultural Society's inaugural summer flower show and fete which had taken place in bright sunshine at Chapel Meadow in Newton Road.

If the 2,500-strong crowd had been expecting Violet Carson to be a mirror image of her fiery TV character, complete with trademark hairnet, they were in for a shock as in real life she was well spoken and very well dressed. Of course, newspapers will always look for an attention-grabbing angle for their reports and the St Helens Reporter's take was revealed in its headline *"TV Star 'Smuggled' In To Open Billinge Flower Show"*.

Those running the show were concerned that if Violet Carson had arrived at the main entrance to the showground, many people after seeing the TV star would not bother visiting the actual flower show, thus denying the organisers badly needed income from their admission fees. The Show secretary was Mr C. Brown and he was quoted as saying:

"Our first show has cost us quite a bit of money, and we could not afford to make a loss. Therefore we decided to get Miss Carson into the ground without drawing a lot of attention, and this is what we did."

And so a crowd of several hundred outside of the main entrance – many carrying cameras – missed Violet Carson being brought through a side entry. Some waited for two hours before realising that they had wasted their time. The Reporter described the flower show's opening ceremony:

> Dressed in a white coat with floral hat and matching white accessories, Miss Carson drew gasps of admiration from the crowd gathered around the dais as she prepared to declare the show officially open, her elegant and smart appearance presenting a vivid contrast to her usual drab appearance on the television screen. Her remark, "I have left my hairnet in Coronation Street," brought a roar of laughter from the onlookers. In more serious vein, Miss Carson told the crowd that if people would concentrate more on the pleasure to be gained from growing flowers instead of crossing frontiers and developing atomic weapons and worrying about outer space, the world would be a far happier place to live in.

Of the hundreds of show programmes that had been sold, fifty had been printed with one page upside down. Those who had purchased such a programme were allowed to enter a tent, where Violet Carson added her autograph to the page. After presenting prizes to the winners of the children's fancy dress competition, the TV star was driven away from the showground. The Reporter said:

> Show officials and police formed a human chain completely encircling her as she approached her car, where a large number of fans had gathered to say goodbye. What were Miss Carson's impressions of her first visit to Billinge? Asked if she had enjoyed her visit as she was making her way to her car shortly after 4 p.m., she said: "Very much indeed. I would not have missed it for worlds."

Violet Carson returned to St Helens on October 5th 1963 after signing a contract with Telefusion to promote their many stores.

These mainly specialised in renting out black and white television sets to customers. But they also sold TVs and offered "slot TV" – sets fitted with meters that needed sixpences inserted to work.

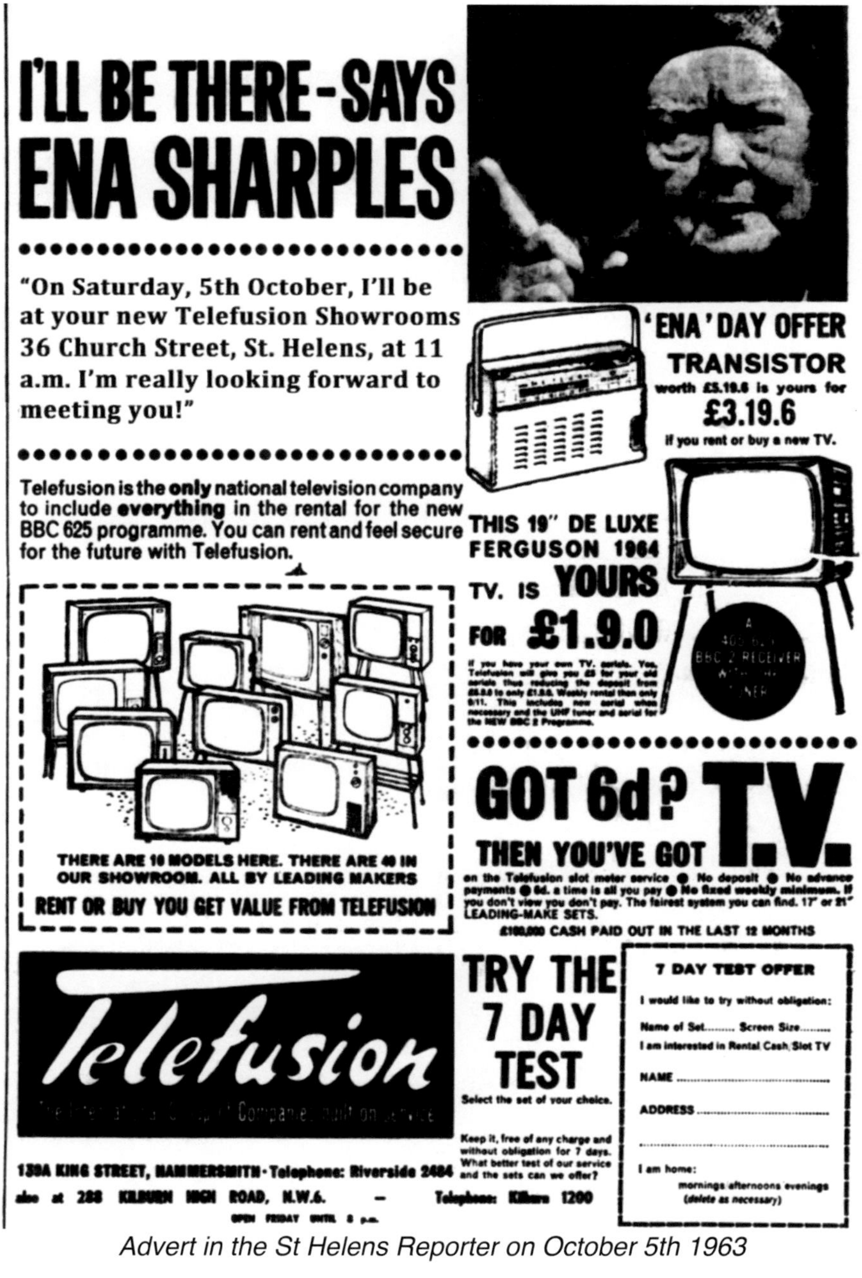

Advert in the St Helens Reporter on October 5th 1963

In a preview of Violet Carson's return visit to the St Helens district, the Reporter published this article which also referenced the forthcoming launch of BBC 2:

> Ena Sharples, the famous personality of "Coronation Street," will be visiting St. Helens this morning to open the new showroom of Telefusion at 36, Church Street. Miss Violet Carson will arrive at 11 a.m. She will sign autographs for her many fans and entertain customers who have become subscribers to Telefusion since the showrooms opened some weeks ago. There will be balloons for the children, and leaflets giving full details of the new BBC programme and how it affects viewers in the area will be distributed. Anyone who purchases or rents a television on Saturday can purchase a radio only £3 19s. 6d. For those who will not be able to see their favourite star, Telefusion will let them have a signed photograph of Ena Sharples if you send a stamped addressed envelope to the Public Relations department, Telefusion Ltd., Telefusion House, Preston New Road, Blackpool.

On the following day Betty Alberge – who played shopkeeper Florrie Lindley in Coronation Street for five years from 1960 *(and later Edna Cross in Brookside)* – appeared at the Hippodrome Bingo Club in Corporation Street to present one lucky player with her or his winnings. Many other stars of the Street also made personal appearances at the former theatre, as well as the Rivoli Bingo Club after its conversion from a cinema in 1965.

HIPPODROME – ST. HELENS

"SUREWIN" BINGO & SOCIAL CLUB

CONGRATULATIONS!

TO MRS. DORIS BATE OF ST. HELENS, WHO ON SUNDAY EVENING AT THE ABOVE CLUB FOR 1/- ON THE NATIONAL LUCKY SCOOP CARD WON

★ £1,292.6.0 ★

SEE THE BIG PAY OUT THIS SUNDAY EVENING AT 8-15 BY

★ FLORRIE LINDLEY ★

Of Coronation Street.

SORRY. MEMBERS ONLY ON THIS NIGHT, NO GUESTS

TWO INCREASING SNOWBALLS CAN BE WON AT ANY SESSION

★ No. 1 £129 No. 2 £158 ★

SUNDAY EVENING ON 50 NUMBERS.

And in Addition

★ TONIGHT (SATURDAY) IS GIFT NIGHT ★
★ TOMORROW (SUN.) IS GROCERY NIGHT ★

St Helens Reporter October 5th 1963

However, Ena Sharples was soon back in St Helens – doing the twist in a Haresfinch hotel! It was a fundraiser for the charity now known as Scope but then called the National Spastics Society. This is how the St Helens Reporter of October 12th 1963 described Violet Carson's appearance, under their headline *"Ena – 'How Beautiful!' Did The Twist!":*

> "Isn't she beautiful?" was the cry which went up from crowds outside the Woodlands Hotel, Haresfinch, on Thursday night as they saw actress Violet Carson (Ena Sharples, of Granada TV's "Coronation Street") arrive in a gleaming grey Jaguar. Few people had originally been told that she was to be there, but the secret had leaked out a few days beforehand and the hotel was packed with fans, eager to see the first lady of ITV. An hour late, and rather tired after a "hard day at the studios," Miss Carson could still manage radiant smiles and waves for the patrons as she entered the lounge to knock down a pile of pennies – donations for Spastics' funds. Before the knocking-down ceremony, Miss Carson answered questions about "Coronation Street."
>
> She was introduced by Dr. W. H. Rout, a local general practitioner, who made an appeal on behalf of the Spastics. He invited patrons to boost the pennies pile by donating the price of "a drink with Ena." Miss Carson knocked the pennies into a blanket and looked on as the patrons tossed in gifts of silver. Total – £27 10s. Twenty minutes and many autographs later, she toured the rest of the hotel before moving to the private apartments for a cocktail party given by the licensee, Mrs. G. M. Lawrence, who was assisted by her daughter, Mrs. M. Barnes. Earlier, Mrs. Barnes' 10-years-old daughter Susan, had presented Miss Carson with a bouquet. At the party were a dozen or so of Miss Carson's personal friends, including her hairdresser, and Mrs. E. M. Critchley, of Mere Road, Newton-le-Willows, who makes

Miss Carson's dresses. As the evening wore on, Miss Carson allowed herself to relax a little, and relaxing, for her, meant playing the piano, singing a few verses of Auld Lang Syne, and – Twisting!

c) PAT PHOENIX (aka Elsie Tanner)

This is Pat Phoenix, alias Elsie Tanner, pictured in 1962 opening a new shop. By then the two-year-old soap was firmly entrenched as a viewers' favourite, with many confusing the real-life actors with their on-screen characters. That seemed to extend to the St Helens Reporter as on April 7th 1962 the newspaper described Pat Phoenix's appearance at a charity function in St Helens Town Hall.

Strangely, the article referred to Pat exclusively by her character guise in Coronation Street and did not even once state her real name. The event was a dinner and dance held in aid of Haydock Old Folk's Treat Fund. The Reporter wrote:

After an express taxi service from her home in Sale, Cheshire, Elsie was rushed past a few curious children at the Town Hall steps and into the main hall, where the 350 dancers had started dinner. After dinner, pretty nine-years-old Elaine Worsley, 100, Bleak Hill Road, presented a bouquet of tulips and freesia to Elsie. Organiser of the event (County Coun. Mrs. Susan Pimblett) welcomed Elsie. "The old folk of Haydock belong to an age which is now more or less, forgotten," she said. "I am glad that at least one day in

> the year they are remembered." Elsie said she hoped the old people of Haydock would be pleased with the proceeds. On display in the hall was a 24lb. cake of Coronation Street, specially made for the occasion by a Morecambe confectioner, who made a wedding cake and christening cake for Princess Margaret. During the evening, practically every dancer paid 1s. for Elsie's autograph. Dancing demonstrations were given by Miss Margaret Howarth and Mr. Keith Holmes.

Later in the year, Elsie Tanner visited Ashton-in-Makerfield, although the Reporter had now realised that she was really Pat Phoenix! Their article was published on October 13th 1962 under the headline *"Coronation Street Fans Chanted 'We Want Elsie'":*

> More than 200 "Coronation Street" fans chanted "We want Elsie" outside the Regent pet stores, Bryn Street, Ashton, on Wednesday evening, as they waited impatiently for the arrival of Elsie Tanner (Pat Phoenix) one of the stars of the show. Miss Phoenix had been invited by the secretary of the Ashton branch of the British Empire Cancer Campaign, Mrs. W. Hayes, 40, Town Fields, to knock down a pile of pennies collected at the stores for the Campaign. When she arrived, half-an-hour late, Miss Phoenix had to have a police escort through the large crowd. Mrs. Hayes greeted her on behalf of the Campaign Committee and six-years-old Jean Lavin, niece of Miss M. Johnson, manageress of the store, presented Miss Phoenix with a bouquet. Before knocking the pennies over, Miss Phoenix spoke to the large crowd. This, she said, was a fine effort from the people of Ashton, and she hoped other shop-owners would emulate the example set by the pet stores. "I am very proud to represent Coronation Street, not forgetting Ena, on this occasion," she said, as she pushed the pennies into a blanket. Later, Miss Phoenix signed autographs for the many youngsters who

crowded into the shop. The total realised for the Empire Cancer Research Campaign was £24.

d) BILL ROACHE (aka Ken Barlow) and FRANK PEMBERTON (aka Frank Barlow)

A few weeks prior to Pat Phoenix enjoying a good nosh up at St Helens Town Hall, William Roache and Frank Pemberton had attended a similar event in Haydock. Frank played Ken Barlow's father – also called Frank – in Coronation Street for four years.

Frank Pemberton and Bill Roache in Coronation Street

Under the headline *"Coronation Street Stars Impressed By Haydock"*, the Reporter on February 3rd 1962 described the dinner. The jokey reference to Ida's life insurance concerned Frank Barlow's late wife who, in the soap, had been run down by a bus:

> Before their first visit to Haydock last Friday, Frank and Kenneth Barlow (Frank Pemberton and William Roache, of Granada's 'Coronation Street') thought of the town as "a little ramshackle place beyond the outback." On Friday, when the two actors were guests at Haydock's Old Folk's Treat

Committee's dinner and dance at Cromptons Recreation Club, they both agreed that they were very impressed by Haydock, its people, and in particular its organisations for the old folk. In an interview with the Reporter, Kenneth Barlow said: "These are a credit to the local council, and we earnestly believe that other councils should take a lesson from Haydock." More than 500 people attended the function, organised mainly by County Coun. Mrs. Susan Pimblett, Clipsley Lane Post Office. After dinner, and a few dances, a half-hour long cabaret was staged by Miss B. Anderson's school of dancing. Mrs. Pimblett, who thanked the famous guests, and all connected with the event, said: "Your help is very much appreciated by everyone. The old people of the town are thrilled by everything that is being done for them."

The Chairman of the Council (Coun. W. Tickle) said: "We are honoured to have two artistes from Coronation Street here. You are supporting a very worthy cause. In this town, there are more than 1,000 people past the age of 65, and we are going to do everything we can for them." With pipe in hand, Frank Barlow began: "Other actors from Coronation Street have had the honour of attending similar functions before, and have arrived in evening dress. The fact is Ida's insurance money hasn't come through yet!"

e) PHILIP LOWRIE (aka Dennis Tanner)

Philip's first spell in the Street as Dennis Tanner was from 1960 until 1968 and the actor visited St Helens on August 10th 1963 to crown the Pilkington Gala Queen. The annual festival at Ruskin Drive was for all staff of the glass giant that were employed at their various factories throughout the country. The Parr Public Prize Band led the parade through the town as it wended its way from Bridge

Street to Ruskin Drive, along Ormskirk Street, Baldwin Street, Duke Street and Dentons Green Lane. Philip Lowrie rode on a float decked with thousands of crepe paper flowers and sitting alongside the gala queen, Mary Mounfield, who was positioned on a swing. The Liverpool Daily Post described how the couple had been given a "terrific reception" from cheering crowds.

Another float featured a gigantic picture book that had children sitting between its pages dressed as characters from nursery rhymes. The St Helens Newspaper described how two rockets had also added a "topical touch" to the floats with one of them carrying two spacemen. A further float had been transformed into the Merseysippi Ferry and featured a jazz band.

The Newspaper described Philip Lowrie's entry into the Gala at Ruskin Drive as "triumphant". Dressed in a charcoal grey suit, the Coronation Street star told the cheering crowd:

> "Come to sunny St. Helens, they said, for your holidays. So I've come. I am glad to see you, anyway. I couldn't bring my mum because she's busy feeding Walter. He eats quite a bit. I couldn't bring Ena because you can't take her anywhere. But we have someone much prettier than Ena – Mary Mounfield, whom I am to crown Queen."

The Walter reference concerned window cleaner cum wannabe singing star Walter Potts who in the Street was lodging with Elsie and Philip Tanner in Weatherfield – and had a voracious appetite! Mary Mounfield was a well-known local singer who at one time had been offered a job by the George Mitchell Singers and she told the crowd how happy she was to have been crowned by "our Dennis ".

The Weird & Wonderful Things St Helens Folk Have Said Part 2

This chapter is devoted to another compilation of quotations from St Helens people that have appeared in local newspapers.

...ON THE BOYS OF THE 1920s – James Gordon was the long-standing secretary of St Helens YMCA, a man with plenty of experience of youngsters – although not all of his encounters had clearly been positive ones. In October 1924 the 44-year-old made this stinging critique of the typical boy at a meeting of the St Helens Rotary Club held at the Fleece Hotel in Church Street:

"He is selfish, inefficient, unambitious. Goodness, beauty and truth do not appeal to him. In sport he is an unmitigated pot-hunter. Music, religion and politics bore him stiff. Leave him to his purely animal pursuits and he is happy, like the swine, to wallow in the mire. Urge him to anything in the nature of brain study or mind exercise and he will flee from it as he will from the plague."

...ABOUT STINKY ST HELENS – In the St Helens Newspaper of August 29th 1919 an unnamed woman was quoted as commenting on the need to keep windows shut:

"When I first came to St. Helens I wondered why the great majority of the bedroom windows were kept closed. In the first week I soon found the reason. The first night I opened my window to its limit. During the hours of darkness I was entertained by the shrieking of cats. That I expected. And I was kept awake by the whistling and chaffing of engines. I expected that also. And then sundry revellers serenaded all and sundry sleepers with unmelodious songs – which did not surprise me either. What did astound me, however, was

> the abominable stink of chemical gases pouring in through the window the whole night through. When morning light was heralded by the chirrup of the sparrows I got up to find a thick layer of smut and dirt lying upon everything in the room, and the metal ornaments oxidised by the chemical action of the atmosphere."

...ABOUT ST HELENS BARBERS – In the Daily Mirror on September 15th 1960 Charles Holland of Eaton Road in Dentons Green lamented the loss of really short back and sides hair cuts:

> "It seems to me that barbers have forgotten how to give a real "short-back-and-sides" these days. Remember how they would bend your head forward as though trying to dislocate your neck; dig their clippers in as if trying to skin you alive; and then keep clipping away past any bit of "parting" you might have had? But what a fine, clean feeling your neck had when they finished!"

...ON GETTING OUT OF ST HELENS – John S. Ward was a writer on the Daily Express who in an 1932 edition of the paper said he had been born and bred in St Helens, the "most depressing industrial town" that he knew. In the 1921 census John Stanley Ward was living in Keswick Road, the 15-year-old son of a joiner and was studying at Cowley Boys school after winning a scholarship. In his article he described a recent meeting with his former headmaster, Gerald Dowse, and discussing with him other old boys who had done well in their chosen field. But in order to become successful, all had needed to leave the town of their birth, which led Ward to say:

> "I have no illusions about my native town. The advantage of being born and bred in a town like St. Helens is that it makes you dead keen to get out of it – to get on in the world that lies beyond its dreary streets and its pathetic, smoke-begrimed, tumbledown dwellings."

...ABOUT BLEEDING TO DEATH – On October 6th 1939 the St Helens Reporter described how a "victim" in a first-aid exercise had got fed up hanging about:

> During the recent test of ambulance workers, a "casualty" in the Thatto Heath area was left duly labelled in the street to await instructions and attendance from the first-aiders; his was a case of "bleeding to death," according to the label pinned to his raincoat. In due course the rescue squad found him – or what was left of him. What they did find was not a man at death's door, but this message written on his label: "Have bled to death; gone home."

...ABOUT SEX FILMS – In September 1971 the Capitol Cinema screened the controversial German sex education film 'Female Sexuality'. The Roman Catholic Dean of St Helens, Canon Hugh Fitzpatrick, denounced the picture as "revolting" and walked out of a special preview after only ten minutes. Since then cinemagoers had flocked to see the film that showed frank, lovemaking scenes, with one group of patrons particularly attracted as cinema manager Alan Peel told the St Helens Reporter:

> "Business has been fantastic. I have never seen so many pensioners, including couples, in the cinema since we showed 'The Wife Swappers' in February."

...ABOUT BEING ARRESTED – On November 2nd 1923 the St Helens Reporter described how some coal stealers at Ashtons Green Colliery in Parr had appeared in St Helens Police Court. The police said that when Margaret Crompton had been arrested the pragmatic woman had said, "Nowt I say will mend it". Mrs Crompton was fined 5 shillings.

And when Frederick McKeode of no fixed abode appeared in St Helens Police Court on March 8th 1920 charged with breaking into the billiard hall in Bridge Street, PC Manser said the 21-year-old had told him: "I have nothing to say. Tell the magistrates I hope it keeps fine for them". He was sent to prison for one month with hard labour. And then there was Henry Meek. This is how the St Helens Reporter on November 30th 1923 described the poacher:

> Apparently having read the prophecy that the meek shall inherit the earth, Henry Meek, of Havelock-street, set out to obtain his share by instalments, beginning by the modest seizure of a hare in the meadows of Eccleston. Curiously enough, he had Meadows with him as well as around him, and on Tuesday Henry Meek and Henry Meadows faced the County Bench on a charge of poaching.

When a gamekeeper and Police Inspector Curran had visited Meek's house and told him he was going to be reported the man had replied: "If you saw me, you saw me". But in court he changed his mind and denied the offence and he and Meadows were each fined £2 or 14 days.

...ABOUT A WOMAN AND A WIND-UP GRAMOPHONE – A dispute between two neighbours in Fern Street in Gerards Bridge in September 1923 led to James Byron and Margaret Pearson being summoned to St Helens Police Court. They were both charged with breach of the peace and PC Glover told the magistrates that when in Byron's house he had asked the man for an explanation of the row to which he replied:

"I could not sit here and have her tantalising me all night." And in court Byron compared his antagonist to a wind-up gramophone, saying Mrs Pearson was: "...the same as the new Edison Bell record. When she is wound up, you cannot stop her." Both were bound over for six months to keep the peace.

...ABOUT RECEIVING A CLEAWT FOR NOWT – When in August 1925 Mary Beardsmore summoned William Seddon to St Helens Police Court alleging assault, Mary admitted that she wasn't too bothered about the thumping she had been given: "I don't mind being smacked, but I dislike to hear filthy language in front of children." However, the defendant claimed he was the real victim of the late night affair in Thatto Heath, telling the court:

> "I was like a football in a Rugby scrimmage. All her brothers and sisters and the whole family came rushing and kicking at me, and I was knocked up and down the place."

When George Barnes from Sandon Street went into the witness box to give evidence, William Seddon was reported to have looked him over and remarked, "Good Lord, tha' owt to ha' bin i' bed at half-past eleven at neet." He also accused Mrs Beardsmore of behaving "just like a wild cat". A witness called Ralf Tabern claimed the trouble had begun when Mrs Beardsmore had said: "Tek no notice o' me Uncle Bill". Mr Tabern insisted that he had taken no part in the bother but he still happened, as he put it, "to get a cleawt for nowt". William Seddon was fined ten shillings.

...ABOUT GHOOASTS – On August 21st 1925 the St Helens Reporter described rumours that a ghost haunted Sutton Monastery by making a nightly walk around its long wall. The paper dispatched a journalist to search for the spectre or, as they put it, to "track it to its den". Near the monastery was the so-called "Pudding Bag" district of St Helens Junction. The origin of that name was that puddings used to be made in narrow-necked muslin bags and the Pudding Bag houses were enclosed by a triangle of railway lines. It was a cul-de-sac containing Woodcock Street and Railway Terrace with a single means of ingress and exit, like a pudding bag with an opening at just one end. The unsuccessful hunt for the ghost contained this lively encounter with a Sutton miner, as the paper described:

> Late that night a wait was made by the long, monotonous wall at the rear of the monastery. To while away the time one chatted to a collier who was passing by and asked him "Why do they call the place "Pudding Bag?" The collier removed his pipe, spat prodigiously and retorted, "Becus tha' con only get eawt same road as tha' cum in. But wot art dooin'

hanging' reawnd here?" he queried. "I'm looking for ghosts," came the halting admission. The collier shrugged his shoulders, and rejoined his mate higher up the road, murmuring, "Ah wonder if yon feller's canned? Aw he'll hear is grass growing' and th' moggies dancin'. Ah've no faith in ghooasts."

...ABOUT THE POLICE – PC Higson told St Helens Police Court on August 10th 1931 that he and PC Murray had entered Havelock Street at 10:40 pm and found fifty people assembled there after some trouble had occurred. The police saw Gertrude Duffy and told her to go home but she had replied:

"The police are never here when murder is going on. I will stand here as long as I like. I have paid rates and taxes and helped to keep the likes of you for years."

...ABOUT THE SIZE OF POLICEMEN'S FEET – In April 1922 Joseph Johnson of Park Road in St Helens was accused of having "impeded a tram conductor while in the execution of his duties" and using offensive language. Joseph Bennett gave evidence that when Inspector Mercer had boarded the tram the policeman had accidentally stood on Johnson's toes. That was after hearing his friend say: "Keep them there great feet off mine!"

...ABOUT YER WORKSHOPS – And finally, in a court case in January 1874 in which a man called Bracken was accused of threatening a neighbour called Mrs Bowles, the St Helens Newspaper described these pearls of wisdom spoken to their Worships on the Bench:

Mrs. Bowles paused here, and concluded by telling the bench that she was "as quiet a woman as was to be found about the diggins." Then came the defendant's story. "It's all spite yer Workshops," he said to the magistrates in a mechanical sort of a way.

Acknowledgements / Credits

Eccleston Library, St Helens

St Helens Archive Service

British Newspapers Archive

Newspapers.com

FindmyPast

Royal College of Physicians – (2016) 'Beef tea, a very 19th century remedy' – Accessed March 15 2024 through https://history.rcplondon.ac.uk/blog/beef-tea-very-19th-century-remedy

Most images are from the author's own personal archive or reproduced from newspapers on microfilm at Eccleston Library.

Sir Samuel Brighouse picture courtesy Lionel Taylor. Clock Face Colliery Band courtesy George Houghton.

Thanks to Diane Charnock and Gyles Charnock for their proof reading and support.

Newspaper Sources: Edinburgh Evening News, Guernsey Evening Press, Illustrated London News, Liverpool Albion, Liverpool Daily Post, Liverpool Echo, Liverpool Evening Express, Liverpool Mail, Liverpool Mercury, London Daily News, Manchester Courier, Manchester Evening News, Northwich Guardian, Nottingham and Midland Catholic News, Nottingham Journal, Prescot Reporter, Stalybridge Reporter, St Helens Examiner, St Helens Newspaper, St Helens Reporter, Wigan Observer, Wigan Times.